NATIONALISM AND THE CULTURAL CRISIS IN PRUSSIA, 1806-1815

NATIONALISM
and the
CULTURAL CRISIS
in
PRUSSIA, 1806-1815

By Eugene Newton Anderson

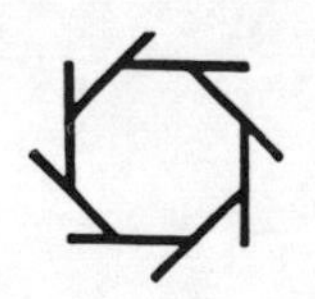

1966
OCTAGON BOOKS, INC.
New York

Reprinted 1966
by special arrangement with Holt, Rinehart and Winston, Inc.

OCTAGON BOOKS, INC.
175 FIFTH AVENUE
NEW YORK, N. Y. 10010

LIBRARY OF CONGRESS CATALOG CARD NUMBER: 66-29328

Printed in U.S.A. by
NOBLE OFFSET PRINTERS, INC.
NEW YORK 3, N. Y.

To My Sister

JESSE MAY

PREFACE

A NUMBER of years ago the author began to read the sources on the subject of nationalism instead of the scholarly monographs. He discovered nationalism to be, not a vague influence in the nineteenth and twentieth centuries, not something for political theorists devoid of historical knowledge to dissect, or for historians devoid of theoretical knowledge to arrange in time sequence, but a vital cultural form peculiar to the last one hundred and fifty years. At about the same time the emergence of National Socialism stirred the author to view nationalism with realistic concern. In his study of the beginnings of German nationalism he sought answers to new questions. How and under what conditions did individuals make the transition from cosmopolitanism or provincialism into nationalism? What were and are the characteristics of nationalists and of nationalism? Why did nationalism rather than state-ism or some other "ism" appear? It was manifest that the solution of these problems demanded the correlation of ideas and society, for the major fact to be examined was that of the birth and institutionalization of nationalism. The clarification of the ideological-socio-institutional unit called nationalism imposed upon the author the necessity of setting this cultural form off against other and competing forms, those of the *ancien régime,* of autocracy and caste, and of liberalism. The student of cultural conflict must delimit his objects by way of contrast and try to draw a general portrait of them. While time and place vary the details of nationalism and the proportion of its strength with respect to other cultural forms, the essential elements of nationalism persist. The author recognizes the dangers of this kind of approach; but he used it as the only way he saw for satisfying his curiosity.

Since the studies of nationalism have been on the whole either too theoretical or too factual, the author had to approach the subject in its simplest form. He selected seven individuals, contemporaries in the first period of German nationalism, to represent types of caste, or class, and occupation. Four of them, of diverse backgrounds and professions, reached and practiced the common cultural ideal of nationalism—Fichte, son of a poor artisan, a philosopher and professor; Arndt, born of peasants, a folklorist-historian and professor; Kleist, an aristocrat and writer; Gneisenau, a half-aristocrat, half-burgher army officer. A bureaucrat-statesman and a peasant might well have been included in the list; but the two outstanding representatives of the former type, Stein and Hardenberg, could not satisfactorily be compassed in an essay, while the lowly peasant has left little or no individual record. The fact that the four figures selected came to hold similar views leads one to accept the further use of types, that of a nationalistic situation and that of a process of nationalism. The idea of nationalism, if one may employ the term "idea" in Meinecke's sense of a living, molding cultural force, has exercised its own power over varied persons and conditions and put its stamp upon them. The first chapter contains an endeavor to describe this idea and the situation in which it flourishes. While the generalizations in it are drawn from these and other studies, they do not pretend to definitiveness and are offered as the frame of reference for the author's thought. Nathusius, burgher and businessman, represents liberalism rather than nationalism; whereas Frederick William III, a king, and Marwitz, an aristocratic country squire and army officer, typify the *ancien régime* which nationalism was supplanting.

The author does not mean to imply that all philosophers, folklorist-historians, poets, and officers turned nationalists, or that kings and aristocrats opposed the new ideal and businessmen were indifferent to it; he is endeavoring to show how in a situation of cultural crisis at the beginning of the nineteenth century certain elements in occupation, caste, or class contributed toward or against a person's development into nationalism. The historical course of events, that is, the unique factors in each life, must likewise be taken into account. And, in the end, one must confess that he does not know why these figures acted with respect to nationalism as they did; one can only describe the fact and explain some of the conditions affecting it.

The bibliography lays no claim to completeness. Using primarily the sources, the author refers to only those secondary works which were especially helpful. He has read more works than he cites.

These essays constitute a by-product of a year's work in Germany in 1930-1931 made possible by a fellowship from the Social Science Research Council. The author wishes to express his thanks to that institution for making this study possible. He feels likewise a deep gratitude to his colleague, Professor Ernst Correll, and to his wife, Dr. Pauline R. Anderson. The value of their criticism and encouragement cannot be adequately acknowledged.

E. N. A.

Washington, D. C.
October, 1939

CONTENTS

NATIONALISM AND THE CULTURAL CRISIS IN PRUSSIA, 1806-1815

I. NATIONALISM AND THE NATIONALISTIC SITUATION

NATIONALISM is devotion to the nation in an intense degree. It means the cultivation of feeling for the nation-group and the subordination of the individual to the interest of that group. While it endeavors to enrich, not to say perfect, the life of the individual by merging him into the nation, it approves of individualism only in so far as it serves the nation. It exalts the welfare and glory of the nation as the end and goal and criterion of all human and divine endeavor. The nation takes on those attributes usually associated with God and Heaven; it assumes superhuman qualities and becomes eternal.

Although nationalism arises out of feeling for the nation, the two manifestations can be distinguished. Love of nation characterizes the normal course of European history, particularly since the late eighteenth century; and, although it is felt in different degrees depending upon the individual and the situation, it does not renounce the sense of devotion to or defeat activity for other than national interests. The individual marries, rears a family, worships God, power, or money, and seeks congenial groups for his leisure hours. He is a practicing pluralist who divides his affection between those persons and institutions which come within the orbit of his daily life. Among them he will sometimes find the nation, which he loves comfortably, resignedly, tolerantly, sometimes ardently, as he does his business or his wife. He is not a nationalist, for he does not regard the nation as the supreme object of his loyalty. He remains a citizen who, in his capacity as private individual, adjusts his life to fortune and does not become exclusively or predominantly nation-minded.

Nationalism must be differentiated from other and often competing forms of group loyalty. A person may give his main allegiance to a monarch, a caste, a religion, a state, a family, a race, a corporation, or another business form. He may believe passionately in liberalism, democracy, socialism, communism, or some other variety of collectivism. In case he is primarily bound to one of these institutions or fundamentally dedicated to one of these ideals, he cannot be a nationalist, for he does not bestow most or all of his love upon the nation. He turns it toward some other social form or ideal and must be called, as the case may be, a corporation-ist, a church-ist, a family-ist, a liberal-ist, and so on. He may combine any of these loyalties with love of nation; but if he places any of them above or even on a par with the national good, he cannot be regarded as a nationalist. He may employ some of the terminology of nationalism for defending or furthering his primary interest or may adopt some of its ideology without thereby accepting its obligations. The person who misuses nationalistic phraseology for selfish purposes can be distinguished from the nationalist by ascertaining the motives for his concern about the nation and by perceiving the extent to which he is willing to sacrifice his private interests for the good of the nation. He cannot merely assert that supreme devotion to the nation includes supreme devotion to liberalism or a corporation. Nationalism entails a large degree of opportunism in the choice of instruments. The nationalist must be willing to utilize every means for the furtherance of the nation, and if liberalism or a corporation does not meet the test it must be crushed and replaced by another instrument which will.

Whereas love of nation has become a usual manifestation, taking precedence over the former love of ruler, locality, province or state, nationalism has been the product of cultural crises. During the past century and a half nationalism has arisen in society when the slow conflict involved in the transition from one culture to another is brought to a head by some general disaster caused by a foreign enemy. Love of nation has grown as the individual has found himself more closely tied to the nation-state, as the number of problems demanding public solution has augmented. It has spread with democracy and the increasing complexity of organized living. From a time when few persons felt any relation to the nation, European society has reached a period in which almost everyone depends more or less on public authority and is therefore group-conscious. Popular education, the printing press, and other means of disseminating information, compulsory military service, industrialism, and the facilities for quick and cheap travel and transportation, have pulled the members of a nation closely together, and the expansion of governmental services has taught and enabled them to employ collective, national action. The growth of national feeling has been paralleled by that of nationalism; although there have been few nationalists, they have increased with the number of those conscious of the value of the nation. Since the last century and a half have been as a whole a period of rapid cultural change, especially in Europe, the number of crises generating nationalism has been large. The sense of nation has grown so acute that the distinction between normal devotion to the nation and abnormal manifestation of it, or nationalism, has dimmed.

The society in which nationalism arises may roughly be divided into three large groups, the conservative defenders of the existing social order, the center holding to what it has while advocating the initiation of certain fundamental reforms, the proponents of complete cultural transformation. The first group consists usually of those at the top of the social order who are content with the *status quo*. It will adhere to a psychology, metaphysics, and social philosophy appropriate to its conservatism and fundamentally opposed to those of the third group. Although accepting those aspects of the new ideology that appear useful to it, this group defends tenaciously the institutional structure and the existing balance of social forces. It may manifest love of nation but never nationalism; for nationalism demands the sacrifice of institutions in favor of others more able to promote the welfare of the nation. The second group embraces diverse elements. In it are to be found the many special interests which understand and advocate in the main only those new ideals favorable to them; but this group, whether consciously or unconsciously, has moved out of the old milieu into the new one. The members share in common the desire for freedom, but will disagree over the amount of it, the restrictions to be abolished, and the guarantees of freedom to be set up. Subject to intellectual and emotional limitations and guided by material interests more than by ideals, they will be unable to perceive the composite meaning of all the new ideals. They will compromise and partake in varying degrees of the interests and ideals of the conservatives and the radicals. They will, depending on native ability, education, and circumstances, love the nation, again in varying degrees, without becoming nationalists; but in case of desperation, they may approach nationalism very closely. The third group, the nationalists, comprises those who wish to reform society according to the pattern of a model culture. They act as the advance guard in the process of love of nation and its concomitant, the collectivization of society, although some of them are more in advance than others and few approach the ideal type of Hitler. Their opportunity to be effective occurs only when a crisis upsets the second group and forces it to comprehend the value of quick reforms in accordance with more of the nationalists' ideals than it would otherwise accept at one time, when a much larger proportion of the population than is ordinarily the case becomes concerned about public affairs and needs and demands a public solution for its problems. The nationalist is a person who, living in a period of social transition, desires to reform thoroughly the structure and spirit of society and who is stirred to ardent and vigorous reformistic endeavor in his nation by the menace to his ideals from a foreign enemy. He becomes a nationalist when he perceives in a crisis that the nation must be saved as an instrument for realizing his ideals. He lives for the future, the middle group essentially for the present, the conservative more for the past.

While not attempting at this point to explain the rise of devotion to the nation, one may distinguish between a character-nationalist and a situation-nationalist.[1] The two types cannot be precisely separated from one another; but the former, exempli-

[1] This distinction is adapted from Dr. Karen Horney, *The Neurotic Personality of Our Time* (New York, 1937).

fied by Hitler and to a less extent by Fichte and Arndt, represents the more extreme manifestation. Both types turn nationalistic in a crisis, that is, the former as well as the latter is nationalistic because of the situation; but the feeling of the character-nationalist for the group is the product of his personal difficulties extending over a long period of time and the immediate situation created by international conflict merely turns him to the nation-group. In the case of the situation-nationalist the preliminary preparation for excessive devotion to the nation-group is much less complete. Character-nationalism arises in those individuals acutely affected by the insecurity and uncertainty of the period of transition who become fearful, hypersensitive, emotional, restless, dissatisfied and inclined to impetuous action. Eager to be at ease and happy in society, they wish to reform it according to their needs. They seek aid and assurance from others and develop an unusual concern about the group. They try to balance their feeling of superfluity in the present order by a belief in their divine mission to save the world and lead it into a new culture; and having acquired the habit of insecurity and therefore of social criticism, they prefer to live in a dream world of the future rather than to endure the distasteful realities of the present. Uncertain of themselves and their purpose in life, they long for orientation and seek it by way of dogmatism, intolerance, and service to the group. They are exaltedly ambitious and fear that their great abilities are going to waste, that the development of their personality is being blocked. The discrepancy between ambition and achievement excites their fantasy, wherein they conceive a society appropriate to their genius. Their nationalism affords an escape from a society into which they do not fit.

In the period of social transition new opportunities open up and wants increase. Even conservatives recognize the value of certain new proposals, but at the same time they augment their resistance to fundamental change and accentuate the confusion. Conflict and competition grow in vigor and the example of the success of other nations in executing reforms or of members of one's own nation in breaking through existing obstructions spurs individuals to intense activity. Certain ones, however, may feel the strain acutely and desire aid from the group. They may endeavor to sublimate competition by demanding that everyone compete only in service to the group. Personal success must mean success in rendering more to the group than another. The individual transfers his private needs to the group and expects that at some future time the group will satisfy them. Group-feeling becomes a way of postponing the day of material contentment without acknowledging one's inability to achieve happiness in the present. Above all group-feeling gives a sense of freedom to the insecure individual devoting himself entirely to the whole. He feels himself to be powerful beyond all limits; his inferiority complex is overcome. He knows that he has the aid of millions of brothers; their strength being his, he can accomplish anything.

In its initial stage a period of cultural transition produces individualism, for each active person must cultivate his abilities without much direction by precedent. Individualism in this social situation encourages the use of reason, which by nature tends toward egocentricity. When the individual applies reason to existing conditions of society, he finds so much to condemn that he is inclined to repudiate the age and to formulate a new social ideal. The contrast between actuality and ideal stirs him to strive to achieve a new society; but in order to do so he learns that reason does not suffice. If he fails to reach more than pseudo rationalism, his disillusionment sets in quickly. Furthermore, as the period of transition continues, danger and uncertainty grow; the individual's mistrust of reason receives continual confirmation, until he decides that human reason cannot guide him with accuracy, in fact, that it offers a poor compass in an uncharted sea. Not knowing what the future will bring and wishing for help, he substitutes for the guidance of reason that of emotions and finds that feelings have the added advantage of offering a means of firm and secure union between himself and the group. He reverts to elemental traits, warmth, love, enthusiasm, naïveté, qualities of the child which in a mature person permit mystical union with an outside force. Being at a level attainable by everyone, these emotions enable all members of the group to feel alike. The individual discovers that certainty and assurance are arrived at by way of the emotions rather than reason. Having exaggerated rationalism and individualism, he goes to the other extreme and seeks to lose himself in something greater than himself, a group. Thereby he rediscovers the penumbral parts of himself, the subconscious areas of mind and feeling relating to group life and regains strength. He enriches his personality while merging himself in a whole. Since he is crossing social frontiers in an era of transition, he longs for group support, which can be had only by way of the emotions. He sympathizes with the masses because he feels that he and they as underdogs face enormous odds. In them he seeks allies who, being fellow sufferers, will understand him in his efforts to create a new society. He claims their sympathy in the same way that he gives them his and deduces from the community of feeling an infallible right to guide them.

The qualities of a character-nationalist are ingrained by years of experience in the slow and difficult process of social transition. The character becomes permanently affected. The case of the situation-nationalist, exemplified by Gneisenau, is different. While the latter undoubtedly shows some effects of the uncertainties of the period, he preserves a degree of the realism of the middle group. The ideals and habits which the character-nationalist acquires over a long period of years are aroused in the situation-nationalist more by the exigencies of a sharp international crisis threatening his existence and that of the group. When in this crisis the character-groupist concentrates his excessive group-feeling upon the nation and becomes a nationalist, he discovers an ally in the situation-nationalist. The qualities of the character-nationalist become those of the situation and are imposed by it upon the situation-nationalist. The two types of nationalists blame the existing social order for the defeat and believe that the crisis cannot be met by palliatives but that, in order to stimulate the desire to fight and to provide the appropriate means for doing so, thorough reforms must be inaugurated. They are encouraged to think so by the loss of morale among the conservatives themselves because of their failure to defend the country. The nationalists perceive that to defeat the powerful enemy the group must fight as one and feel as one, that it is composed of brothers and that God is on its side. They both realize that the emotions must be so excited as to induce man to risk his life, that rationalism and mere knowledge are inadequate to life, that the individuals must love their fellow members of the group and hate the enemy, that any means is legitimate in the fight. They both judge all competition in terms of service to the group and wish to imbue all members of the group with ideals for the future that are worth defending. They both maintain that each person must be freed from existing bonds in order to develop himself fully and serve the group with all his abilities, that each must cultivate his will power and initiative and be active, that a moral regeneration must occur.

The difference between the two types of nationalists grows out of the difference in personality and social background. The character-nationalist, embittered at his own group for neglecting him, finds the enemy a convenient object upon which to vent his double anger; the situation-nationalist hates the enemy alone. In contrast to the former, the situation-nationalist disclaims any divine power or mission for himself or the nation, but agrees with his more exalted colleague that God is helping their nation. The character-nationalist knows little of politics or public affairs and runs easily to extremes; the situation-nationalist relies upon more practical means for overcoming the enemy than the character-nationalist and knows that ideals must be instrumentalized. He puts his trust in this generation, refusing to believe that it is too thoroughly corrupt to overcome the enemy. He does not share the character-nationalist's ultimate solace, the power of education to transform the young, who will then save society. For the defense of the group he is willing to coöperate even with opponents of his reform program, and is far less dogmatic than the character-nationalist. Once the situation which produces nationalism is eliminated, the situation-nationalist returns to normal acceptance of the *status quo,* subject to slow, peaceful reform, while the character-nationalist seeks some other instrument than the nation for realizing his ideals.

Since group-feeling does not necessarily mean national feeling, the question arises as to why devotion to the nation-group.

The explanation varies slightly with circumstances; but common to all nationalistic situations is the threat of destruction by some foreign power of the culture of the entire nation, its political, economic, and social organization, its language and achievements in literature, the arts and knowledge, its morals and ideals. The unity of the nation is perceived through the unity of its cultural heritage, whether the basis stressed be language or blood. In case the nation is divided into states, the lines of separation are quickly obliterated, for culture is a national and not a state creation. The states within the nation being too weak to cope with the enemy, the individual seeks the support of the next largest practical and natural group, the nation. The nationalist regards the state as merely an instrument for preserving and furthering the national culture. He is not a state-ist but a nationalist. The state bears for him the character of something artificial, man-made, whereas the nation seems to have been an organic growth. To the nationalist the state lacks the biological-historical unity and the mystical qualities of the nation. The members of the nation seem to be a blood-brotherhood; the members of a state seem forced into union by accident or policy irrespective of whether they belong together. The nation can be the object of the deepest emotion, common to all its members; the emotional response to the state is based on some calculation of self-interest. In an elemental situation of danger both character-groupist and situation-groupist turn to the elemental group, the nation.

Nationalism arose at the end of the eighteenth century in rebellion against the forces within the nation hostile to it, absolutism and caste. It hated both for restricting the freedom of the individual to serve himself and the nation. Neither absolutism nor caste held out much inducement to the lower classes to further the national culture and defend the existing society in which they played so humble a role. Absolutism and caste allowed some freedom to the individual within caste lines but not on the broad plane of the nation; they interposed allegiances prior to those of the nation. The nationalist demanded that these be abolished. Instead of privilege, he asserted the right of each person to equal opportunities; instead of docile subjects, each person must become an aggressive, active citizen eager to participate in public affairs of the nation. Instead of rights, there must be duties to the nation. The mercenary army must be replaced by a national army, irresponsible government by responsible rule, private education by national education, cosmopolitan or provincial culture by national culture, private or mercantile economy by national economy, private charity by national obligation. The criterion for social action must change completely. The social scale must be determined no longer by birth but by service to the nation. The king at most might say, "I am the first servant of the nation," provided he were; if he were not, he should be forcibly subjected to the nation's will or eliminated.

Hostile to any interest disadvantageous to the nation, nationalism disliked in turn liberalism, its ally in the overthrow of absolutism and caste. They coöperated for a time only because of opposition to common enemies and adherence to a superficially similar ideal of freedom, that is, particularly in the early phase of the nationalistic process when nationalists like the four analyzed here were, in different degrees, inclined to identify freedom with their ideal. Between Fichte, the most extreme of the four figures, whose social beliefs were close to those of liberalism, and Hitler, who detests this bourgeois force, lies a century of the process of nationalism, during which the essential antagonism between the two ideals has become apparent. Nationalism has come to reject flatly the cosmopolitan elements of liberalism, its rationalism, individualism, emphasis upon rights, suspicion of group-authority. Liberalism may suit the rootless intellectual and the businessman capable of readjustment to any situation, but the nationalist denies that it can defend a group weakened by internal conflicts and menaced by foreign threats. Liberalism inclines toward cool compromise, while the nationalist asserts that there are situations in which society can be saved only by the power of ecstatic group action. The liberal believes in freedom as a rational, absolute right of the individual which should be infringed upon as little as possible by a central authority and never beyond certain broad limits. For the nationalist the concept of freedom acquired meaning during a social crisis when the individual could survive and develop his powers only in intimate coöperation with the group. Freedom became not merely an individual right but a social one, and for the sake of individual and group the rights of the individual as conceived by the liberal had to be sharply curbed. The individual must find freedom in devoting himself entirely to the group. He must live not as he wished but as the group wished, or rather the authority controlling the group; he gained freedom by obeying group authority. This is the Hegelian conception of freedom applied to the nation instead of the state. A product of a time of social stress, it reflects the need of society in a period of this kind.

Nationalism, particularly character-nationalism, grew as orthodox Christianity declined, replacing the latter with belief in a mystical experience of its own. It is significant that nationalism arose immediately after the Enlightenment and that it first acquired a stronghold among the continental peoples most influenced by the Enlightenment, the French and the Protestants of North and Central Germany. Superficially nationalism and Christianity share common ideals. Both denounce vigorous individualism, adhering to a conception of freedom which curbs it and sets a goal above the welfare of the individual in present time and space. They both preach love, fraternity, self-sacrifice, devotion to a savior, and both endeavor to unite feeling and reason. Both assert the duty of being "my brother's keeper." Both acquire moral regeneration, constantly watch to preserve the faith, and strive to satisfy similar wants in man. But these analogous qualities and ideals should not conceal the fundamental difference. Orthodox Christianity places its heaven, the objective of man's striving, in the next world; nationalism seeks its heaven on earth in the perfect nation. Christianity works to save men's souls for the next world; nationalism devotes its efforts to saving the nation for this world. Christianity offers a divine savior; nationalism wishes human saviors filled with divine power. Christianity preaches resignation, meekness, humility, peace, and forgiveness; nationalism arouses pride, the will to act, hatred, vengeance, and war. Christianity preaches universal virtues and regards all men as equal in the sight of God; provided men believe in Christ, it accepts them irrespective of birth, race, nationality, or any other condition. The nationalist approves only of national virtues and devotes his attention only or primarily to members of his nation. He believes in a chosen people, and maintains that God is not a universal Deity for individuals but a God of his nation. Christianity is a missionary religion for all mankind; nationalism seeks to convert in the first line the members of the nation, but it thinks that because God works through this nation, it must carry its ideals to other nations, if necessary by the sword, and guide them into a new era. Then all mankind will be organized into nations, naturally with the mother nation still leading and perhaps controlling the destinies of the others. Nationalism is optimistic about the nature of man and society; orthodox Christianity holds that man is born in sin and cannot progress. The practices and beliefs of Christianity conform to the needs for realizing the ideal of salvation in the next world; those of nationalism derive from the task of saving the nation in this world. Through nationalism the individual who has lost his faith in orthodox Christianity will satisfy his emotional need of belief in the future, in the eternal, in the salvation of the individual by self-sacrifice for the nation. Orthodox Christianity regards this sinful life as hardly worth struggling over, and promises solace in the eternal rewards of the next world. These rewards are of little use to the nationalist, eager to defend his nation. If he were an orthodox Christian he would not be so determined to act on his own behalf. He needs God on his side, fighting in the unequal battle against the nationalist's enemies both within and without the nation's frontiers. Nationalism becomes a new mystery religion: the Kingdom of Heaven is among the nationalists, in this world. Service to the nation justifies every act; martyrs for the nation will live forever; divine revelation comes through the history of the nation; national leaders are the new saviors; the mysterious union of God, the national leaders and the nation, of spirit and matter takes place. In this age of democracy and collectivism the idea of salvation through the God-man gives way to that of salvation through the God-group, the nation. The nationalist believes literally in the assertion, "The Kingdom of Heaven is within you." By "you" he means the nation. He applies to the nation the Christian injunction, "He who will save his life must lose it"—for the nation. The Beatitudes are replaced by *Mein Kampf;* Christ by Hitler.

II. FICHTE

THE history of nationalism teems with intellectuals or pseudo intellectuals who seek to impose their ideals upon the nation. The function and role of the intellectual have been especially notable in the early period of nationalism, but from Fichte to Mazzini to Barrès to Masaryk to Hitler, from the first to the last nationalistic outburst, ideologues and idealists have exerted a profound influence. It should be clear that not all intellectuals tend toward nationalism. Many merely criticize society; others are loyal to the *status quo* or some other régime, often as passionately as the nationalist to the nation. In the degree to which the intellectual turns nationalist, he rejects the essential basis of his way of life, reliance on human reason, and becomes devoted to national reform rather than to the pursuit of clear thinking. Furthermore, to turn nationalist the intellectual must possess an acute social sense; if he studies geology or physics he will not be so receptive to the forces leading into nationalism as the ethicist or historian or folklorist or poet. His nationalism will appear, if at all, particularly in times of cultural crisis; whether the crisis is real or imagined by him does not matter.

Within these wide limits the susceptibility of certain intellectuals or pseudo intellectuals to nationalism remains a fact. They possess qualities which under appropriate circumstances and in the right type of personality may lead them into nationalism. The intellectual in question serves as an advance guard of the social process, feeling out or peering into the future and striving for something better. His tools are ideas, by means of which he sets up criteria for his own society and its future course. Being less related to the material world than others, he is more willing to dare the uncertainties of the future by executing these ideas, and his restless mind urges him to do so. His vested interest, so to speak, lies in experimentation, for thereby alone can he arouse original thoughts. If he can look backward for confirmation of that which he wishes to be accomplished in the future, that is, if he is historically minded, he enhances his longing for creative action. As one who deals in ideas he is able to grasp the fact and significance of the whole, in this case the nation, before other more earthy-minded men; his tendency toward abstraction assists him. Since he devotes his energies to things cultural, a threat to this culture menaces him first. His sensitivity to events affecting it is greater than that of other members of society, and in case of danger to it he becomes more alarmed. Then he helps to awaken the others to defense. But the crisis also arouses his zest for action, because it affords him an opportunity to learn something, perhaps to carry out some of his ideas. He rushes to the front. By virtue of the fact that he is a speaker and writer, he regards himself as a public leader and wishes an audience. He comes naturally to the belief that he is indispensable to society; he seeks a following for his ideals and discovers quickly the possibilities of the nation for this purpose. Since he reads widely and perhaps travels, he learns before his fellow countrymen do what is transpiring abroad and is the first of his nation to be aware of the difference between its cultural level and that of others. The spur of foreign example sets him to reforming; the threat of foreign domination makes him ashamed of his people. Its culture being his, the two rise or fall together; and, as the intellectual is above all proud of his mind and his accomplishments, he wishes a proud and glorious nation. So he borrows, molds, and reshapes for his own people elements taken from foreign cultures and turns into a reformer in order to spread these and his own indigenously national ideals among it. His sensitiveness admirably fits him for the role of nationalist and he easily assumes it. The relationship may be summed up as follows: Given an insecure personality in a cultural crisis, real or imagined, with intellectual interests of a decided social content, intellectualism in Europe since the French Revolution has easily become transformed into nationalism. The example of Fichte brings out the relationship in clear form.

Johann Gottlieb Fichte was born in 1762 in a country village in Saxony. His parents were artisans scarcely differentiated from the surrounding peasantry. Because of his excellent memory the boy Fichte attracted the attention of a local aristocrat, who provided for his early education. After living and studying for several years with a Lutheran minister, he transferred at the age of thirteen to a famous school near Naumburg. Fichte frequently suffered here at the hands of the officials of the school, who were often petty tyrants. At the same time he had an opportunity to associate with boys of the upper classes from whom he learned the ways of gentlemanly conduct. From Naumburg he went in 1780 to the University of Jena to study theology. Before and after he completed his degree he had to earn his livelihood by serving as tutor in private families, and his struggle with poverty at times became so acute that he scarcely had enough to eat and could seldom purchase books and clothes.

Some years later after Fichte had succeeded in establishing himself as a university professor his younger brother asked him for assistance in making his way into the intellectual world of the upper class. Fichte replied by describing the difficulties in the path of social ascent. He spoke of the necessity for learning the classical languages, emphasized the trouble which his brother would encounter in pronunciation, first, because the vocal organs of a person of his years were more fixed than in a child, but, secondly, because he spoke the Saxon dialect in its most corrupt form, that of Upper Lausitz.

Even though I left the region in my early childhood [he wrote] I have had trouble in so purifying my German pronunciation that my native land cannot be distinguished. You will never be able to. Because of this mother tongue, I have never been able to speak French correctly. . . . Another main point is the more refined conduct of society which is now necessary for an intellectual wishing to belong to the upper class and not to remain among the common educated handworkers. This is becoming increasingly necessary. . . . Whoever fails in this respect becomes ludicrous, just because the superior power of the intellectual is regarded with disfavor. . . . You cannot conceive this at all because it lies entirely outside your sphere.

Refined conduct cannot be learned after one is grown; for the impressions of early training are ineradicable. (One no longer notices my conduct, perhaps; that is a result of my early life in Miltitz's home and in Schulpforta among mostly better reared children, my early dancing lessons, and so forth. Nevertheless, even after I left the university some peasant traits remained with me, which much traveling, serving as tutor in different areas and homes, and, especially, the most careful self-observation have eliminated. And I do not know whether even now they are entirely gone.) . . .

First of all you must improve your physical appearance and your manners. Before you have done this I cannot allow you to visit me, because you would put me in a bad light at the university among the students. Also you must test whether your memory and your tongue can handle languages. This may require a couple of years. Above all you need an instructress rather than a teacher. To instill good manners in a young man, the female sex is indispensable. Furthermore, you must live in a city. . . . You must certainly learn to dance. After you are so cultivated that you can appear in society without giving offense, I shall take you in my home and then consider what is possible. But whether you will ever get that far is the question. . . .

You err when you believe that the cost will be small, for you consider that matter from one side alone, that of book-learning. Even on this point you do not realize how much there is to learn of which you have absolutely no conception. Learning is the easiest part; the question is one of your entire deportment; to learn that takes time and money in proportion to the lack of it.[1]

In letters to his brother Fichte portrayed the hardships of his own case. He was a parvenu and felt this all his life, struggling incessantly to overcome the deficiencies of background. The series of self-examinations, especially in the first half of his life, revealed the constant attention which he paid to the question of his social adjustment. In a sense he became decidedly a "social climber," throughout his life he was a democrat more in theory than in practice. Although advocating universal education, he never appealed to the masses and accepted the fact of cultural differences. His pride and sensitiveness, his zest for controversy,

[1] *J. G. Fichtes Briefwechsel* (Gesammelt und herausgegeben von Hans Schulz, Leipzig, 1925), I, 383-85.

above all his colossal egotism may be regarded in part as results of an effort to compensate for his social insecurity. His conception of education as character-building, shared by many others in this period of social transition, may be traced to the same source.

Fichte might never have become a famous professor if he had not been tremendously energetic and aggressive. These qualities gave him self-confidence and supported an exalted ambition. "I will go very high or will lose everything," he wrote to his parents in 1790. In the same year he expressed his ultimate hope in Providence, trusting that God would enable him to find the truth and a proper place to use it in this world. This faith inspired him with the zeal necessary for making history. "The main object of my life is to develop, not my mind . . . , but my character in every way which fate allows," he wrote. "I search for the course of Providence in my own life. . . . I believe in a guiding Providence and I take note of its hints." [2] This trust in Providence enhanced his self-confidence. He wrote to a friend as follows:

> You know that I have had a good deal of confidence in my luck and my powers. Through experience, especially in the last two years, this confidence has become so strong that I consider impossible nothing which I firmly will. God preserve this confidence in myself and my health, which seems very good . . . , and I shall tremble before nothing.[3]

Even in the face of financial distress Fichte expressed confidence. When he had reached twenty-eight years of age, he still lacked a secure post. His initial ambition and that of his family had lain in the ministry and he had studied theology with this in view. But theology enticed him into philosophy and that into doubt until the Saxon government rejected his request for a post as pastor. He needed money to embark upon an academic career, and free-lance writing offered at best an insecure income. Consequently, he continued to find casual employment as a private family tutor, while his brilliant mind and restless, ambitious soul

[2] *Ibid.*, I, 103, 60, 62.
[3] *Ibid.*, I, 93.

chafed at their bonds. Although his tutorial position had aided him in acquiring cosmopolitan manners, its disadvantages outweighed the positive gains. One family tried to compel him, as he put it, to be "a slave to their children." He must devote his entire time to them, the master warned him, and not waste it in reading, writing, or visiting friends. Another vital question for his consideration was that of the social relationship between him and his employers and their guests. Fichte worked out a code of conduct in which he tried to strike a balance between equality and subservience. He sought to be neither peer nor servant, to be present but invisible except when someone wanted to see him, to make no approaches, to speak only when addressed. It is from cases such as his that one perceives why men of the lower classes in the eighteenth century craved liberty and equality. In the year in which the French Revolution broke out Fichte expressed to a friend his disgust with the role of teacher "of the tender sprouts of *petit-bourgeois* or of narrow little *Krautjunker*, by whom after one has taught them the alphabet one is dismissed."[4] Yet, try as he might, he could obtain no pastorate or any other work except that of this hated profession. In the intervals between employments, he borrowed money wherever he could, pawned his own clothing, and, in one instance, the garments of a friend. In Königsberg in 1791, finding no friend to whom he could appeal, he almost reached the end of his resources. Kant and a kindly pastor succeeded at the last moment in obtaining for him another appointment as private tutor. When at the end of the engagement he returned to his fiancée in Zurich—whom he was able to marry because of her private income—he possessed nothing except a deep dissatisfaction with society, a love of freedom, a restless ambition and a mind fermenting with philosophical ideas.

In 1790 Fichte disclosed a frame of mind which might easily lead to the life of a reformer. He wrote to a friend, "I wish not merely to *think;* I want to *act*. . . . I have only one passion, one need, one complete feeling of myself, that is, to work for humanity. The more I do, the happier I feel."[5] Every factor

[4] *Ibid.*, I, 46.
[5] *Ibid.*, I, 61-62.

seemed to encourage Fichte's development along this line. Nature and personal hardships made him aggressive in the defense of his interests and ideas. His reading in the works of Montesquieu, Rousseau, and particularly in the popular pedagogical writing of Pestalozzi and many others provided him with an emotionalized picture of the reforms to be achieved. In addition, his theological training, by making him intimate with God and dogma and assuring him of the existence of absolute truth and of man's ability to discover it, had elevated his self-confidence to the point where he believed himself a prophet. To the end of his days Fichte remained essentially a reformer.

Life dealt so severely with Fichte that he never acquiesced in the existence of an ordinary burgher. Having fought against hardships from his earliest youth, he acquired the habit of resisting and, when circumstances were not contrary, he made them so. He was bluntly honest in a society devoted to etiquette and flattery. When Fichte engaged in a conversation, he became serious and vehement, pressing his opponents, who, particularly if they were aristocrats, refused to be disturbed by things of the intellect and disliked the vulgar strenuousness of such a moralist. Fichte proved troublesome everywhere, often becoming a nuisance. Even his wife hinted that he was temperamental. She tried to soften his imperious and impetuous ways, but with no apparent success. Instead of sympathizing with her troubles, Fichte wrote her, "You should not have married an unusual man." [6] Unfortunately he was almost devoid of a sense of humor to counterbalance his social shortcomings. Since he wished to be a model for humanity, he never forgot himself and his purpose. From his early years his self-consciousness had been feeding his ego until by the time he suddenly secured a professorship, he was ready to tilt his wings at a high angle. Five years in this exalted position convinced the artisan's son of his indispensability to society.

Equally lacking in Fichte was the capacity for contentment. He was never satisfied with himself, with the society in which

[6] *Ibid.*, II, 183.

he lived, with the place or the age. His biography consists of a series of ardent, short-lived friendships followed by as ardent animosities, of enthusiasm about a place and its society and immediate disgust with them. The population of each town or city in which he lived grew repugnant to him. The same restlessness and dissatisfaction with society appeared in his writings and, in fact, made his nationalism possible. Dissatisfaction with one's immediate environment leads to dissatisfaction with the world at large. Fichte perceived a field of activity for his reforming zeal and came to regard the nation as a natural unit with which to begin world betterment. His social maladjustment helps to explain his greatness. The discrepancy between his birth and position, character and training, hopes and actualities induced him to endeavor to transform society in accordance with his ideals rather than to adopt the easy life of his more fortunate contemporaries. It led him to strive for a society in which he would be a perfectly adjusted member. The fact of Fichte's becoming a nationalist is not thereby fully explained. He might have turned his energies to another sphere of reform such as the church, the guild, the local community. The question of why he devoted his efforts to the nation must be asked after further elements conditioning his life have been considered.

In 1788 Fichte, still a wandering tutor, spent a sleepless night writing down some random thoughts. The resulting document proves that Fichte's character and experiences fixed the essentials of his philosophy before he had read Kant and before he had the encouraging example of the French Revolution. In it he pictured society as corrupt. He found the position of women low, the upper classes tyrannical, especially to the peasants, mankind in misery and decline, laws inadequate and absurd, religion disregarded, understanding in eternal conflict with the heart and with morality.

Would there not be place for a book [he asked] which would portray the complete depravity of our governments and customs, both from its ludicrous and from its horrible side, a book which without exaggeration would express the necessary results of this and which would outline principles of better government and better customs and the means of achieving them? [7]

There followed a summary of the main points which he would make in this book. Under the heading, "The Condition of Knowledge," he wrote, "Speculations about unnecessary things and neglect of the generally useful. Nonsense of the merely speculative intellectual without knowledge of the world and of men." [8] The memorandum formulated the problem with which Fichte wrestled for the rest of his life: society as it was versus society as it should be. At times even the details were identical with, or at least similar to, those of his later works. His criticism of existing society, his objection to mere speculation without any practical bearing, and his deep concern, not with the individual as such, but with him as a member of the social group, remained the same throughout his entire life. The three points almost contain the gist of the ripe Fichte—the will to reform, the growing inclination to formulate a set of ideals for which to work, a keen appreciation of the value of the group. They afforded the means of developing him into a nationalist. In the main this document expressed the aversions of a young man; the positive deductions from his condemnation remained as yet undrawn. But the principles in accordance with which they were to be drawn were implicit in these thoughts. They can be summed up fairly well in the famous slogan of liberty, equality and fraternity.

In 1789 came the French Revolution. In 1790, almost by accident, Fichte discovered Kant. These two events brought about a revolution in Fichte's thinking, which led to the formulation of his own system of thought. The effects of the two upon him were practically inseparable. When Fichte began to study Kant's philosophy, he proclaimed the fact in exalted phrases:

Since reading the *Kritik der praktischen Vernunft* I live in a new world. Statements which I believed were irrefutable have been overthrown; things which I thought would never be proved, for example, the concept of an absolute freedom, of duty, etc., have been

[7] *Ibid.*, I, 11-12.
[8] *Loc. cit.*

proved, and I feel all the happier. It is incredible what regard for humanity, what strength this system gives us.

A few pages further he continued:

I now believe with all my heart in the freedom of man and perceive that only with this belief are duty, virtue, in fact, any ethics at all possible. . . . It is, furthermore, clear to me that results extremely harmful to society proceed from the acceptance of the principle of determinism and that the great moral depravity of the so-called better classes mainly flows from this source.[9]

Fichte was so stirred by the Kantian philosophy that for a time he planned to devote his life to its propagation, attributing to it the same social value as to religion. He traced the "humiliation and degradation" of mankind back to a deficient feeling for the ego, which, he wrote,

is the basis and the creator of all sublime feelings. And here, I believe, lies the true service of the Kantian philosophy. It elevates the soul; I will assert without previous investigation that anyone who shows a trace of petty egoism has not yet plumbed the depths of this philosophy. It is still a small seed; but it will and must become a tree which will give shade to all humanity. It will produce a new, nobler, worthier race.[10]

Kant's philosophy confirmed for Fichte the belief that the concept of freedom should be made the focal point of a philosophical system. In a letter of 1793 Fichte wrote to Kant:

My soul is afire with a great thought—to solve the task set by the following statement out of the *Kritik der reinen Vernunft:* "The idea of a constitution affording the greatest human freedom in accordance with laws which enable each freedom to exist alongside other freedoms is necessary not only to the first draft of a state constitution but to all laws."[11]

This assertion posed but one problem connected with a philosophy of freedom, but it reveals the line of thought which Fichte followed and his wholehearted devotion to the ideal. Kant gave him

[9] *Ibid.,* I, 123, 142-43.
[10] *Ibid.,* I, 329.
[11] *Ibid.,* I, 275-76.

the philosophic justification for that which Fichte's natural inclination and his experiences had led him to desire, namely, freedom.

The first important work in which Fichte elaborated his ideal was, significantly enough, entitled *Beiträge zur Berichtigung der Urteile des Publikums über die französische Revolution, 1793.* To analyze completely the defense in this volume of Rousseau's Contract Theory would go beyond our present purpose. It is sufficient to note that the experiences of the French Revolution substantiated Fichte's objections to absolutism and supported his faith in freedom. In this volume he defined the objective of mankind as being the "culture toward freedom"; in this way, he said, humanity might achieve its higher spiritual purpose of complete harmony between its will and the law of reason. To attain cultural freedom it was necessary for individuals to participate actively in all those affairs which concerned them, including the destruction of absolutism. The effects which the execution of this doctrine would have had upon the society of Fichte's age were manifest, and Fichte drew attention to them frankly and bravely. They constituted later a part of his program of reform for the nation and will be considered in connection with the content of his nationalism.

Two years later, when Fichte was working on his *Wissenschaftslehre,* the chief exposition of his philosophy, he wrote to a person with French connections, asking for a stipendium from the French Republic until he had completed his philosophic study. Although the letter may never have been sent, it manifests the intimate bond between his philosophy and the French Revolution. His argument in favor of an annuity from the French government ran as follows:

> Mine is the first system of freedom. As that nation [the French] emancipated man from external chains, my system frees him from the bonds of the thing in itself, of the external influence, and establishes him as an independent being. It arose in inner struggle with myself, with all my deep-rooted prejudices, during the years in which it [the French nation] fought with external forces for political freedom and not without its [the French nation's] assistance. French

example encouraged me and developed in me the energy which was necessary for conceiving this system. While I was writing about the Revolution, the first hints of this system came to me. Thus my system already belongs in a sense to the nation, and the question is whether this nation will openly accept it by giving me the funds with which to erect it.[12]

Fichte was willing to write the work in Latin and, if France wished, to become a French citizen. While the hyperbolic devotion to the French Republic may have been caused in part by pecuniary considerations, Fichte's intellectual obligation to the French Republic should not be underestimated.

Fichte's wholehearted acceptance of Kant's philosophy depended upon the enthusiasm of fresh acquaintance; it was soon shaken by the writings of other men. A person of his independent character could never be reconciled to the role of unoriginal propagandist. His keen and active mind brought him into contact with the works of two opponents of Kantian philosophy, Maimon and a philosopher known under the pseudonym of "Nicodemus." The writings of these two men dispelled the Kantian charm and permitted Fichte to create his own body of thought. To follow out the ramified sources of his philosophy would be irrelevant for our purposes. Fichte himself declared that his temperament exercised great influence upon the character of his philosophy and that his system of thought had to satisfy both his head and his heart.

The qualities of preacher, theologian, democrat, and passionate activist were all sublimated into Fichte's philosophy. Freedom provided its keynote: freedom for the artisan's son, freedom for the hungry scholar, freedom for the humiliated private tutor, freedom as exalted by Kant and the French Revolution. But the artisan's son must struggle to gain and develop this freedom for himself and humanity; his philosophy must preach the necessity of doing as well as of thinking. Action and thought must assist and control each other, for by that union alone could the new era of freedom for Fichte and humanity be ushered in. Furthermore,

[12] *Ibid.*, I, 449-50.

one would scarcely expect him, a former theologian, an ardent reformer, an aggressive hothead to take his philosophy lightly. Fichte believed in it as an absolute truth. He alone had evolved a means, so he said, by which the will of God could be known to mankind, by which the ego might unite with the eternally unfolding deity in whom all life and all history were organically combined. He alone could answer the question: How can philosophy be made into a science as clear and certain as geometry? Fichte was convinced that in his *Wissenschaftslehre* he had succeeded where Kant had failed. When another philosopher protested against his dogmatic manner, he replied:

> My discovery seems to me true and important, but it never occurs to me to ascribe credit to myself for it or to say that Fichte created it. The age, nature, God made it. . . . The real discovery is—a fortunate inspiration, a stroke of genius. But to conceive that I, Fichte, am especially deserving because of this genius is a folly of which I was incapable even in my youth. . . .
>
> You say that the philosopher . . . should consider that he as an individual may err, that he can and must learn from others. Do you know . . . what attitude you are describing? That of a man who in his entire life has never been convinced of anything. . . . I am so certain of the principles of my system that as long as I remain sane I can never doubt them.[13]

These words seem more appropriate to an Old Testament prophet or to Luther than to a modern philosopher. A colleague, in fact, did call attention to the similarity between Fichte and the founder of Protestantism, and it seems indubitable that Fichte was conscious of the likeness. Both Fichte and Luther thought themselves to be vessels of divine truth, and both possessed the reformer's temperament. Like Luther, Fichte through the years worked out the practical applications of his philosophy, but unlike the former, he came more and more to assume the role of a new Messiah. He gave to his philosophy the function which he had formerly ascribed to the Kantian, that of entirely reforming culture. His ambition was, he wrote in 1793, "to justify my

[13] *Ibid.*, II, 267-69.

existence to humanity by deeds, to achieve for humanity and the entire spiritual world eternal results."[14] In a request for assistance to the Prussian government in 1804, he declared:

> For a short time a system has been in existence which is complete in its external form and which prides itself upon the fact that in itself it is complete, unchangeable and clear. Furthermore, it gives all other branches of knowledge their first principles and guiding lines and thus abolishes forever all strife and misunderstanding from the field of knowledge and unerringly directs the human spirit, which can be strengthened by it alone, into the only field of its progress, into ever greater clarity, the *Empirie*. If this discovery is what it claims to be, it will bring about an unprecedented regeneration of humanity and of all human relations.[15]

These words were written two years before Fichte became a nationalist. They are of the greatest significance in showing why he made that turn. With the increase of his devotion to his philosophy he felt a corresponding need for a proper means to implement it. This led him slowly to the discovery of the nation.

The change to nationalism might not have occurred without the impetus of the continued rough course of Fichte's personal history. After his appointment in 1794 to the chair of philosophy at Jena he felt his responsibility to God and to mankind more than before. The intellectual, he wrote in one of his books, must guide and inspire society, a role which he always attempted to fill literally. As an act of duty as well as of temperamental inclination he sought the vanguard. At Jena he immediately tried to put his teachings into social action, first, by holding popular lectures during the regular hours of worship on Sunday morning; second, by inducing the student clubs to give up their practices of fighting and drinking in favor of humanitarianism and liberty.

The story of Fichte's efforts at reform need not be repeated. It would include such items as broken windows, temporary retreat before the anger of students and the usual run of academic quarrels with students and colleagues. One episode alone deserves mention because of its effects upon Fichte's career. In 1799 he

[14] *Ibid.*, I, 266.
[15] *Ibid.*, II, 375.

aroused a religious controversy in which he was accused of atheism. He attacked with such Fichtean ardor that he offered the government good provocation for dismissing him. Neither religion nor philosophy caused his sudden fall; rather, the authorities disliked his fiery ways. As for Fichte himself, he contended that his democratic beliefs were responsible and interpreted his dismissal as an indication of rising reaction in Europe. Since he had long admired the French Republic, he thought of seeking refuge under it, but hesitated.

> Although no reasonable man [he wrote in 1799] can doubt that the principles upon which rest the French and similar republics are the only ones in which the dignity of humanity is upheld, nonetheless, it has been clearly evident that through arbitrariness on both sides the practices of the two opposing groups [Republican and monarchical] resemble each other. Indeed, the Republican often appears worse than the other. In this state of affairs I must regard it as risky to entrust myself to the Republic except in extreme necessity.[16]

Before he finished the letter, the news arrived of the assassination of the French representative at Rastatt. This made Fichte doubly certain that reaction was ruthlessly advancing and he continued in the same letter as follows:

> It is clear that from now on the French Republic alone can be the fatherland of an upright man . . . , since from now on not only the dearest hopes of humanity but even human existence depend upon its victory. . . . I dedicate myself and all my abilities to the Republic.[17]

Again in the same year he wrote:

> I am more than certain that if the French do not acquire a dominance and make changes in Germany, at least in a considerable portion of it, in a few years no one in Germany who is known to have practiced freedom of thought will have a haven. I am more than cer-

[16] *Ibid.*, II, 100.
[17] *Loc. cit.*

tain, therefore, that even if I find a corner somewhere, I shall be driven out within two years at the most.[18]

When Fichte made these remarks, he was negotiating for a position in a proposed German university to be established at Mainz, that is, in the German area controlled by the French. Although the plan for the school never took form, the event revealed Fichte's cosmopolitanism, or, to put it negatively, his indifference to the fate of his own nation.

In the eighteenth century the terms "patriotism" and "fatherland" were used without any particular feeling. Saxony was the state of his birth; but Fichte had traveled so widely over Germany and had so often encountered difficulty in finding a position that he had never acquired a special love for any spot. At most he belonged to the German Republic of Intellectuals (*Gelehrtenrepublik*), a company of self-confessed heroes of thought, who scorned the mob and magnified their own quarrels. Revolutionary France touched Fichte's heart and satisfied his judgment; she seemed to be the country of freedom, where Fichte's democratic aspirations were most likely to be fulfilled. She promised to be the state which should lead mankind into a new epoch. As a man, a philosopher, and a world-citizen he approved her.

The loss of his position at Jena had a deeper meaning for Fichte than the material result of economic insecurity. It struck him at a moment when the hope of winning disciples to his philosophy had begun to wane. He realized with anger that students persisted in misunderstanding him and in evolving their own systems. The sudden conclusion of his academic life forced Fichte to try a new method of gaining followers. He determined to renounce the pen in favor of the platform. From that date to the end of his life he continued to clarify the thought of his *Wissenschaftslehre* and endeavored particularly to popularize its social application. Of these series of public lectures, which will be discussed later, the most famous in chronological order were *Der geschlossene Handelsstaat* (1799), *Die Grundzüge des gegen-*

[18] *Ibid.*, II, 104.

wärtigen Zeitalters (1804-5), and their continuation in *Reden an die deutsche Nation* (1807-8). The three subjects were closely related. In the first series Fichte formulated for society the economic program which he repeated in the *Reden,* and in the *Grundzüge* he worked out the philosophy of history which later supported his faith in the advent of a nationalistic age.

After the personal crisis of 1799 Fichte's confidence in the value of his philosophy was deepened by an increased concern with religion. At the darkest periods of his career he sought profounder understanding of God and remained convinced that history proceeded toward his goal. Although he saw the practical realization of his philosophy postponed, he did not doubt that ultimate victory would be his. When one means failed, he tried another; when one support fell, he found a better; when the present denied him, he looked to the future. He grasped every chance, for his self-esteem was impregnable. In 1804 a Bavarian professor negotiated with him over the possibility of entering the service of that state. Fichte immediately proposed that the government establish a philosophers' school for him, writing as follows:

> This plan could perhaps be carried out without any assistance from a government; nonetheless, this is difficult. If an intelligent government would support it, that government, in my opinion, would gain undying fame and at the same time be a benefactor to mankind.[19]

Unfortunately, the Bavarian government did not aspire to "undying fame." The call failed to materialize and Fichte had to fall back upon his project of winning disciples through popular lectures.

During the winter of 1804-5 Fichte delivered in Berlin the first series of lectures of importance for showing how his devotion to his own philosophy led him into nationalism. His subject was *Die Grundzüge des gegenwärtigen Zeitalters.* The lectures proposed an interpretation of the past to explain why the phi-

[19] *Ibid.,* II, 385

losophy of freedom was not being accepted. Soon after Fichte had lost his position at Jena, because, so he thought, of his democracy, France succumbed to the despotism of Napoleon. France had therefore rejected this philosophy which in Germany was being ignored. Fichte's fate, that of the French Revolution, and that of their common philosophy seemed identical. In both its abstract and its practical form freedom seemed threatened with collapse. Fichte wanted to know why and in his lectures offered the answer.

Fichte divided the past and the future into five epochs. The first was that of unconditioned domination of reason by instinct; the second, that in which reason-instinct had become transformed into external authoritative systems devoid of profundity but characterized by absolutism; the third, the epoch of liberation from absolutism, reason, and reason-instinct, had brought about the age of complete sinfulness; the fourth, the period of reason-knowledge, in which truth should receive recognition as the highest good; and the fifth, the epoch of reason-art, when mankind would be completely justified and sanctified. Fichte regarded his own age as the third, a period of pure negation, of clever rationalism for no other purpose than mental calisthenics. It opposed, toyed, and ridiculed. It adored freedom of the will, in which Fichte refused to believe, for, he said, its end could only be anarchy. He considered an age like this more suited to the despotism of Napoleon than to idealistic philosophy, expecting it eventually to exhaust itself. Thereafter would follow the fourth epoch and after it the last and perfect age. Fichte made it clear that the fourth era would be ushered in and dominated by his own philosophy, contending that it alone combined thought and action and offered suitable reforms for attaining freedom. After humanity had accepted its guidance, the fifth and final epoch would follow of itself. From then on mankind could only advance in excellence.

When Fichte delivered the lectures on his *Grundzüge* he was still an ardent cosmopolitan. The defiant passage in which he proclaimed his cosmopolitanism is famous.

What is the fatherland of the really educated Christian European? In general it is Europe, in particular it is in each age that European state which leads in culture. . . . Let the earth-born ones who think of their fatherland as the soil, the stream and the mountain remain citizens of the decadent state. The sun-loving spirit will be attracted irresistibly to the place where light and justice dwell. And in this cosmopolitanism we ourselves and our descendants can remain indifferent forever to the affairs and fates of states.[20]

The freedom of the roving intellectual from national bonds was celebrated by these words of Fichte in terms as glowing as any used by Lessing or Schiller. But what if the cause of humanity should become identical with the cause of Germany? In 1804 Fichte seemed to be far from that view. In fact, he was eager to leave Prussian service and to accept a call from Russia. The Prussian government had not appreciated him to the desired financial extent and he hoped for more recognition from Russia, writing to the Russian negotiator that if the government would make him a member of the St. Petersburg Academy of Science and pay him a salary of not less than four hundred roubles, "I would be theirs until death." [21] The expression is characteristic of an ardent builder of palatial dreams. In spite of Fichte's hopes the project collapsed and a nationalist was saved for Germany.

In the same year the first sign of Fichte's interest in the German nation appeared. It seems to have been the direct result of disappointment over France. Napoleon stood for everything which Fichte opposed; the French conqueror had destroyed the promise of the French Revolution and killed freedom. France, thought Fichte, remained infected with the poison of rationalism and too ill to lead mankind into the fourth epoch. Who was competent to assume the role? Fichte acknowledged his fitness, but he needed support. In the year in which he delivered his lectures on the *Grundzüge* he expressed privately the belief that Germany was destined to be the world leader, not because as a nation she ranked superior to the others, but because she was less ruined by empiricism. France's acquiescence in Napoleon's

[20] *Die Grundzüge des gegenwärtigen Zeitalters* (Leipzig, 1908), p. 222.
[21] *Briefwechsel,* II, 395.

despotism helped him to draw this deduction from his own genetic philosophy.

Two years later, by 1806, the transformation of Fichte the cosmopolitan into Fichte the nationalist was completed. On the eve of the Battle of Jena the philosopher still scorned patriotism for a particular state or nation, but in his thoughts cosmopolitanism and nationalism were merging. In *Die Patrioten,* a dialogue composed before Jena, Fichte wrote:

> Cosmopolitanism is the will that the purpose of humanity be really achieved. Patriotism is the will that this purpose be fulfilled in that nation to which we ourselves belong and that the results spread from it to entire humanity. . . . Cosmopolitanism must necessarily become patriotism.[22]

A few pages further he declared that the distinction between Prussian and German was artificial, whereas that between Germany and the other European nations was natural. A good Prussian was a good German, he said, and vice versa. Prussia must take care that German character developed both in its own population and in all Germans. Fichte also explained why the Germans comprised the great people. "The source of genius from which up to now humanity has drawn its life has been exhausted; that is, the age of reason-instinct is past. Knowledge has taken its place." He referred to the new German philosophy of idealism.

> The German patriot [he wrote in the dialogue referred to] . . . wishes that this purpose [the acceptance of the new philosophy] be achieved first among the Germans and that the effects then be spread from them to the rest of humanity. The German can will this because this knowledge began with him and is written down in his speech. The greatest ability for understanding this knowledge lies with that nation which had the strength to create it. The German alone can will this; for he alone can, by means of the possession of this knowledge and of an understanding of the age through it, perceive that this is the next objective of humanity. This objective is the only possible patriotic one; the German alone can, therefore, be a patriot; he alone can for the sake of his nation encompass entire humanity;

[22] Johann Gottlieb Fichte, *Sämmtliche Werke* (Herausgegeben von J. H. Fichte, Berlin, 1845-46), XI, 227-28.

contrasted with him from now on, since the extinguishing of reason-instinct and the entry of pure egoism, the patriotism of every other nation must be egoistic, narrow and hostile to the rest of mankind.[23]

How had it come about that even before the Prussian defeat at Jena Fichte had unfolded into a nationalist? His philosophy was genetic, its purpose being to reveal the dialectic of freedom. Since his philosophy alone disclosed this, he must be its missionary. The genetic nature of his thought led Fichte away from rationalistic cosmopolitanism to freedom, and the necessity of finding a group in which to spread his philosophy brought him to an understanding of the importance of the nation. The first enabled him to perceive that the experiences of the past had molded the Germans of the present; the second provided a strong personal motive for discovering the nation. The concept of progress, which he accepted, assisted in the work. The aggressiveness of his action in endeavoring to achieve his ideals urged him forward and external events favored the completion of the process.

Fichte first became aware of the difference between the French and German nations when he noted the difference in their philosophies. His philosophy had profited greatly from the French Revolution and so long as he thought that France fulfilled his ideals, he was devoted to her. Perceiving that France was unworthy of the new mission, he transferred the role of leader to the people which had produced Transcendental Philosophy. The excellence of the German thinkers was, in Fichte's opinion, reflected in the nation; therefore the latter possessed more than any other people the faculty for taking over this philosophy. His nationalism was not aroused by Prussia's military defeat and humiliation, for these had not yet occurred, but resulted from devotion to his own philosophy. Through disappointment in the French he turned to the German nation as the instrument for fulfilling it.

The war of 1806 deepened Fichte's feeling of nationalism and gave him an opportunity to propagate his ideals. He called it a holy war rather than one of *Kabinettspolitik,* and in the

[23] *Ibid.,* XI, 234.

hope that he would inspire the fighters with his teachings, he offered his services to the Prussian government as official orator to the soldiers. The government's refusal did not crush his ardor. When the French pursued the Prussian forces east after Jena, Fichte joined the court and the army in their flight. He refused to bow to the enemies of mankind or to permit them to acquire any control over him. His pride was too great to allow him to meet Napoleon or flatter the French. The collapse of Prussia seemed to him a personal affront and he identified himself with the Prussian state and the state with the German people, feeling himself the humiliation which was the nation's. He united his own fate and that of Germany so completely that it is impossible to distinguish between the hurt done his pride as a person and his pride as a German. His extraordinary social sensitiveness to the fate of the nation-group to which he belonged pierced his thoughts and forced him into action. His excitement during these months resembled the emotionalism of a boy. His nature drove him from Berlin and his philosophy approved his flight. He did not allow his retreat before the French, however, to remain unnoticed by the Prussian king and government. Even in moments of exaltation, Fichte retained interest in material things. He could not have fled if he had not been fairly sure that the government would maintain him financially, as it did, although not so amply as he wished. And he left his wife and child in Berlin to defend with the assistance of less idealistic friends the family possessions. Fichte had no intention of sullying himself by French contacts; his wife's pride was of less consequence; and to the friends who remained behind and aided her he applied the epithet of "Rhine Unionists." A letter from Königsberg to his wife reveals the loose combination of idealistic and material, personal, and patriotic motives in his action:

I do not envy Müller and Humboldt [they had been received by Napoleon]; I am glad that I did not obtain that shameful honor; I am glad that I have breathed, spoken and thought freely, and have never bent my back under the yoke.

It makes a difference in one's conscience and apparently also in one's later success if in troublous times one has openly shown devotion to the good cause.[24]

As a matter of fact, he did profit; undoubtedly his call to the University of Berlin resulted from this episode. This does not detract from the patriotism of his act, but merely places it in its proper light.

The defeat of Prussia shook Fichte out of a mood of pessimism, not about the fate of his philosophy, for he rarely doubted its ultimate success, but about his own future. He had expected some trouble, writing in 1804 to the philosopher Jacobi as follows:

> I believe that by my recent work I have completed the *Wissenschaftslehre* . . . but I shall never lay it before this age in print. I shall only impart it orally to those who have the courage to receive it. What is happening does not move or astonish me; I expect much worse; for I believe that I have understood our age as that of absolute corruption of all ideas. Nonetheless, I am of good spirit; for I know that new life can only emerge from complete decay.[25]

In July, 1807, he told his wife that he had long been determined to renounce the present world. But resignation was alien to his nature. How could his philosophy, he asked himself, reach fruition while a people ruined by the Enlightenment dominated Europe? How could the philosophy of freedom hold sway under a despot? In Fichte's belief his own fortune, his philosophy, that of Germany and of humanity were interdependent; if one was endangered, all were endangered. He conceived of himself as fighting for them all and the struggle against the French touched him personally. On the other hand, he thought that in the crisis his philosophy would have better chance of being accepted. The Prussian defeat seemed to him to bring anarchy, thus marking the close of the third epoch. He thought that the dialectic was working out as he had predicted. The course of events pointed toward the dawn of the new era of reason-knowledge, he hoped, when he and his philosophy would guide humanity into this age.

[24] *Briefwechsel,* II, 444.
[25] *Ibid.,* II, 381-82.

Fichte was pleading for a new form of loyalty. He endeavored to arouse the German people to a sense of their nationhood, a feeling which, except in the case of rare individuals, was unknown. Cosmopolitans, Prussians, Hessians, Bavarians, peasants, Junkers, princes, cowards, the indifferent—all must be transformed into nationalists. The problem of discovering and instilling a new group-loyalty had lain central in Fichte's thought at least since the publication of the *Wissenschaftslehre* in 1795. He was endeavoring to reconcile the needs of individualism, stressed by the Enlightenment, and the needs of efficient social organization, freedom, and the overcoming of freedom—questions still perplexing to the western world today. Fichte asked them, as did other thinkers of his period; but he was one of the first to conceive of the nation as the means of uniting the individual, the group, and God, and to preach the gospel of national love as the binding, harmonizing force. He believed that he would be a new Luther.

In spite of his vows not to return to Berlin while the French were still in occupation, Fichte was compelled somewhat shamefacedly to do so. He took the edge from his indignity by living in a garden house and studiously avoiding the enemy. In the quiet of this retreat his wrath smoldered and he expressed as much of it as he dared in his famous work, *Reden an die deutsche Nation*. He delivered these lectures to small audiences in the course of the winter of 1807-8 under the eyes of the French.

The *Reden* considered alone seems to consist of the words of a great patriot thinking of the nation and its salvation. Placed in the author's intellectual biography, the essays are revealed as a plea to the nation to accept his philosophy. Their origin and purpose do not necessarily diminish the patriotism of the *Reden;* Fichte was offering to the nation his best gift, a program by which, he believed, humanity could be resurrected. Every great theoretical document of nationalism is a summary of the author's ideals for the nation and of the ways of realizing them. The value of these plans depends, not upon the quantity of emotion contained within them, but upon the caliber of the reforms advanced. In the case of Fichte the heroic vigor of his thought cannot be doubted. The *Reden* substantiates the thesis that Fichte turned nationalist first of all through devotion to himself and his philosophy. Because of his burning faith in both he discovered the nation. His nationalism consisted of patriotism to himself, his philosophy, and the nation, and he hoped that the last would be guided by the first to accept the second, thereby creating a new human race. The Fichtean Germany of the future, not the present Germany, was the object of his ultimate adoration. Immortality, said Fichte in the *Reden,* should begin on this earth. That is what he expected for himself and for the nation, provided the latter accepted his philosophy.

Fichte gave the key to the *Reden* in his second dialogue on the *Patrioten,* written after the Battle of Jena and before the *Reden.* In this he identified patriotism with the acceptance of his *Wissenschaftslehre* and made the salvation of Germany and of humanity dependent upon their embracing his philosophy. The present Germany, he added in this dialogue, could not understand his teachings. The pedagogical method for training the younger and unspoiled element of the population lay at hand in Pestalozzi's writings, but the education must be given to the entire people, not merely, as Pestalozzi had in mind, to a class or group. Once this method had provided a foundation, the *Wissenschaftslehre* could be comprehended.

Fichte carried the thought further in the *Reden.* In speaking to Germans, that is, to the educated part of the nation, he developed the thought that Germany was threatened with the loss of her identity; a new world must arise, he said, if she were to be saved. He indicated the *Reden* as designed to show how this could be achieved, namely, by educational reform along Pestalozzian lines. The proposed new education, he said, would bring about "an entire transformation of humanity." [26] More would be achieved by it than mere national patriotism. "Man," he said, "will be perfected in all respects. . . . Spiritual nature has made our complete recovery from all the evils which oppress us depend-

[26] Johann Gottlieb Fichte, *Reden an die deutsche Nation* (Halle a. d. Saale, Verlag von Otto Hendel), p. 119.

ent upon the recovery of our nation and fatherland."[27] The pedagogue, a favorite among nationalists, was represented as the savior of the world.

In the *Grundzüge* Fichte used the phrase "permeation of the burgher by the state." By reading "nation" for "state" one possesses the most concise formulation to be found of his proposed process of nationalizing. The idea of integrating the population and the nation, of making it "nation-conscious," formed the core of his thought in the *Reden*. Educational reforms leading to economic, social, and political ones supplied the means by which this end was to be attained. To regard his nationalism as merely a matter of feeling or of shallow pedagogy ignores the profundity and breadth of Fichte's intelligence and the dynamic, reform-like quality of nationalism. Only by this broader approach can the grandeur of Fichte's nationalism be appreciated and the enormous implication of the phrase "integration of the burgher and the nation" be perceived. It was, with the possible exception of communism, the most revolutionary social ideal of the nineteenth and twentieth centuries, and much of its meaning has still to be disclosed.

Fichte regarded as the object of the history of humanity the realization of freedom according to reason. The life of past, present, and future humanity could be judged according to whether man was free or unfree. It followed that history fell into two parts, that of mankind as unfree and as free, and Fichte had no hesitation in branding the past with the present as unfree and in prophetically designating the future as the age of "freedom according to reason." With this simple formula he constructed a philosophy of history which placed his own age at the crucial point of division and imposed upon him the role of a Moses. He took upon himself to lead man out of the bonds of slavery into the realm of freedom, inaugurating the epoch of the kingdom of Heaven on earth.

The bald antithesis of freedom and unfreedom is almost meaningless without the analysis which Fichte made of his own

[27] *Ibid.*, p. 120.

period and his description of that to come. Only the boldness of his pen and the bluntness of the distinction rendered this possible. Fichte stood on a high mountain from which he could view the eighteenth century on the one side and the nineteenth and twentieth centuries on the other; the age of absolutism and cultural, rationalistic individualism on the one, the age of liberalism, nationalism, and organic collectivism on the other. With the glass of freedom he could peer far into the future; but, as is to be expected of anyone using so limited an instrument, he saw only a part of his own age. He was fundamentally a reformer, not a historian.

Before going into particulars Fichte liked to reduce his analyses to philosophical terms, in which metaphysics, epistemology, and especially ethics blended into a whole. He characterized his own age as "the age of direct emancipation from all authority and indirect freedom from the control of reason-instinct and of reason in any form, the age of absolute indifference to all truth, of complete absence of restraint or guiding lines, one of complete sinfulness." [28] Lacking control by any form of reason man had degenerated, he said, into a mere individualist, whose life was dominated by the desire for self-preservation and personal happiness. The period was utilitarian, materialistic—concerned with housing, clothing and food, comfort and fashions. It hated or scoffed at the historical, loved abstractions, and tried to frame its institutions according to ideals without root or sap. Experience furnished its criteria and sole source of knowledge. In morals it sought guidance only from personal advantage and professed to find an ignoble motive for every act. Religion had become to it a means for achieving happiness, reminding man that he must enjoy moderately in order to enjoy long. God was looked upon as a human creation whose function lay in satisfying human needs. The old religious systems were, he charged, kept as soporifics for the masses.

Fichte dissected out the disintegrating effects in every aspect of a life of selfish individualism. In *Der geschlossene Handelsstaat*

[28] *Grundzüge, op. cit.*, p. 21.

he showed those upon economic life, denouncing in terms which might have come from Karl Marx the competitive blood-sucking of the producers and traders.

> There arises an endless civil war of the entire trading public, a war between buyer and seller; and this war becomes fiercer, more unjust and in its effects more dangerous as population increases, the commercial state grows in size, production and the mechanical arts improve and as the volume of wares in circulation and the demand for them multiply. That which in a simple economy could go on without great injustice and oppression, with increased needs changes into the most crying injustice and a source of great misery. . . . In short, no one has any assurance that continued labor will preserve his status, for individuals want to be absolutely free so that they can destroy each other.[29]

He called it "an anarchy of trade."

In the social and constitutional spheres Fichte found conditions just as distressing. According to existing theory and practice, he maintained, the function of the state consisted, not in correcting it, but in preserving this anarchy. In fact, he believed, everything about German society was evil, and after the Prussian defeat at Jena his philosophical criticisms changed into sharp denunciations. Since, however, he was endeavoring in the *Reden* to convert the nation to his ideals, he had more or less to let the past bury itself while he devoted his energy to assisting at the birth of the future. In the *Reden* he made a blanket charge: we are all responsible. But an unpublished manuscript from the winter of 1806-7 reveals the bitterness which he felt about the sins of the existing order of society. It must be used as an extensive footnote to the more diplomatic and purposive *Reden*.[30]

Fichte introduced the memorandum with a statement about the tendency of individuals to become, as they advance in years, mentally and morally immobile and of the period to deteriorate. The early years of a life may have shown promise, he held, but with time the tender buds have soon shriveled up. In the army

[29] *Werke, op. cit.*, III, 457-58.
[30] *Ibid.*, VII, 519 ff.

"bravery, versatility and alertness" were found only among the lower ranks; laziness, carelessness, ignorance, cowardice, and "shameful capitulations" characterized the upper groups. The higher a child stood by birth, the sooner his environment corrupted him. Such an individual despised the lower classes and exploited them; and since he had the power, he gave his selfishness free rein. The state did not curb him; the laws applied to him in small degree; he did as he wished. The lower classes were unable to protest against this abuse because they were too ignorant or because they were kept in obedience by both state and religion. At the top stood the prince, educated in French, riding, a bit of military drill and, in case of very careful schooling, music and drawing. He was never told of his duties toward his subjects and learned nothing about the functions of the state or the needs of the nation. He was kept in a hothouse surrounded by useless courtiers or ministers trained in "gallant studies" and salon-statesmanship. The conduct of foreign affairs consisted of eavesdropping, telling anecdotes, avoiding decisions, and waiting for one's hand to be forced. The art of domestic administration was still simpler: it consisted of accumulating gold in the easiest way possible. With a large part of these funds an army was dressed, equipped, and fed in such a way that in the first battle it surrendered. The officers' positions were reserved for the aristocracy, which considered the appropriate requisites for this vocation to be avoidance of a polite and academic education and cultivation of a bold bearing and a haughty disregard for all other classes. Without bad grammar, it thought, an officer could not be brave. In time of danger, Fichte continued, officers were first to throw away their standards and flee or surrender. Their kinsmen at home practiced the same kind of patriotism: they gave their country's soldiers little and that with an ill will; but when the enemy appeared they feted it as a hero. Many of the princes, continued Fichte, were even eager to assist it at the expense of their neighbors in the hope of selfish gain. That Germany was being ruined by their acts never troubled them; they were too circumscribed to recognize that they were destroying themselves. Rulers and ruled had become thoroughly corrupted by utilitarian individualism, thus sundering the bonds holding together a state or nation. Society had been reduced to a mob of whimpering cowards. The collapse of Germany, Fichte thought, had been inevitable.

It could be inferred from Fichte's condemnation of his age that society suffered from too much freedom instead of too little. Fichte met this criticism by defining the concept of freedom in a form which suited his purpose. He retained the idea from the Enlightenment, but changed its mechanistic, individualistic content to a social one. He began with the proposition: "By way of freedom the life of human society develops into a pure expression of reason." There can be, he concluded, only one life, "that is, there is everywhere only one thing living, the one living reason. . . . Reason is the only possible living, self-dependent, self-supporting existence; everything which appears to be existing and living is only the modification, condition, alteration and intrinsic form of that." The individual is nothing in himself; "he is but a single unit of being thought out of the one general and necessary thinking." [31]

Freedom exists when it is relinquished for an idea, Fichte declared. No general answer can be made to the question whether or not man is free.

> Because man is free in the lower sense [Fichte wrote], because he begins in indecision, he can become free, or in a higher sense of the word, unfree. In reality the way each person answers this question reflects clearly his true being. Whoever is nothing more than a link in the chain of appearances can indeed imagine for a moment that he is free; but this delusion will not stand further inspection. Man thinks that the rest of humanity is like himself. On the other hand, he whose life is gripped by the real, whose life has come directly from God, is free and believes in his own freedom and that of others.[32]

In this statement Fichte aimed to distinguish between two ways of life, the one consisting of passive resignation, a fatalistic

[31] *Grundzuge, op. cit.*, pp. 27, 33-34.
[32] *Reden, op. cit.*, p. 96.

acquiescence in that which is, a renunciation of every effort to improve, an egoistic manner toward the rest of society. A person who adheres to this social philosophy may imagine that he is preserving this freedom by rejecting that which is troublesome and concentrating his world upon himself. But, as Fichte said, a little clear thinking will disillusion him. In the second and true state of freedom man believes that he contains an absolutely original life within himself; he finds humanity can be improved to infinity; he avows a faith in progress. Man is therefore free if he has ideals toward which he strives, if he is willing to sacrifice himself for these ideals. He is free, not in the lower sense of carefreeness or irresponsibility, but in the higher meaning. Since the plan of history is revealed through the nation, Fichte declared, man must for the nation's sake, his own sake and God's integrate himself and the nation.

Freedom and reason offer individualistic, universal standards. Nonetheless, since Fichte was trying to liberate Germany from the Napoleonic domination, he must also defend the right of the nation-group to exist. He did so as follows:

> Spiritual nature was able to realize the character of humanity only by making both individuals and peoples greatly different from one another. Only as each people and each individual within the group develop and form their own individualities do they realize the Godhead as it should be. . . . Only in invisible and unconscious characteristics of the nations, through which they are connected with the source of original life, lies the guarantee of their present and future value, virtue and service. If through intermingling and friction these should be weakened, separation from spiritual nature will occur and all will come to a common ruin.[33]

Thus Fichte justified the division of society into nations, among them the German. He could not prove his assertions that nature demands national differences in order to realize its many forms; that the eternal reveals itself in these forms and binds the realm of the senses to that of ideals. He postulated them as bases for his German nationalism. The place of the individual was in the

[33] *Ibid.*, p. 176.

nation and his purpose was to serve that group, even to the point of self-destruction.

Fichte defined the nation as follows:

> In a higher sense of the word, taken from the standpoint of the whole spiritual world, a folk is a people living together in a society and biologically and spiritually reproducing itself and subject to a particular law in accordance with which it reveals the divine.[34]

What does this statement mean? A few further quotations will elucidate it.

> The natural . . . instinct of man is to find Heaven on this earth and to fuse the eternal with mundane, daily work; to plant and cultivate the imperishable in the temporary, which is connected with the eternal, not merely in an incomprehensible way, but in a manner apparent to mortal eye.[35]

What could satisfy this demand for the eternal on earth?

> Only an order of things could do so which [one of noble mind] is able to recognize as eternal and as capable of receiving the eternal in itself. Such an order is . . . the special spiritual nature of the human environment out of which, with all his thinking and acting and with his belief in its eternity, he has come; this environment is the folk, from which he derives and in which he has grown to what he is. For it is undoubtedly true that his work, if he can legitimately claim for it an eternal character, can in no way be the result merely of the spiritual law of nature of his nation or be absorbed in this result, but that it also must flow directly out of original, divine life. Yet it is likewise true that this larger element in accordance with this special spiritual law of nature must in the first instance accommodate itself to a visible appearance and take on sensuous form. So long as this folk exists, all further revelations of the divine will appear in it and receive form in it according to the same natural law.[36]

The significant points in this formulation are: first, that the individual seeks the eternal on earth so as to have something permanent for which to work; second, that in the nation he finds

[34] *Ibid.*, p. 104.
[35] *Ibid.*, p. 102.
[36] *Ibid.*, pp. 103-4.

the assurance of the survival of his efforts; third, that the people as a means of expressing the eternal natural law participate in the molding of individual life; fourth, that this life has its source and its sanction partly in divine law, but that its results can be preserved only through the nation; fifth, that so long as the nation endures, the individual will be assured of his own endurance. His life is stretched to the infinite.

> His belief and his effort to plant the imperishable, his conception of his own life as an eternal life are the bonds which tie his nation and through it humanity . . . to his expanded heart. This is his love for his people, above all respecting and trusting it, made happy by it, honoring himself through his origin. The divine has appeared in it and the creative has honored it by making it the direct channel into the world; the divine will therefore continue to appear in it. Therefore, be active, effective and sacrificing for it. Life, merely as life, as a continuation of changing existence, has never possessed value for the individual without this; the individual has wished life only as the source of the eternal; but this eternity alone assures him the independent survival of his nation; he must be willing to die so that his nation may live and that he may live in it the only life he has ever longed for.[37]

The right of the nation to exist and to dominate therefore rests upon eternal natural law; the nation is the expression of God; through it the divine is given form. One can speak, not of the divine right of the nation, but of its divinity. The nation is original; it is a divine source. It is the means and instrument of progress.

That man could achieve freedom by way of the nation was Fichte's idealistic faith; but ideal and reality stood in such glaring contradiction that only a person with Fichte's rare confidence in himself, in humanity, and in God would ever have envisaged their meeting. Fichte faced the necessity of explaining why man had been and still was wicked and at the same time of showing why in the future he could perfect himself and society, especially why Germans and the German nation could do so. For that pur-

[37] *Ibid.*, p. 105.

pose Fichte assumed certain characteristics of God, nature, man, and the German nation, representing them as fulfilling a Fichtean dialectic.

Man is born good, Fichte declared, and rational nature keeps him free from evil during his early years. Nor does caste cause differences in ability at birth. Man acquires bad traits from his social environment. Hence Fichte believed that by isolating children from society and educating them properly one could develop them into model citizens of a future, ideal society. How was this possible? The two component parts of man are understanding and will; these complement each other and must be cultivated together. Would the individual cultivate them if properly directed? Fichte replied in the affirmative, explaining that man was endowed with the instincts to seek heaven on earth, to arrive at clarity and order, to be respected by others and to respect others. He selected for man those instincts which would assure the possibility or even certainty of the cultivation of Fichtean social individuals and the coming of the fourth and fifth ages in the history of mankind.[38] Since Fichte wished absolute assurance, he assigned to each individual a core, a general instinct defining his character and establishing the law for his own personality. This instinct, he said, manifested itself in two basic forms of consciousness, that of obscure feeling and that of clear perception (*Erkenntnis*). The former, as the more primitive and dependent on the emotions, led to selfishness. It might in exceptional cases overcome egoism and awaken longing for another order of things; but essentially it accounted for wickedness. The second form of consciousness, that of clear perception, led, not to contentment with the present, but to a desire for a more perfect world. It should be developed in order to realize the nation and to guide mankind to glory. Since it was supported by a fundamental law of man's spiritual nature, the striving toward spiritual activity, and by man's instinct toward clarity and order

[38] In mentioning another instinct, that toward selfishness, he violated the course of his thought and explained man's egoism in another way. If man were selfish by instinct, manifestly no amount of education or environmental perfection would secure him against falling back into egoism.

and the kingdom of heaven on earth, it would triumph over the other form of consciousness. Man need only be sure that the educational and environmental order of society permitted this form of consciousness to be cultivated.

Fichte divided the world of senses from that of the spirit, the eternal from the ephemeral, man from society. His problem in developing nationalists lay essentially in finding a means of binding all these elements together into lasting union. How could he do so? Into the first place he put the instinct of respect for oneself and for others. This caused the individual to act in such a manner as to obtain the respect of others and to pay others this respect because he wished it himself. Furthermore, Fichte united the sensuous and the spiritual worlds by way of a metaphysics of transcendentalism. God was immanent in the world; the senses furnished material with which the spirit worked; the nature of man demanded development from the material to the spiritual; the ideal had its genesis in reality and gave it a future incentive and goal as the nationalistic ideal did to the Germans.

The essential bond of union was love. Fichte called it a fundamental part of man. "Man can will and achieve that which he loves," he wrote.[39] And he continued:

> The direct appearance and revelation of God is love; first, the manifestation of this love through knowledge postulates a being and, indeed, such a being as will eternally develop and this as the only true world, in so far as there is any truth in a world. On the other hand, the second world given and known to us as existing is only of shadow, from which the perception of its manifestation of love constructs a firm form and a visible body; this second world is the means and condition for perceiving the higher world which cannot be seen of itself. God does not enter into this latter higher world directly but likewise comes here only by means of the one pure, unchanging, and formless love, in which love alone He directly appears.[40]

Love, the revelation of God, united heaven and earth, ideals and reality; it was pure, changeless, and formless. Love had its own dialectic. Intuitive perception produced a picture from the visible

[39] *Reden, op. cit.*, p. 21.
[40] *Ibid.*, p. 40.

world in which it clothed the invisible object of love; but since love was the direct expression of God and pertained to the realm of the ideal, it contradicted the visible form and drove the mind to seek a new and higher form, which in turn was rejected by love. Thus, an eternal movement originated, through which love also became eternal and through which man strove toward the creation of heaven on earth. Love served as the binding and driving force in two ways: there was a love "whereby each one is bound to the world of thought; this is the bond between the world of the senses and that of the spirit." Through it man easily and eagerly cultivated his mind and turned to knowledge. Without love the form of consciousness of pure knowledge remained cold and useless and soon gave way to the other form, that of obscure feeling. With it the individual was led to act on the basis of his pure knowledge and to help his fellow men. The love of pure knowledge induced him to seek ideals and to realize them for society, for knowledge without action was not knowledge. The transference of knowledge into action arose out of the other love, that of man for man. By means of it men united into a "reason-community of like-mindedness." [41] Thus love overcame the lower means of union, fear and hope for the present life, and bound man to man and man to the eternal. By way of it man could feel one with others. Through it the "quickening breath of the spirit realm" blew into the world.

By means of love alone could the individual become a nationalist. "He who does not regard himself first of all as eternal," Fichte wrote, "has not love and cannot love a fatherland; in fact, he cannot even have a fatherland. He who regards his invisible life as eternal but not his visible may indeed have a Heaven and see in it his fatherland, but here below he has none." [42] Since man could love only that which endured, he must believe that his nation fulfilled this requirement. He must love it so deeply, so completely, that he could not conceive of existence without it and, since the nation was eternal, he did right in devoting his whole being to it. He must transfer his religion to the divine

[41] *Ibid.*, p. 131.
[42] *Ibid.*, pp. 105-6.

nation of the eternal fatherland on earth. "Whoever has inherited a fatherland," Fichte asserted, "whoever unites in his soul Heaven and earth, visible and invisible, and thereby creates a real and genuine Heaven will fight to the last drop of blood to transmit undiminished to his successors this precious possession." [43] Fichte longed to develop an individual who would fight Napoleon to the last drop of blood and believed that the acceptance of his ideals would bring that about. He envisaged the perfect man as the product of the new kind of schooling, an eager universalist, an ardent nationalist, receptive, original, active, perfect as to will power, perfect in his love of the ideal and in his devotion to society. Fichte portrayed in the *Reden* the manner in which these qualities were to be developed in the novice.

> The constitution of the new nationalistic school [he wrote] must be so arranged that the individual not merely sacrifices for the sake of the whole, but that he can be active and creative for it. In addition to intellectual development, physical exercise and the mechanical arts . . . of agriculture and of many handicrafts must be carried on. It is a fundamental rule that everyone who excels in one of these branches shall assist in training the others and assume responsibility for them. Everyone who discovers an improvement or grasps quickly and clearly one suggested by the teacher must execute it with his own efforts without being excused from his regular individual tasks of learning and working. He must do this, not from compulsion but of his own accord, and must expect no reward, since in this society all are equal with respect to work and pleasure. Nor must he even expect praise, since it is the ruling manner of thinking in this community that each merely does his duty thereby and that he alone will enjoy the satisfaction of having worked for the group and, in case of success, of having accomplished something. In accordance therewith under this constitution the work will inevitably evoke new effort and increased efficiency and the more capable in particular will often watch when others sleep and meditate when others play.
>
> The novices who . . . show certainty of joyously accepting responsibility and of working and growing in strength by this work, can be turned out into the world with assurance. Education has achieved its aim with them. Love has been ignited in them; it burns

[43] *Ibid.*, p. 106.

down into the roots of their living impulses, and from now on will grip everything which touches this living emotion. And in the greater society of the world the students will never be able to be otherwise than they were in the small society which they now leave.[44]

In another passage Fichte extended his description to include an analysis of the economic and social organization of this miniature society.

The fundamental law of this little economic state [he wrote] must be this: that in it no articles of food, clothing, and so forth, and so far as possible no tool shall be used which has not been made in it. . . . For this self-dependence and self-contentedness of the whole each individual must work with all his power and without keeping account of the amount he does or making claim to any article as his own. Each must know that he owes all to the whole and must enjoy or suffer, as the case may be, with the whole. Thereby the honorable self-dependence of the state and the family into which he will enter and the relation of their individual members to them will be made clear to his mind and will be forever rooted in his soul.[45]

The protégé of this education [Fichte asserted] is not merely a member of the human community on earth and for the short space of life here, but he is also . . . a link in the eternal chain of spiritual life under a higher social order. Undoubtedly for understanding this higher order a training which comprehends his entire nature must be given him. Just as this training leads him to picture a moral world order which never exists but which is always becoming, so it must lead him to picture in thought a likeness of that supersensuous world order in which nothing becomes and which has never become, but which eternally is there and to understand that it cannot be otherwise. He will, if rightly trained, succeed in forming such a picture and will find that there is nothing other than life and, indeed, spiritual life which exists in thought. . . . Thus he will see his life as an eternal link in the chain of revelation of the divine life and every other spiritual life as such a link and will learn to hallow it. And only in direct contact with God and the immediate pouring out of his life from that life will he find light and blessedness; but through

[44] *Ibid.*, pp. 31-32.
[45] *Ibid.*, p. 141.

remoteness from immediate contact with God he will find death, darkness, and despair.[46]

These quotations describe Fichte's conception of the means by which freedom should be introduced into the world. The school community was a microcosm, a training ground by virtue of the fact that its organization and functioning were to be, on a suitable scale, those of the larger society outside. Here was the incubator of the nationalist, of the complete man who would emerge innocent of sin, mighty in virtue, invincible in devotion to his ideals. The unreformed society into which he came could not corrupt him; for strength of will, love of the good for its own sake, habits of original thinking and a compulsion toward action had suffused his soul. He was to have acquired the deep religious feeling of being a unit in the divine process; he was to have absorbed Fichte's philosophy of the Idea; he was to have become another Fichte, bearing witness in his life to the Godly purpose and, like Christ on a charger, rushing the world toward the Heaven of Fichtean nationalism.

Fichte proposed the same program of education for everybody. The government was to assume charge of it and make it possible for every member of the nation to enjoy its benefits. In fact, the state should compel everyone to be educated after this manner. Fichte criticized severely the existing custom of abandoning this fundamental function to private families or to the church, attributing much of Germany's disaster to neglect of this duty. Where church and family determined education, he said, only a few received instruction and even these few served private rather than national interest. He thought it inevitable that under existing circumstances these interests clashed.

The social and economic consequences of the educational reforms which Fichte proposed would have been enormous. If everyone were educated up to the limit of his capacity, as Fichte demanded, caste distinctions soon would be obliterated. If each caste were given an equal start, the outcome of life would depend upon ability rather than birth, and the material basis for caste

[46] *Ibid.*, pp. 33-34.

and privilege would soon be destroyed. The entire educational plan rested on freedom, that is, freedom to serve the nation. The pupils, reared in a community where freedom, equality, and fraternity received material as well as spiritual form, would work for the group, love each other and the group, seek no selfish advantage, share all alike with all. If an aristocrat were ever subjected to this type of education, provided the effects were those which Fichte anticipated, he would not emerge an aristocrat. How could one, after having lived in this almost socialistic society during his most impressionable years, return to caste, castle, and privilege? Nationalism implied a common feeling among the members of the nation; it created bonds, inculcated in the individual a sense of responsibility for the others of the group. Where there was devotion to the nation, there would exist a will to make that nation great, cultured, and perfect. Each part of the nation would be important by virtue of the fact that it was a part. Each part must be offered every opportunity to develop. Since the nation consisted of individuals and since the health, wealth, and culture of the nation depended upon the condition of the component members, these individuals must be allowed to expand their lives. Nationalism, a leveler of classes and castes, should also elevate. It imposed group responsibility and forced the nation to realize the ideals of the French revolutionary slogan. Since an unfree being could not love his nation, he could not work for the nation unless he were freed. So with privilege and nationalism: no obstacle should be left to impede the development of the individual for the sake of the nation; no legal restrictions should endanger the life process of the entire body. Inequality and absence of liberty make for staleness, desuetude. They do not belong in a nation of brotherly love and must be eliminated like disease. National consciousness must be aroused in every being to fulfill the purpose of the world process. Participation in service for the Ideal must be universal and unanimous; each person must conceive of himself as a part of eternity, of God, of world evolution. And in order to have this consciousness instilled in him, he must be educated to the fullest of his ability, placed where he can work and achieve to capacity, be treated in such a way that he will take pride in his efforts, in his nation, in his divine mission. Living, not being, is the principle of his earthly stay. As the instrument of the divine, the nation should function perfectly; therefore, it must be reorganized in accordance with freedom in reason. Caste must go, privilege must go, an organic, national society must take their places.

The analysis above does not exaggerate Fichte's thought. Fichte perceived the implications of his central idea. He advocated every reform described and fully expected to reach the goal of freedom in an organic, functional society. The only condition which needs to be made concerns the germinal source of these reforms: not the feeling of nationalism but the Fichtean ideal of freedom in the group constituted it. The tremendous conception of a society organized in freedom and working at its fullest capacity first induced him to follow out the details of his vision. When Fichte had discovered the nation, he wished to endow it with this constitution. By a remarkable coincidence the characteristics of his ideal society harmonized perfectly with the idealistic requirements of nationalism. Freedom, love, devotion to the group, equality of opportunity, full development of the individual, progress, active living instead of passive being, fulfillment of the divine purpose through the group—all these could be equally true both of nationalistic society and of society organized on a basis of freedom according to reason. The idea of the nation and that of freedom in society might point in different directions. It so happened that they did not; in fact, Fichte became thoroughly nationalistic as a result of his earlier vision of a society living in freedom. History still attests to the unity of the two ideas. The only difference between them lies in the fact that in nationalism the specific nation has taken the place of society at large as the vehicle for achieving freedom for humanity.

The ideal had to be given reality by some nation; and all of Fichte's argument led to proving the German nation divinely called for this purpose. The Germans alone, Fichte preached, had the ability to accept the new education and achieve the age of perfection. Their superiority lay in the fact that they possessed a living language in place of one derived from a dead tongue.

Without stating so, Fichte referred particularly to the French, who must first learn the meaning of the words they used.

> Man is far more shaped by language than language is by man [Fichte wrote]. . . . Man does not really speak; rather, human nature speaks in him. . . . The language of this folk is necessarily what it is and the people does not actually express its knowledge [*Erkenntnis*], but its knowledge speaks of itself out of the language. . . . Since language does not relate arbitrarily but breaks out as a direct, natural force from intelligent life, a language developed consistently according to this law has the power directly to lay hold of life and to arouse it.[47]

The German language, Fichte declared, had grown within the nation. In it thought became part of the being of the people because of the organic nature of the medium. An idea aroused German feeling so strongly that execution had to follow. The Germans alone were creative and genial; they alone constituted a body of patriots, a nation. "To possess character and to be German are the same thing," Fichte declared,[48] and he endowed his people with all the finest qualities. He spoke of their seriousness, depth of thought and feeling, clarity, enthusiasm, their thoroughness and good nature. They were faithful, honest, open and simple; they were pious, modest and reliable; they had public spirit. "When a German seeks something, he finds more than he sought."[49] Thereby Fichte explained how the Germans had become the mother folk of the modern world. Antiquity had left to mankind a rich and varied cultural heritage, which in each age had attracted humanity and induced it to clothe this culture in its own form. Thus the union of old and new made possible the development of mankind. In this process antique culture furnished the initial stimulus, to which foreign countries responded in a superficial manner. The Germans, aroused by these foreign adaptations, completed and incorporated them into life. While receiving the stimulus from foreign peoples, they must become like them. This was, Fichte said, the condition of Germany at the

[47] *Ibid.*, pp. 48 51.
[48] *Ibid.*, p. 159.
[49] *Ibid.*, p. 77.

present, that is, of most of her intellectuals, and explained their imitation of the foreign, especially in the field of philosophy. Fichte declared that the German philosophy of idealism was re-inaugurating as the harbinger of a revival of mankind the age of creativeness. He described the rare quality of German philosophy as follows:

> The true philosophy . . . proceeds from one pure, divine life—as absolute life, which it remains in all eternity, but not as of this or that life. And the true philosophy sees how finally in appearance this life unendingly opens and closes and how only in accordance with this law does it become being or anything at all. From this philosophy arises being, which that [the philosophy] postulates. And thus this philosophy can only be German, that is, original.[50]

The dialectic, moving toward the age of creativeness and perfection for the Germans, this time led by Fichte and the philosophers as previously by Luther and his aids, once more turned their genius to finding more than they had sought. Fichte felt reassured by this belief.

In the eventuality that the German nation should lose its identity, Fichte saw ruin ahead.

> If in their blindness for such things [German genius] and carried away by appearance [he wrote] foreign countries should ever rob their mother country [Germany] of its independence and thereby destroy and absorb it, they would, in case of success, cut the last vein by which they have maintained contact with nature and life and would succumb to spiritual death. . . . In that case the hitherto steady flow of the culture of the race would cease, barbarism would begin anew and advance without hindrance until we should all live again in caves like wild beasts, consuming each other. The German alone can and will perceive that this is so and must necessarily follow; to the foreigner, knowing no other culture than his own and having an unrestricted field in which to marvel at himself, it must and will appear as blatant, ignorant slander.[51]

The implication is clear if one remembers that Fichte's philosophy was necessary to save Germany. In fact, Fichte reduced the

[50] *Ibid.*, p. 87.
[51] *Ibid.*, p. 71.

conflict to one between German and foreign philosophy. The fate of Germany and of western civilization depended on the acceptance of Fichte's philosophy and Fichte, made of Promethean stuff, did not shrink from responsibility. At the end of the *Reden* he grew apocalyptic again:

Centuries have passed since you were called together as today in such numbers, on such great, urgent, common business, so entirely as a nation and as Germans. This opportunty will never be offered you again. If you do not heed, if you let these words pass you as empty sounds in your ears or as a curiosity, no human being will trust you longer. Do not go from this hall undecided; let everyone who hears this voice resolve this . . . as though he were alone and must do all himself. . . .

It depends on you whether you will be . . . the end of an unworthy race . . . or the beginning . . . of a new age glorious beyond all your dreams. . . . Remember that you are the last in whose power this great transformation lies.

Since affairs stand thus you will not overcome them with material weapons; your spirit alone must rise against them. The greater fate is yours to found the empire of the spirit and of reason and to destroy crude physical force as the ruler of the world. . . .

The old world with its splendor and greatness as well as its defects has sunk. . . . If that which has been expressed in these *Reden* is true, then of all peoples you are the one in whom the germ of human perfection most clearly lies and to whom the vanguard in its development has been assigned. If this quality in you is ruined, all hope of salvation for the entire human race in the depths of its evil will be destroyed. . . . There is no alternative; if you sink, entire humanity sinks with you, devoid of hope of future resurrection.[52]

Fichte's nationalism was that of a philosopher. It is significant that he based national differences, not on geography or race, but on language, willingly dispensing even with the last in case his philosophy was accepted.[53] Since his main object was to ex-

[52] *Ibid.*, pp. 191, 199, 201-2.

[53] See *Reden*, p. 98, where Fichte declared that anyone accepting and understanding the new German philosophy was a German no matter what language he spoke; and those who did not accept it were not Germans in spite of the fact that they might speak German.

plain why the new philosophy of transcendental idealism had arisen in Germany and why the German nation, which had produced this philosophy, alone was creative, he found sufficient the linguistic theory of nationalism. He had no special love for a territory or group except as it provided the necessary material foundation for the acceptance of his thought. He never felt the pull of a home, loved because of its trees, its gardens, its dialects. He never struck root in any soil. His imagination did not conceive of Germany in terms of a people living and working in a humdrum way with its failings, its petty happinesses and sorrows, its births and deaths. Fichte envisaged a Germany of intellectuals, a people who like him would all be philosophers, in short, a Germany of a Fichtean future. The nation's ability to think abstractly and its spiritual mission endeared it to him. The nation afforded the setting and vehicle for his idealism. It was not Being but Becoming. Fichte loved it because he wanted to make it over. He had not objected to the French so long as they had followed the path of his own desires and ideals. He had been willing, if not eager, to serve them. But as soon as they deviated from the path, his admiration turned to hate. He did not become a good German when first disillusioned by the French, but remained what he was, an intellectual idealist. Since he wanted Germany to fulfill his ambitions and hopes, he perceived that she must be saved and in turn save humanity. His German national feeling was aroused by loyalty, not to Germany as she was, but to his own ideals. Fichte primarily felt concern for his own ideals as an instrument to improve mankind. Except in so far as his own interest coincided with that of the nation, this aspiration lifted him above nationalism. He combined cosmopolitanism and nationalism, but he subordinated both to the universal acceptance of his philosophy, the abstract expression of himself.

The *Reden* enjoyed little contemporary popularity. They first came to be widely read some years later. No one made a move to put the proposals into effect. Fichte's plan for organizing the University of Berlin along national lines and making it a center of light for the new philosophy lay forgotten in a governmental cabinet. But Fichte could not be discouraged. In 1810 he asserted as boldly as ever: "The true *Wissenschaftslehre* remains in the world and I am also still here and the time will yet come when I shall be listened to."[54]

The constellation of events seemed to favor Fichte again in 1813. The fate of Prussia and of Fichte had converged in 1806, when the defeat seemed to open for the idealist an opportunity to lead Germany and mankind into the fourth epoch. The hope had failed to materialize; but the War of Liberation revived it and Fichte immediately offered his services to the Prussian government. The proposal he made resembles closely the one of 1806. Fichte worded his request to the Director of the Department of Religion and Education as follows:

My plan is to attempt by oratory to elevate those of authority and of action into the spiritual mood and views of . . . Christianity. It is true that thereby I will be doing what every pastor should; but I believe that I can do it otherwise than the ordinary pastor because I have a higher and more practical conception of Christianity. Since the task is one of long standing with me and the present time offers the best opportunity of achieving it and since after careful consideration I can at present do nothing better, I regard it as a call of duty to make the attempt. If I succeed, the gain will be immeasurable. If I fail, the benefit will have been demonstrated and someone after me will succeed. . . .

I wish to elevate into the spiritual world; where I cannot do this through speculation, I must accomplish it through Christianity. But thereby the passages will often acquire a deeper meaning than is customary. . . .

My place should be at the Royal Headquarters, where the guards and volunteers of the guard, among whom the most are students, are stationed.

I request the privilege of being subordinated to no one except the King or his representative at Headquarters. In case I am not permitted to remain there, I wish the right of returning to my present position. Also, in case I perceive that my attempt has failed, I wish the right to leave.[55]

[54] *Briefwechsel, op. cit.*, II, 550.
[55] *Ibid.*, II, 600-1.

Fichte was accustomed in crucial moments of decision to note arguments for and against. A few of his memoranda have been preserved, fortunately the one in this issue. It reveals how fully he lived his philosophy and how his ambition for it was mated with his actions. A few quotations will manifest this.

> First duty is to advance my knowledge; if I cannot do this by reading, I can by solitary meditation; but just as well at the front. It is also a duty to participate in the great movements of the time, to advise and help. . . . If I could arouse a more serious, holier mood in the leaders, that would be a great gain and such is decisive. . . .
>
> Is the latter duty more important than the former? It accelerates at least my effectiveness, which in any case will result later. . . . The question is . . . whether at the present time and for the immediate purpose to bring the higher view to humanity, to submerge the war leaders in God. Secondary question: Do I wish thereby to further religiosity in general or the better success of the present objective? Certainly the latter, and who says that I cannot further it? . . . All my activity aims at the creation of a new humanity. If I succeed, would it be of advantage to immediate action, to the present objective? Why not? Some will be strengthened and the Idea will be held before them, for instance my students; others will be brought closer to the Idea. . . .
>
> The *ratio decidendi* is: *to test the power of living oratory* and perhaps to acquire for myself this new effectiveness. . . . If I fail, perhaps I shall not lose all. . . . My principles will find entrance somewhere.[56]

The long soliloquy shows Fichte eager to be active again and seeking reasons why he should be. He saw an opportunity to gain power for his philosophy earlier than he had expected. When the outbreak of the war offered him a second chance, his fancy immediately took fire and he dispatched his request to the government. The project was intoxicating in its boldness. If he could convert the army, beginning with the leaders and the choice troops, he might see the fulfillment of his mission and be able personally to guide mankind into the fourth epoch; if he did not,

[56] *Ibid.*, II, 597-600. The italics are those of Fichte.

the effort was still worth making. And of one thing he remained certain: even if he failed, "My principles," he said, "will find entrance somewhere." Neither the memorandum nor the letter to the government contains any mention of national feeling. It is implied, to be sure; but the propagation of Fichte's philosophy, disguised in the letter under Christianity, was the author's essential interest. He wanted his teachings spread; then, he thought, the national feeling would follow.

Self-confidence like Fichte's makes a man important, even great. It is a common trait of nationalists, especially those of the pen. Governments, however, rarely share this confidence and the Prussian ministry offered no exception. It had no inclination toward letting inspired professors run loose at Headquarters and felt no need of more spiritual enlightenment or "submersion in God." It refused to allow creators of a new human race to use the army for experimental purposes and probably never informed the military leaders themselves of the opportunity they were missing. Fichte was kept in Berlin, where he joined the *Landsturm,* marched, drilled, and made speeches.

This was the last opportunity Fichte had for persuading the Germans to accept his philosophy. While serving his country in hospital duty, he contracted a disease from which he soon died (1814). One can be sure that in spite of personal failure, he never for long lost faith in the ultimate victory of his philosophy. This faith had led him to nationalism; it had shown him, somewhat astigmatically, the future; it had raised him to fame. The philosopher, the nation, the future of humanity were interdependent and Fichte thought that, since his philosophy revealed the truth of nature's process, it would unite them. The future would be Fichtean.

III. ARNDT

EVEN after the abolition of serfdom, the peasantry remained more a caste than a class; it has been on the whole indifferent to national affairs and consequently to nationalism. Ignorance accounts in part for this attitude, but its way of life has tended to enable the state easily to neglect its educational needs. The peasant has been less affected by the movements of ideal and material forces during the past century and a half than any other caste or class. His interests are concentrated on the small world of his acres and his village, and he mistrusts the larger society as one of economic enemies trying to buy cheaply from him and sell dearly to him. His routine is fixed; outside it he feels lost and indecisive. His ties with the nation are few, for he knows little of it and perceives slight or no advantage to be derived from a larger concern about it. His mind tends to focus upon the elemental fact of the plot of land; by training and interest it lacks the capacity for soaring into the ideal realm of a nation, something the peasant cannot see or feel or relate intimately to himself. He is rather the defender of localism, the antithesis of love of nation; he believes in and clings to details, the concrete, and he shuns theories. While not necessarily a conservative, he approves changes only when they benefit him; otherwise he is indifferent or hostile. Even at the present day when governmental decisions affect the peasant profoundly, the latter engages in politics primarily with his eye, not on the welfare of the nation, but on that of himself. His piece of ground still comes first, even when he follows a leader like Hitler. His sense of the nation scarcely transcends the simplest feelings of individuals acutely affected by a crisis. And during the crisis he keeps his attention mainly upon his locality, turning toward it rather than toward the national center for criteria for his actions.

In spite of the antithesis between peasantry and nationalism, the one has indirectly but deeply influenced the evolution of the other. The nationalist has found in this rural folk an inspiration for his idealism. First of all, the peasant preserves the mores of the national life as no other group does. He is closest to the soil, the elemental basis of the nation, and by his mistrust of change he guards the abiding character of the nation. Secondly, the peasant thinks and acts as a member of a group. He is not an individualist, but a member of a family and of a community. The nature of his occupation demands coöperation with others and teaches him consideration of them. On a small scale he offers a pattern to the kind of fraternal life essential to nationalism. Third, human reason seems less useful to him than do physique and feeling. He must be strong of body; and, being so close to nature, he develops intuition rather than intellect. By keeping a mean between the qualities of man, he again offers the model for the nationalist. Fourth, he practices the ways of a consumption economy rather than or more than those of a production economy. That is, he adheres to the old habits of producing all or most of the objects which he and his family need and preserves more independence of international capitalistic economy than do other groups. Thereby he foreshadows nationalistic autarchy. Particularly if a member of the peasantry grows out of the group by way of some profession, he may cast the nostalgia for his early life into an ideal for the nation. Persons of other birth may, of course, take up the cult of the simple folk. But Arndt was one of the first of peasant birth to develop into a nationalist.

Ernst Moritz Arndt was born in 1769 on the island of Rügen, then a possession of Sweden. He grew up as a normal boy, suffering from no physical handicaps or unfortunate experiences and subject to the disciplinary influence of a large family. His father, a former serf, exemplified the benefits of emancipation. He had enjoyed the exceptional advantage of learning to read and write and had traveled sufficiently to acquire self-confidence, enterprise, and some knowledge of the world. He had married the daughter of a small tavern-keeper, who had also received an education beyond that of her station. By means of hard work, personal astuteness, the aid of friends more highly placed in the social scale and a rise in agricultural prices he had become the renter of a large estate in Swedish Pomerania, including several villages of serfs, and the occupant of a house which a short time previously had been the home of an aristocrat and had once been visited by a princess of Sweden. The story of his life reveals the relaxing of the economic and social restrictions of caste during the latter part of the eighteenth century and the beginnings of the turn toward the social forms of the succeeding period.

The Arndt family lived in a simple, patriarchal manner, keeping in close contact with near-by relatives and friends. Social intercourse among peasants, burghers, aristocrats, and intellectuals of the district was free and easy. Each person, no matter of what class, was accorded respect; each learned from the other; each assisted the other when necessary. Visiting brought with it enormous eating, dancing, and talk of agricultural affairs, but also storytelling, discussion of literature and, after 1789, even of politics. When one considers that the Arndts lived in a fairly secluded, virtually self-sufficient area, one finds noteworthy the quality and variety of books with which they and their friends were acquainted. The stir of thought and the impulse toward creation among these people seem no less extraordinary. Folk tales remained numerous and poetic impulse compelling. Dreaming throve alongside practical activity. The music and stories of Uncle Heinrich formed as integral an element in Arndt's background as did the oxen and the growing grain. Landscape and people blended perfectly. The Baltic sky, the sea, the many bays, streams, and marshes, the hills and rich soil, the forests and sandy wastes fascinated young Arndt as they had his forefathers. All classes worked and played, kept their dignity and modesty, cultivated goodness and beauty, thus setting a model for the nation which Arndt later conceived.

Before Arndt could sublimate the experiences of his early years into an abstract social norm, he had to develop an independent personality, above all to establish the independence of his intellectual judgments. He had to discover himself by gaining objectivity with respect to the thinking and the standards of society. The son of a former serf had to overcome the insecurity felt by a person crossing the barrier between one class and another, and his growth was slow. Self-assurance came only with wide reading and traveling, with emotional and intellectual adjustment. Even then Arndt never succeeded fully in acquiring it; his nationalism grew out of the effort to do so.

Although the literature of the Enlightenment dominated in the homes of his parents and friends, Arndt early disliked it. Cold rationalism failed to satisfy him. He loved a nature which lived and died rather than one which served as the subject of mathematics or physical science. He felt the push and tug of emotions, fighting his passions by solitary tramping and by swimming in bitter cold water. From his life on the farm he learned that the vagaries of climate and peculiarities of soil blocked the most carefully laid plans. Thus he was led to seek a more balanced instrument and guide than reason.

Experience in society taught Arndt the same lesson. He loved the intimacy among his family, relatives, and neighbors. In order to attend school at Stralsund he had to depend upon the aid of his father's friends and felt no humiliation about doing so, for the friends rendered the assistance gladly and enjoyed his company. He learned early that society did not consist of a loose agglomeration of individuals associated by man-made rational contract, but of a body of people working together, mutually dependent and united by feeling.

Throughout his life Arndt loved to dream. As a boy he began to compose poetry and to gather folk tales, while his enthusiasm for creations of the imagination, whether of his own or of another's in the past, deepened his appreciation of things cultural. According to the standards of the Enlightenment he should have despised this absurd lore of a peasant folk; but under the inspiration, among others, of his Uncle Heinrich, Arndt as a youth fastened upon his deepest interest—in the folk in all aspects of its life. Beginning by collecting folk tales, he developed into a cultural anthropologist, folklorist, and historian. The pattern of his thinking was set; he maintained the tradition of Rousseau and Herder, not that of Kant. The abstract approach to problems characteristic of Fichte or Schelling appealed to him only in so far as he could employ it to interpret the course of the past. Fichte and Schelling formulated a philosophy of history, but their method demanded a minimum of history and a maximum of philosophy. Although Arndt became as much a moralist of history as a historian, his conception of the past bore the imprint of a historian rather than of a trained philosopher.

Arndt's affinity for history cannot be explained. Dreaming might as well have led to philosophic creativeness. One dare not argue that the peasant's son preferred concrete facts to abstractions, for Fichte came from similar stock. History could scarcely claim to be more practical than philosophy, especially when, as in Arndt's most famous works, the two were popularly combined. Perhaps the answer lies in Arndt's early love of folklore, which attracted him to learn the character of the formative age of mythology. The history of the Greeks from Homeric days through Pericles and beyond, a necessary part of the classical education of his time, encouraged the interest. Arndt learned that the peoples of past epochs shared many characteristics with his own immediate folk, that other characteristics had since become vestigial or lost. Puzzled to explain why, he plunged more deeply into history and endeavored to arrange the materials into some intelligible form. The comparison of his own period with those periods of the past which fascinated him threw into relief the evils of his own age, spurring him on to consider reforms for eliminating these evils and for inaugurating another great age in the history of mankind. The vision of a future epoch furnished him with the goal of his nationalism and the efforts to realize it constitute the story of his nationalistic activity.

Folklore and history were studied during the age of the Enlightenment, but basically they both tended toward the acceptance of irrational elements. An interest in folklore aroused in the student a psychological understanding deeper than that of the school of Locke, while history demonstrated the diversity of life and standards and, by way of the concept of development or change, broke up the rational mold. Folklore and history served the same purpose for Arndt as idealistic philosophy for Fichte. They strengthened his native aversion to rationalism and afforded him sympathetic agents for evolving a new ideal for man and society.

Interest in history and folklore led Arndt into the most troublesome problem of his entire life, that of bringing together knowledge and actual existence, of relating contemplation and action. In the study of the past one could see when, where, and how union had been possible; the concrete evidence of experience was available in the story of Hellenic Greece, early Germany, the Renaissance. Arndt felt profoundly moved by the contrast between the harmony of forces in those ages and the discord in his own. The peasant's son with his roots in the soil, living close to his family and folk and desirous of utilizing knowledge for human living, disliked with increasing intensity the intellectual self-satisfaction of the Enlightenment. When he studied theology at the University, he met more of it, and ultimately gave up his first choice of a profession, the ministry, because the cold, pedantic dogmatism of theology as then taught repelled him. Nor could he accept the office of religious guide, for he saw no value in the kind of religion dispensed. While he himself was devoid of religious faith at the time, he appreciated what it was like and what it should do for the common folk. Religion, he thought, connoted mystery, solace, assurance, resurrection. It should lead to warm intimacy between pastor and congregation rather than to separation of an intellectual leader from a docile, conforming flock. It should unite knowledge and emotion for the enrichment of the lives of the people. The pastor and his congregation, as Arndt conceived them, realized in miniature the social dream of the future nationalist.

For at least half his life Arndt allowed mood and circumstances largely to direct his course. Unable to balance his love of action and his love of contemplation, he found difficulty in adjusting himself. From childhood he had struggled with the "hot Arndt blood," as he later called it. Tempestuousness, vehemence, enthusiasm remained characteristic of the man as they had been of the boy. Years of inhibiting his rich sensuousness may have contributed to the unsteadiness of his course. When he graduated from the gymnasium in Stralsund, he fled to the soil, fearing that in an urban environment he would degenerate into a moral weakling and dilettante. After two years of quiet study and work in his parents' home, he attended the Universities of Greifswald and Jena. By the time he had finished his university work he was twenty-five years of age and still without a predilection for any career. The next two years he spent again at home, combining physical work with study; then for a year and a half he taught the small children of a friend. At the end of that time he still lacked any clear plan. In 1798 he determined upon a trip and for a year and a half wandered, often on foot, through Germany, Austria, Italy and France. Running away from books to the knockabout life of a traveler, he associated with persons of high and low position and learned, so he said, to esteem a man for his true character and not for his birth or fortune. Upon returning home, he married the illegitimate daughter of a professor at the University of Greifswald, to whom he had been engaged against his family's will for several years. Through the influence of his father-in-law he drifted into teaching at the same university.

Since he lived in a period of social transition, Arndt was profoundly concerned with questions of conduct. "I do not know whence I came; I do not know where I am going; but how I go, that I must know," he wrote his mother in December, 1796.[1] The statement reflected Arndt's subjectivity and revealed the absence of devotion to any one position or field of work, to a past or existing society. It portrayed the feeling of a person seeking to find himself in a contrary world, a person so emancipated from the routine of a social environment that he was free to envisage a better society. Since he lacked the assurance which comes from the ownership of property or from a fixed place in the world, he felt hypersensitive about his social relations and had to form standards in abstract terms. Idealists are inclined to judge conditions according to absolute values. As soon as Arndt had clarified

[1] Ernst Müsebeck, *Ernst Moritz Arndt. Ein Lebensbild* (Gotha, 1914), I, 44.

his ideals of man and the group, he was to wish to live in accordance with them and, discovering that he could not in the present society, he was to try to reform it.

The years between 1798 and 1806 represented the richest in Arndt's development. During that time he translated into ideas the subconscious inclinations and feelings which had hitherto guided him. With slight modification and expansion these ideas remained henceforth fundamental to him. Although he now took a few hesitant steps out of the academic sphere and experimented in relating knowledge and life, he still endeavored primarily to discover the nature of the age in which he lived, to fit it into a philosophy of history and to elucidate in general terms his positive ideal for man and society. He dealt theoretically with all the questions which later absorbed his full powers, thus acquiring the intellectual assurance to try to aid the world.

The trip through Europe which Arndt began in 1798 opened up to him a world beyond his native North Germany. In several volumes he carefully described the cultures of the lands which he visited and tested his vague ideas against reality. He broadened his view of national psychology and learned to differentiate between nations and to distinguish a true folk from a loosely related mass of people. The European scene enriched his interest in cultural anthropology and in the historical differences among nations and states. The function of politics and the state acquired new meaning, which under favorable circumstances a decade later drove him into nationalistic activity. In France Arndt observed the effects of the Revolution, substantiating his conviction that the Enlightenment, progenitor of the Revolution and guide of its acts, was a curse.

In 1801 Arndt lost his wife in childbed. It is difficult to estimate the significance of this event in the history of his course toward nationalism. Certainly his wife's death loosed the bonds holding him to the University of Greifswald and to his profession. The disruption of his family life revived his pessimism and inclined him toward diffidence and fatalism as much as his energetic and fiery temperament would allow. But the death of his wife likewise enabled him to fall in love again two years later with Charlotte Bindemann, who seems to have stirred his ambition to become something more than a teacher.

During his early married life and subsequent years of misfortune Arndt devoted his energy in the main to scholarly work. In 1802 he finished two books, in which only the choice of subjects and occasional warm passages betrayed the future nationalist. In one Arndt dealt with the history of serfdom in Swedish Pomerania, showing its recent introduction into that area. Although the tendency of the book to favor peasant emancipation appeared only between the lines, the peasant question was so acute that even a scholarly work aroused controversy. Arndt found himself the center of a dispute which, if he had pursued it, would have related knowledge and actuality as intimately as he might wish. He chose to remain the scholar. The same reserve characterized his other book, *Germanien und Europa,* which is much more important for the history of his nationalism. In this work Arndt declared mad both himself and the age, and he endeavored to explain the origins and nature of the ills from which the world suffered and how the ills could be cured. Since the ideas worked out in *Germanien und Europa* furnish the basis of all his future writings, Arndt's answer to these questions will be discussed later.

In 1803 Arndt received permission to study in Sweden during the next academic year. After an unsympathetic stay in Stockholm he traveled through the rural districts. His joy knew no limits. The old Swedish stump, he said, referring to the tradition of the Swedish origin of his family, was beginning to sprout again. He loved the country with its lights and shadows, its mystery, its living folklore and poetry. And then the Swedes themselves! "What men those are!" he wrote. "Such powerful, overwhelming sensitiveness to nature, such poetic love of spring, light and life." [2] He told of his friend, a Swedish professor of law, who sang folk songs on the coming of spring and burst into tears. He described another as "a nobleman, a knight, a rich landowner, a man of learning, an antiquarian, enthusiastic about his gods and

[2] *E. M. Arndts Briefe aus Schweden an einen Stralsunder Freund* (Herausgegeben von Erich Gülzow, Stralsund, 1926), pp. 66-69.

heroes, . . . an active, practical, rural leader, member of all learned societies and of all those for the advancement of industry and agriculture." "That is a proper, complete, happy, knightly, Nordic man," he added, of whom he had seen several examples, "the brave one axe in hand and the pious one with the Bible." [3] Among these people he relived the society of his youth. These Swedes preserved their folklore, loved the land and possessed all the social virtues. They illustrated the union of knowledge and action. Only over Stockholm, where imitation of French culture among the higher classes blighted the ideal, did he feel disappointment.

Arndt saw examples of Germans being assimilated in Sweden with excellent results and would have become a Swede himself if he had found a position. He still lacked feeling for a particular nation, and was intent upon his personal development and the clarification of his thoughts. At the same time that he waxed enthusiastic about the Swedes, he was enlightening them about German romanticism, the one aspect of German culture which inspired him with pride; and he owed some of his popularity in Swedish society to his knowledge of the new cultural movement across the Baltic. His acquaintance with the Swedish folk coincided with his reading of Schelling's romantic philosophy and the two experiences blended perfectly—the organic philosophy with the organic folk, the slightly cosmopolitan quality of Schelling's thought with the crossing of two peoples, Germans and Swedes. He returned to Greifswald with a more fixed social and cultural faith, for he had lived among a folk who personified his emerging ideals.

After a year in Sweden of stimulating association with aristocrats, intellectuals, and peasants, Arndt found the provincial life of the University of Greifswald boring. He prepared himself intellectually for his future writings about his own age by lecturing on a wide variety of literary, historical, and even philosophic subjects. In the next year, 1805, he wrote *Geist der Zeit,* I, which some years later he properly called a continuation of *Germanien*

[3] *Ibid.,* pp. 29-31.

und Europa. This work and a third book written in the same period (1802-5), *Fragmente über Menschenbildung,* contain the gist of his criticism of contemporary life, his philosophy of history, and his panacea for the troubles of his age. Of them all *Geist der Zeit* was written with most passion and dealt most directly with actual conditions and with Germany proper. Since in his later writings Arndt used and expanded upon the ideas contained in these works, the body of his thought will be analyzed at this point irrespective of whether it came from these three books or from succeeding ones.

By 1805 Arndt had developed four deep aversions, one to rationalism and the Enlightenment, the second to the French and their revolution, the third to the vestiges of feudalism, and the fourth to absolutism. He identified the Enlightenment with French culture and regarded the spread of the one as an imperialistic instrument for the other. Since the upper classes in countries outside France, especially royalty and the aristocracy, mainly accepted the Enlightenment, he had double cause for antagonism to each. He likewise nursed a multiple grievance against absolutism, which he considered to be derived from rationalism. The four phenomena constituted a whole to him and cannot be discussed separately. Inasmuch as Arndt was seeking an ultimate solution, he turned to the philosophy of history in order to discover how these forces had gained power and what should replace them. Every philosophy of history, at least of this period, contained the author's criticism of his own age and his dream of an ideal future.

History to Arndt revealed the workings of three forces in life—body, mind, and soul. In the beginning the body scarcely recognized the presence of the other two; not until the age of the Greeks did all three reach harmony and thereby produce the most original and varied culture which history could offer. The Greeks failed, however, he thought, to permeate the entire people with their culture; and for this reason, together with that of political imperialism and a resulting mixture of races, their civilization decayed. Mind and soul failed to preserve union with the body. The results of the split appeared, he said, in early Christianity, when the mind became too rationalistic, the soul too mystical. The

Renaissance recombined the alienated elements, but the division among the three forces persisted and in succeeding centuries widened again. The age of dominion by the mind followed, reaching its peak in the eighteenth century, especially in France. "The highest good," Arndt asserted, "which the intellect could find of itself was expediency and order; it produced artificiality and not art, machinery and not a full life." [4] Rationalism could, Arndt declared, only destroy belief in the group and in God; it crushed all warm sympathy for humanity and could not create but only tear down.

Arndt hated absolutism, a product of rationalism, for its rigidity and violation of freedom. The individual, he said, had degenerated into a mechanical instrument of the royal will, important mainly as a taxpayer. Utility and legality were the highest meaning of despotism, he said. The ruler demanded subordination from every subject and reduced the idea of fatherland to a concept used only in school, signifying nothing more than the spot where chance threw one or the glory which mercenary armies and an honored regent cast upon one. Arndt condemned the court, the bureaucracy, and the standing army for dividing folk and state. Two-thirds of the officials were superfluous, forming a horde of flatterers and spies. As for the mercenary army, Arndt cursed it: the soldier and the burgher stood in hostility to one another; since the latter need not defend his country, he could no longer develop and exercise the virtues of courage and patriotism. The cost of supporting the standing army was destroying the object for which it ostensibly existed. Despotism produced cowardice and avarice, laziness and deception, selfishness and serfdom. "Most men live now like thieves," Arndt wrote, "without the feeling that what one has belongs to all and should be enjoyed by all. . . . A sense of humanity or even of civic duty is entirely impossible." [5]

In this society youth lacked fire and enthusiasm, Arndt complained; it grew old and grey in early manhood. In this society

[4] Cited in Hans Polag, *E. M. Arndts Weg zum Deutschen. Studien zur Entwickelung des frühen Arndt 1769-1812* (Leipzig, 1936), pp. 37-38.

[5] Ernst Moritz Arndt, *Geist der Zeit* (1806), p. 111.

one obeyed the law, not out of duty but because of compulsion; one hurried from pleasure to pleasure, from fashion to fashion. Shallow, poor, and wretched, man felt no love and existed without fantasy, a fatherland, or freedom. He accepted no religion, for slaves could not have "these holy feelings," and he merely toyed with art, poetry, and music. Reason had withered everything living and fresh.

> In my childhood [Arndt lamented] God and the angels moved about the homes of men and the cradles of children; spirits wandered and legends of olden times sounded sweet in the evening; old songs were sung and in spring and autumn fields and heaths resounded with joyful cries. All that is dead; even common people speak of it as childish nonsense and superstition, and have become sophisticated and shallow like the upper classes. . . . Fixity and hollowness are the two main characteristics of the present and in so far as there is movement it lacks continuity.[6]

Man had become nothing and could accomplish nothing; the age was mad and knew it.

Arndt believed in monarchism but the thought of the German princes made him bitter. He could scarcely refer to any period in German history when they had shown nobility and patriotism. He blamed them for having permitted Germany to become the battleground for European powers and condemned their egoistic greed for territory and their cowardice. During the past twenty years, he lamented, they had exposed their "foolishness, blindness and lack of honor" to the entire world.[7] But he sadly acknowledged that they were no worse than their contemporaries. Arndt ranked the aristocrats with the most despicable, for he disapproved of a privileged, hereditary nobility in any case, believing that after three or four generations a noble family degenerated. He maintained that the aristocracy rarely equaled members of other castes in talent and virtue and laid most of the blame on it for the weakness of states and the dissension among classes and for serfdom and misery. The able intellectual son of a former

[6] *Ibid.*, pp. 117-18.
[7] *Ibid.*, p. 364.

serf concealed neither his contempt for these useless aristocrats nor his aversion to the survivals of feudalism. He attributed to the latter, which he called "this antiquated barbarism," the insufficient cultivation of the soil and the persistence of famine, declaring that it prevented the freedom of action to create, so vital in this period of rapid social change.

The originality and independence of Arndt's thinking about the age came out clearly in his attitude toward the French Revolution. One would expect the opponent of serfdom, hereditary aristocracy, and the existing organization of government to greet the Revolution with ardor. Arndt sympathized with much which the Revolution did or tried to accomplish and watched its course with keen interest. Yet from its inception he seems to have doubted a beneficial outcome. He objected to its excesses, the change of constitutions, the wars of conquest, while the confidence of the people in the power of reason to solve all questions shocked him. He hoped that with the advent of Napoleon to power the era of reform would reopen. The turn of the latter to autocracy disillusioned him and caused him to believe that the progressive acts of the French Revolution had been destroyed. By 1802 he declared that the French Revolution furnished the surest proof of the inhumanity of the age. Guilty of bloody deeds, the French revolutionists, he asserted, could not have acted otherwise because they had lost their roots in the earth. The revolutionists had deluded themselves into endeavoring immediately to use in action and in the construction of government that which they had formulated precisely in their minds. They had lost all intimacy with the earth and the farther they separated from it the more they believed in the powers of the mind. Arndt diminished the censure somewhat by attributing to the age part of the responsibility; nonetheless he felt repugnant to both the revolutionists and the age. He hated Napoleon as the embodiment of rationalism, slyness, egoism, cold-bloodedness, cynicism, despotism, as one who violated the sacred rights of man and of society. He hated him for cruelly abusing the Germans, for scourging the common people whom Arndt loved, for shaming Arndt by the ease with which he defeated the Germans and found followers among them. He denied to Napoleon any gift except military genius, at times even questioning that, and he absolutely refused to believe in the invincibility of the French ruler. "Alas, everything appears to have conspired," he wrote in 1805, "to produce an Emperor. Ten years ago the boldest dreamer would not have conceived of such shameless despotism." [8]

If one can trust his autobiography, written years later, Arndt never cared for the French. His aversion dated back to childhood, when he read the history of Louis XIV's invasions of Germany; during the revolutionary wars he mourned over each German defeat. In the measure that he freed himself from the cultural hold of the Enlightenment, his capacity for understanding the French people narrowed. On his trip through France in 1799 Arndt had felt both fascinated and repelled by the French. He thought them charming, esteemed their social graces and admired their national spirit; but he disliked them for these same qualities, excepting only national spirit, which he soon denied them. Their social charm, he thought, quickly turned into love of display and desire for empty externalities, and expressed affectation, weakness, ignorance, and shallowness. When some years later he met French polish among the upper classes in Stockholm, he again was attracted by it. But after his first sojourn in Sweden he never succumbed again to the allure of this culture. "Devoid of religion, poetry, truth," he apostrophized the French in 1805, "too weak to correct yourselves, too cultivated to comprehend your evil, you go about proudly while shamelessly crowing to us others that we are uncouth barbarians." [9]

The criticism which Arndt made of his contemporaries reflected the feelings of an intellectual who had built his ideals around rural life. Arndt inveighed against the evils of caste privileges, the burden of taxation, and serfdom, which oppressed the common folk. Disliking the customs and ideals which had grown up with the bourgeoisie and had formed the culture of the Enlightenment, he lamented the loss of folkways and resented the fact that the upper classes disregarded them.

[8] *Ibid.*, pp. 348-49.
[9] *Ibid.*, pp. 356-57.

In condemning the French Arndt eliminated a vigorous competitor of the German nation for the role of cultural guide for mankind. Nonetheless, he had not as yet fixed upon the Germans as the chosen nation. While he became infuriated at the French for taking parts of Germany and denounced their methods of warfare, yet his anti-French sentiment did not arise out of the desire to exalt the Germans. The fact that Pomerania, the home of the Arndts, was populated by Germans and governed by Sweden, conditioned Arndt's public ideals and political loyalty throughout his life, more especially through the first period of it. Arndt belonged to both Germany and Sweden. He did not feel exactly as a Swede, because Sweden lay across the Baltic and spoke an alien language; he could not regard himself completely as a German, because Pomeranians revered the Swedish king and, living on the periphery of Germany, failed to receive the full influence of German culture. When Arndt traveled through Europe in 1798-99, he called himself a Swede because, as he said, the name German "stinks in the world," not, he added characteristically, through the fault of the common people. In 1802 he entitled his book *Germanien und Europa* and among the Germans he included the Scandinavians.[10] Arndt's first trip to Sweden in 1803-4 served in part to reconnoiter for a new post. The opposition to peasant emancipation among the Pomeranian German aristocrats angered him, whereas in Sweden he found a folk without serfdom. In Sweden the elite of the country received him heartily, honoring him to an extent undreamed of by the Germans of Pomerania. He frequently compared the two peoples, always to the detriment of the Germans. "These northern fellows," he wrote, ". . . once in motion attack with words and fists. . . . I have often been ashamed of our soft and crumbly Germanism. . . . I feel every day that there is nothing more paltry than this miserable German thing called good nature or even mildness and humanity, but which in reality is the fear to say 'yes' or 'no' and is merely the conceit of weakness."[11] The Swedes gave Arndt a

[10] He used the word *"Germanien"* here to refer to the Teutonic peoples, the word *"Deutsche"* to refer to the Germans proper.

[11] *Briefe aus Schweden, op. cit.*, pp. 42-46.

profound experience of a people with a national spirit. Their culture appealed to him, a man of the people who revered the past and loved to see a people united and self-contained. It satisfied every part of his nature; but it saddened him to think of German disunity and its disastrous effects.

> Not merely all nature but the history of the people are a thousand times more alive than with us, and this consciousness of Swedish happiness and German deficiency often weighs heavily on my German heart. In the first place, how many memorials of the earliest time they have preserved, not only in marvelous sagas, but in existing realities, in hillocks in which gods and heroes slumber, jagged cliffs, from which they have plunged to the immortal tables of the gods in ever-green meadows, in time-honored, stone-girdled landmarks of popular assemblies, in runes, and the like. We Germans have hardly a stump or a pale saga left of all these things; our people neither sees nor understands anything of this. Every Swede is rooted in the tradition of his past and looks up to the shining halls of his gods and heroes. We have had too many foreign floods roll over us, foreign peoples and robbers have come; even the first missionaries of Christianity were allowed . . . to destroy them and let them rot. In the second place, Sweden is a unified kingdom and has long been under one rule; her great kings, heroes, prophets, soothsayers and poets belong entirely to her, belong to every man, and every man is proud of them. For many centuries we have had only division of territory and of hearts and in many places are so divided from one another that great German names are only known in one locality and one even curses what another blesses.
>
> Why should we longer regard as a higher humanitarianism our miserable German disunity, our so-called humane all and nothing, through which our country has become so much a nothing, the despised of foreigners? [12]

Arndt felt loyal to Germany and to Sweden because the two peoples formed one group, the Nordic race. Loving them both he had no occasion to choose between them, for he still thought in terms of a cultural folk, not of a political nation. He evolved a racial theory to justify his hatred of the French and love of the Swedes, which ran as follows: the South European was char-

[12] *Ibid.*, pp. 42-46.

acterized by buoyancy, the North European by gravity and firmness; the Southerner was the classicist, the Northerner the romanticist; the Southerner created easily and naturally, the Northerner with effort. The Northerner must first train himself to become that which the Southerner already was, an instinctively artistic man. The Northerner, more a prey to feeling and passions, easily exaggerated; he seldom gave himself up to that inner stillness from which art springs. The Northerner was joyous, gallant, strong of physique; he was good, courageous, possessed resolution and cleverness; but, since he lacked the richer fullness of life of the Southerner, he must seek to live in clarity and order. Arndt attributed to the North European the characteristics which he himself possessed. To the Southerner he gave those which he had observed in studying the culture of the Greeks and the Italians of the Renaissance. He placed these two groups as basic types in the European world. The Northern group contained peoples of different degrees of perfection; but the model of the Nordic existed as a finished, ultimate thing which Arndt thought he had found in the Swedes. When after 1806, he turned from the Swedes to the Germans, he reversed the order of excellence until the Germans either ranked superior in quality to the Swedes or had the capacity and the mission for doing so. Living between North and South, the French, according to Arndt, were doomed to be uncreative. A mixture of North and South in speech and character, they approached the excellence of neither. Mediocrity of this kind should not be trusted with the hegemony of Europe.

In tracing the emergence of Arndt's nationalism one must keep in mind three lines of his thought: condemnation of the age, its culture, and its institutions; belief in the regeneration of mankind; and the search for some people to lead in this work. Each was essential to making Arndt a nationalist. In pursuing the first line of thought Arndt had rejected the culture of the upper and middle classes. It is now necessary to ascertain whether he expected the common people to effect a revival of civilization, and if so how soon he expected it, what it would be like, and by what means it would occur. The answer to these questions leads to the heart of Arndt's nationalism.

A writer of Arndt's imaginative depth and energetic temperament could not rest content with a mere condemnation of his own period. "He who lacks enthusiasm now and cannot build for himself a seventh heaven over this earth and this heaven is nothing," he wrote in October, 1805.[13] He had to console and reassure himself and others by prophecy. In *Germanien und Europa* (1802) Arndt wrote that his age could only prepare for that one which would perhaps be possible after centuries had passed. Three years later he believed that he himself was living in the period of crisis, out of which would emerge a glorious age, and his certainty grew with the intensity of his nationalism. The idea that man must be purified by "death by fire" remained an abiding belief with him. He used the phrase in a figurative sense, denoting any form of severe punishment. Just as Goethe seemed to him in 1802 the harbinger of a new humanism, so the Napoleonic victories impressed him as the work of destruction, presaging the resurrection of man and society. Like the Christian, society must lose its life in order to save it. Arndt added to his dialectic of history a Christian character which put God on his side. "The French Revolution will make the third great epoch of Christianity," he wrote in 1808. "I do not herewith declare Marat, Danton, Robespierre and Bonaparte to be followers of Christ. Devils must also serve God." [14]

An age like that of the French Revolution and Napoleon may allow a person to surpass himself. Arndt was of mediocre talents; yet by virtue of qualities which suited the time as a nationalist he ranks alongside his more gifted contemporaries. He lacked the supreme and persistent conceit of Fichte; it took longer to stir him to action and he was more modest in his demands for personal authority. Nonetheless, he felt a profound sense of mission and never doubted that he possessed infallible truth. In *Geist der Zeit* he placed himself in the line of succession to

[13] E. M. Arndt, *Briefe an eine Freundin* (Herausgegeben von E. Langenberg, Berlin, 1878), pp. 36-37.

[14] *Geist der Zeit* (Herausgegeben von Heinrich Meisner, Leipzig), II, 135.

Pythagoras, Socrates, Christ, and Luther, and arrogated to himself the task of diagnosing the disease of his age and proposing the remedy.

Arndt looked beyond the political revolution to the spiritual blight which had attacked the vitals of civilization. He believed that Kant had destroyed all previous philosophy, leaving the world clear for the creation of a new one. He avowed that no one had comprehended the significance of the Reformation until a few years previously and included himself among the very few who did so. Whether a definitive philosophy would ever be evolved, whether the true meaning of the Reformation would ever be realized, depended, Arndt thought, upon the acceptance of his ideals as the basis for complete reform of man and society. Even more was at stake. "The two worlds are divided, it seems forever, the spiritual one here which the spirit has now forsaken, and the heavenly one above which should light and bless the one below."[15] Arndt heard a call to unite heaven and earth, spirit, soul, and body, to bring the ideal and material together, to teach the wise and the good man the necessity of intimacy with the earth. He prophesied and preached revolution in every phase of life. The times have been in movement, Arndt said apropos of the past twenty years, but men have stood still. Writers and scholars have become feeble and sterile. What was formerly a gift of prophecy (that of the writer) has become a degrading handicraft. Arndt wanted to restore the high position of his profession. "Whoever wishes to move the world," he said, "must have clear understanding, a forceful hand, a moving speech and Pythian anger, the power to denounce and prophesy with a divine voice."[16] His feelings drove him to attempt this role. "I wish to speak to relieve my heart," he wrote.[17] Nature, his creator and queen, gave him these feelings, he said, and he would remain true to her as long as he lived, not permitting "this holy freedom of nature" to be taken from him. He wept over the times and the degeneration of man, who had been created upright and godly, to look toward the light of the stars, to understand justice.

[15] *Ibid.*, I, 51.
[16] *Ibid.*, p. 8.
[17] *Ibid.*, p. 3.

In his effort to teach others to fulfill that duty Arndt turned to nationalism.

Arndt believed that the next great epoch, the third stage just beginning in the history of mankind, would see the three forces of body, mind, and soul united again in even more complete harmony than among the Greeks. This stage would know the ideal man and the ideal society; for all of man's powers would be released and would enrich each other. Body would not overshadow spirit or spirit crowd out soul. The mystery of the Trinity was to be repeated. The kingdom of heaven would come to earth, but would be a kingdom in which a strong body would house and keep in balance a powerful mind and a rich soul. Neither asceticism nor hedonism, neither rationalism nor mysticism would acquire predominance. In 1808 Arndt added a Christian element to his vision: it would be the age of the religion of light. In his search for a group to realize the third age he turned to the nation.

That man might fulfill his purpose Arndt demanded complete liberty for him. By temperament Arndt loved freedom and made the ideal the focal point of his philosophy. "Man loses all with loss of freedom," he said,[18] and he realized that in order to enrich culture in this period of the breakup of old forms and customs the individual must be allowed to set his own goals. He learned early in life, however, that complete freedom was impossible, and the perusal of Schelling's philosophy between 1803 and 1805 confirmed the idea of union between spirit and nature, in which he had longed to believe. This philosophy satisfied his own desires for universality and inclined him for a time to accept an all-inclusive world-soul. By assuring Arndt that he served powers beyond his understanding it lent him security and self-confidence. A few years later the return to belief in a personal God had a similar effect. In 1810 Arndt wrote:

The freer we are to be in the endless and heavenly kingdom of the sun, the more firmly and more simply must we bind ourselves in the closed and earthly kingdom and the more every man and every

[18] Langenberg, *op. cit.*, p. 34; Polag, p. 22.

folk must be self-dependent so that they can enter without danger into divine freedom, whereby all peoples and tongues of the earth shall finally play and compete in the highest unity.[19]

When Arndt tried to explain the power which ultimately controlled the destiny of all, he sometimes spoke of a Providence outside the course of the earth and sometimes of a God immanent in human affairs. While always recognizing with awe an incomprehensible divine force, he did not excuse man from struggling to fulfill divine purpose and maintained that man held Providence in his own hands. Freedom did not exist for the individual alone, but for the individual in society, where he performed the work set for him by the Deity. Life partook of both freedom and predestination, a belief which constituted the metaphysical basis for nationalism.

When Arndt portrayed the ideal individual, he grew ecstatic. "What is man without enthusiasm and love?" he once demanded.[20] He believed in the essential goodness of man and patterned his ideal after his own model, a peasant who had heightened and expanded his qualities by intellectual and social experience while preserving intimacy with the soil. Everything and everyone, Arndt maintained, would be improved if men of the sword, the oar, and the plow also knew how to use the pen. They would be sound, joyous, understanding human beings, shaped by life for life. They would combine body, mind, and soul as the ancient Greeks and the men of the Italian Renaissance had done and as Arndt tried to do. They would be citizens and statesmen, farmers and poets, men of books and of action, dreamers and creators, and would revive the age of poetry, of myths, and of heroes. They would all be practical mystics, for mysticism, Arndt declared, was the force of life of the finest natures. The noblest spirits will be born only among the folk, he said with himself in mind, and they must have "the heart and eyes of a child." [21]

Arndt appreciated the fact that the group was necessary to

[19] Ernst Moritz Arndt, *Hoffnungsrede vom Jahre 1810* (Greifswald, 1921), pp. 46-47.

[20] *Geist der Zeit*, I, 50.

[21] *Ibid.*, p. 66.

develop individuals of this type and he easily made the transition from individualism to group-consciousness. A sense of union with his people animated the child, he once declared, and, although the statement is not universally true, it fitted him. Except perhaps for a brief interval Arndt always recognized the dependence, like that of the peasant upon the family or the community, of the individual upon the group. Even during this interval he merely shifted the emphasis. He preferred the man to the citizen, he declared, adding that man did not exist for the sake of achieving the best state, but the state existed to help in forming the most perfect individual. While he disliked the regime of Frederick the Great, he did not object to man's being a citizen nor did he wish to weaken the state; he believed that a completely developed individual would make a model citizen. He accused the French and English of stressing political education far too much and asserted that it was good to love and to serve one's fatherland but far better to be a man, esteeming everything human above the merely patriotic. His historical sense showed him that the ideal could not always be achieved. So long as the universal, that is, the human and free could not live, he declared, the national should hold sway. By national he meant partisan loyalty to national institutions and ideals as they existed, irrespective of their quality. He approved of the fact that the French lived temporarily by this standard and was not prepared to reject all devotion to political interests. After having witnessed the tragedy of political disunity in Italy, he wrote in 1798, "Poor disunified Germany. What shall I prophesy for you?" [22] A few years later, in 1803, he feared that Germany might suffer the fate of Poland or Italy. A people, he said, lost all power and ambition with the loss of its political basis. Man could not create out of air. "Only when we have a fatherland, when we have the exalted human and political ideas of a strong people will we attain abiding customs, firm character and artistic form. Then only can the highest and most glorious of humanity grow out of these earthly

[22] Polag, *op. cit.*, p. 21.

roots toward the shining sun." [23] Without the fold, he declared in 1805, there could be no humanity and without the free citizen no free man.

Arndt never accepted the current cosmopolitanism. He believed that a person was most completely a citizen of the world when he served his own country. Because Arndt loved multiplicity, he defended the right of the Germans and other nations to exist alongside the French. As he grew older, he searched in each folk or nation for something individual and eternal. His interest in all aspects of the culture of a nation fed his desire. Although the outward forms changed, he said, the spirit remained the same and during the distressing times of Napoleonic victories its presence lent him confidence that the age of glory would come. He even knew who was keeping the spirit alive, he wrote in 1805, for in cultured society it appeared only in extraordinary men during crises. That the description fitted himself and his period scarcely needs to be noted.

In order to unify the body, soul, and mind Arndt had to bring into intimacy man, God, and the world. It was manifest that the union could not be achieved by the intellect, which deceived itself too easily. A more reliable instrument must be discovered and Arndt, who believed in the goodness of man's nature, found this in feeling. "It is an eternal rule," he said in September, 1805, "that when one speaks of the highest, of love and friendship, one should not think but let the heart reign. What can art do? Leave to God the guidance and all will go well." [24] He denied that life could be planned rationally and despised the system-building philosophers. Necessity and love should direct one's education, he thought, "guidance by the invisible hand of wisdom and innocence, a listening and understanding." [25] Arndt was remembering his own education in the fields, along the shore, at home listening to folk stories. For creating new ideals and goals nature and feeling had served him better than intellect. He did not stretch his confidence in feeling so far as Kleist did; in Arndt

[23] Ernst Moritz Arndt, *Notgedrungener Bericht aus seinem Leben* (Leipzig, 1847), pp. 198-99.

[24] Langenberg, *op. cit.*, p. 34.

[25] Müsebeck, *op. cit.*, p. 140.

the cautious peasant always kept the poet in leash; but during personal or social crises Arndt relied upon the voice of instinct. By way of the heart he could enter into intimacy with the folk as no rationalist could. If he could bring all men to believe and act in accordance with the dictates of the heart, a nation of brothers would arise who understood and, above all, loved each other.

Arndt learned that only certain feelings gave him assurance of performing God's work. "When I feel, act and strive for the general," he wrote, "I feel in myself the power to change the fate of the world." [26] In 1810 he declared again: "Only the person whose life has taken a steady course toward God, who wills and does all through and for God and for the whole wherein God is, who daily forgets himself and sacrifices himself for the people and the world—only in this brave and faithful one are mirrored heaven and its invisible powers, only to him will the glance, the word, the sound, the consecration be given to influence the people powerfully and prophetically and in friendly and gentle manner to bring back to the soulless earth the spirits that have fled." [27] Arndt felt most himself when he forgot himself in service for others. In another age religious devotion might have lent him the certainty for which he longed; in this one, nationalism—the merging of individual and nation—did so.

After Arndt returned from Sweden in 1804, he took up his work at the University of Greifswald. During 1805 war broke out between Sweden and Napoleon and Arndt composed *Geist der Zeit,* I, in its shadow. Disgusted at the hopeless situation in Germany, he denied that the Germans formed a nation. For centuries they had lacked a common feeling. "I myself," he wrote in *Geist der Zeit,* I, "live among a folk which in its best periods had only a half-German sense; now no one speaks any more of this sense." [28] That Arndt was relatively indifferent to the Germans was evident from the fact that he allowed the Germans only the humble honor of being brothers to the Scandinavians and that he wrote the first part of *Geist der Zeit* not merely for

[26] Cited by Dr. Paul Hermann Ruth, *Arndt und die Geschichte* (Munich and Berlin, 1930), p. 147.

[27] *Hoffnungsrede, op. cit.,* p. 57.

[28] *Geist der Zeit,* I, 212.

them but for all Europeans. He was searching for any people competent to defeat the greatest menace to his ideals and to realize and spread these ideals. In 1805 and the first half of 1806 he thought the Swedes capable of this mission. "The world builders and the world destroyers always came from the South," he wrote in 1805; the North sent the avengers and liberators.

When all Europe falls because of laziness, cowardice, and despotism [he wrote], when there is no longer any country free from tyranny and cunning, when there is no longer any voice raised in praise of freedom and truth and no arm to draw the sword for these, there will still dwell in Scandinavia's woods and mountains a free people who will punish and bring salvation to the suffering world; dominion and victory will proceed from here and the cowardly will tremble and serve.[29]

The writing of *Geist der Zeit,* I, did not imply that Arndt was turning from contemplation to action. He preferred, so he said in 1805 and 1806, the quiet existence in Pomerania of a scholar and poet. He found trouble in living according to his wishes, for the distress of the Germans and the revolutionary times upset him. "The accursed political activity and the misery and pitifulness of man," he complained, "penetrate every breast and push one out of the happy life that one could have into rude and fearful reality. To learn to endure bravely is something but is not to be compared with vigorous action."[30] Few persons were quiet, happy, and free, Arndt said to a friend, and he lamented that the age was not conducive to history and poetry. Hardships were teaching him that before he could make a name for himself in these fields he must help overcome the present conditions and create the third age in the history of mankind; nevertheless it required several more years for the lessons of Napoleonic despotism to destroy his hope that he could enjoy a quiet life and to force him into active nationalism.

In September, 1806, Napoleon crushed the Prussian army,

[29] *Ibid.*, pp. 298 99.

[30] H. Meisner and R. Geerds, *Ernst Moritz Arndt, Ein Lebensbild in Briefen* (Berlin, 1898), p. 55.

advanced into Pomerania, established control, and, in raising money and supplies, threatened the land with ruin. Arndt fled into Sweden, for his vituperation against Napoleon and the French made it dangerous for him to risk falling into their hands. He remained in Sweden until late in 1809, longing for someone to lead the struggle in Germany. For a person with as great a need for freedom as Arndt, enforced sojourn even among a people he loved became identical with harsh exile. His sense of union with the German folk, the people of his language, was denied a normal outlet and the separation intensified his suffering. When one adds that while in Sweden he was parted from his son and relatives and from the woman he loved, one comprehends the high pitch of his feelings. Confronted with an ever more successful enemy, he needed all the encouragement that the Swedes could give. Yet he met nothing but disappointment. A position in a university was never offered him and his task of assisting in the preparation of a new legal code for Pomerania proved dull and tedious, more particularly as he disagreed with his colleagues. Worst of all, greater intimacy with the Swedes brought him disillusion. Devoted to the Swedish king, who hated the French and wished war as much as Arndt did, he longed for the former to lead a crusade for the liberation of Europe. To Arndt's astonishment and sorrow he discovered that the Swedes opposed the war against Napoleon and regarded indifferently the fate of Pomerania, not to mention Germany; he realized that the brotherly Nordic feeling was all on his side. When the king began war, first with France, then with Russia and Denmark, his officers opposed it and betrayed their troops in order to harm their ruler. Arndt felt isolated, lonely and useless, and when early in 1809 the nobles and the army deposed the king, he was eager to leave Sweden. By that time he had concluded that the Swedes lacked public spirit, courage, and initiative. They were not a nation.

As the other man's pasture always looks greener, so the Swedes attracted Arndt more when he lived in Germany, the Germans when he stayed in Sweden. He needed a people to influence, to lead, one which would fulfill his ideals, and as danger augmented, the need became more pressing. As early as 1802 he had noted a unique quality about the Germans. "There is rising throughout Europe but especially in Germany a new living spirit," he wrote.[31] As time passed he saw this spirit concentrating itself in the ideal of a folk or nation, a group of kinsmen bound by ties of love and devoted to the common welfare. That people most capable of comprehending an idea, he thought, would first become a nation, and he found evidence among the Germans that they possessed this capacity. They were still a youthful people, less tainted by the evils of the age than others. "In our customs, in our art, in our life, in our poetry and our costumes," he wrote, "there is something which reaches to the highest ideal, something that in this age burns like a bright flame and if only the fiery strength could be concentrated into one point must kindle us and others."[32] By July, 1806, Arndt was so sensitive about the Germans that he fought a duel with a Swede for having insulted them in his presence. In the autumn he felt proud of the Prussians for having the courage after their defeat to resist Napoleon. Within another year he wrote to a friend as follows: "I shall never desert my German fatherland and its holy cause so long as there is a drop of blood left in me. I feel now more deeply than ever before that I belong to the Germans and could not or would not like to belong to another people."[33] He perceived essential qualities in the Germans which the French lacked, qualities which he had formerly attributed to the Swedes. And by considering German negligence rather than French superiority responsible for defeat, he assured himself that Germany could recover her freedom. A people with so glorious a past could not die; "we," he declared, "live in a beautiful, large, rich land, a land of glorious memories, undying deeds, unforgettable service to the world in remote and recent times. We are the navel of Europe, the center of North and South. . . . We are as good as the best. . . . German! What a name and what a people!"[34] If Napoleon conquered Germany, he predicted, entire Europe would become "a lifeless and soulless slave heap."[35]

[31] Polag, *op. cit.*, p. 52.
[32] *Geist der Zeit*, II, 186-87.
[33] Langenberg, *op. cit.*, pp. 56-57.
[34] *Geist der Zeit*, II, 87-88, 93.
[35] Polag, *op. cit.*, p. 107.

Arndt realized that he could not rely on the Germans without leadership to grasp and fulfill the ideal. He must inspire them. "O fatherland," he lamented in 1806, "you do not lack brave, bold hearts, you lack brave and bold voices which will proclaim with seriousness and love your need and your salvation." [36] This was his mission, to be a prophet for a new age, one of "the mighty army of writers," for, he declared, through the indifference or caution of other leaders writers must begin the work of saving the folk. In this uprooted, tumultuous age they bore the enormous responsibility of the age to come. They felt the misery and shame of the entire folk. Arndt, fresh and vigorous, was certain that divine power inspired him, that he would live long and achieve "something significant for my German folk and fatherland." [37]

In assuming the role of guide for the Germans Arndt began by preaching one elemental fact. Germany must unite, he declared, or go backward: she could not stand still. All Germans, high and low, must appreciate their mutual dependence and become one people, a spiritual unit. German character must change —teachers like Arndt would attend to that task; it must acquire moral as well as physical courage so that national unity would last. The German name must be restored to honor and fame. Higher than religious difference there must be one belief, the faith in the fatherland. "I am not ashamed of the gospel of my people; may it not be ashamed of me," he wrote in 1810.[38]

In the autumn of 1808 Arndt listed the causes which he defended. "I love my fatherland and its honor and freedom above all; I love my freedom, I love the monuments which past ages have transmitted to us to preserve; I love knowledge and light, which despotism wishes to wipe off the earth." [39] The list is significant. Arndt loved his fatherland and wished everyone else in Germany to do so; for wherever he went, he lived under the menace of Napoleon. In an age like this, he said, "we must all be armed, for today does not know what tomorrow will bring." [40] One must be a complete man in order to survive. The love of

[36] *Geist der Zeit*, II, 9.
[37] Langenberg, *op. cit.*, pp. 55, 58.
[38] *Hoffnungsrede, op. cit.*, p. 18.
[39] *Geist der Zeit*, II, 188.
[40] Langenberg, *op. cit.*, pp. 56-57.

honor and freedom appealed especially to the foot-loose peasant's son, sensitive as regards his personal honor and freedom and those of his nation rather than as regards those of caste or locality. Without freedom he could not exist, for it was as vital to an intellectual as caste privilege to an aristocrat. The historian and folklorist cherished the monuments of the past and set an exalted value upon them and the nation creating them. Arndt joined the illustrious line of historical scholars who have developed an ardent love of the nation through their work. The protest against endangering knowledge came from a passionate intellectual defending his vocation. Without knowledge, without the freedom to seek it, he thought, man would degenerate into a slave or brute, while through them humanity could reach the goal of history, Arndt's third epoch. The professor, molder of ideas, and writer upheld the life which his aspirations craved. "How the political tramples down the poetic in me!" he once lamented.[41] In his future world the two would complement each other.

It is difficult to reconcile Arndt's words with his acts during the years of his stay in Sweden. "O day of vengeance, you will, you must come," he wrote. "When I see your holy flame arise, I shall throw myself in with the first and joyously die."[42] These were easy exclamations from one who remained in Sweden conversing sentimentally about Germany with Baroness Munck. Ecstatic phrases about the nation and the times afforded solace in exile. Mysticism and passivity fitted his mood, and by adding to his essential pantheism a belief in a personal God he secured divine approval of his conduct. While Gneisenau and others left Prussia in fury to join the English, Spanish, or Austrian army against Napoleon, Arndt wrote poetry and advised others to fight. If Napoleon had not deprived him of his comforts, he would have turned into a restless, vociferous, pedagogical reformer or a banal poet of trivial mysticism. Fortunately, Napoleon forced upon Arndt the opportunity to become famous, and it is to his credit that he seized it.

[41] Cited by Polag, *op. cit.*, pp. 86-88.
[42] *Geist der Zeit,* II, 72.

The explanation for the dualism between Arndt's words and conduct lies in the fact that Arndt served his ideals rather than any living fatherland. Even during the years in which he exalted the German nation and condemned the Swedes, he still appealed in his writings to both peoples. His disappointment in the Swedes was paralleled by his doubts of whether the Germans were or ever would be a nation, and he complained that he could not find his fatherland. In 1807 he said bluntly, "If you [the Germans] are deaf to the warning voice of this age, to the wail of your mutilated fatherland, to the complaint of freedom which fears slavery, I despise you deeply and shall seek to forget myself and your speech and the place where I was born." [43] Shortly thereafter he exposed his ultimate loyalty even more clearly: "Whether it be Germans or Samojeds [who establish this ideal society] is the same to me." [44] He was a nationalist in theory before he became one in fact, a nationalist for either Sweden or Germany or any other people before he turned to active German nationalism. If he had loved Germany as ardently as he often declared he did, he would have joined the Austrian army in the war of 1809. Far from thinking of doing so, in January, 1809, on the eve of his return to Germany, he denied that political problems worried him greatly. He wished to live and die among Germans free from foreign domination, but was otherwise reconciled to playing a modest role. At a time when Gneisenau, Stein, and the nationalists were plotting war to death against the destroyer he declared that he would be content as a publicist for the common people. The prophet and leader, the idealist who thought his ideals vital to the future of the world, had become depressed and humble. He would start the spread of his ideals among the lowly folk, from whom he sprang.

Marwitz, the conservative aristocrat, would have damned Arndt as a foot-loose, erratic, subjective scribbler, and ideamonger. The historian must judge him differently. Lack of foothold enabled him to disregard caste and provincial ties, a necessary condition for developing loyalty to the nation. His sub-

[43] *Ibid.*, p. 78.
[44] Cited by Ruth, *op. cit.*, p. 130.

jectivity, which resulted from or was accentuated by the absence of a fixed place in society, inclined him to plan a future society in which he would be a normal, happy person. His pen served as his gun and his ideas as his ammunition. A person might be filled with his own importance, completely devoid of social ties; if he lacked the power to dream, to form an ideal, he could never become a nationalist. If he lacked courage, ambition and perseverance, he could not become a nationalist. It took a world crisis to force this Swedish-German Pomeranian out of his routine into the world of strife; it required hard personal experience and thousands of self-intoxicating words before he felt nationalistic. All other outlets for his activity had to seem closed before he threw in his lot with the German nation.

When late in 1809 Arndt returned to Pomerania, then still under French occupation, he kept silent for fear of being captured and shot. Toward the end of the year he left for safer quarters in Berlin. Sojourn in Prussia's capital during the winter brought him into contact with the reformers, but their example did not immediately affect him. When the French restored Pomerania to Sweden in 1810, he went back to his position at the University of Greifswald and accepted with equanimity, not to say satisfaction, the political loss of a province of Germany. He praised Sweden for having left her German subjects entirely free to preserve their cultural unity with the rest of Germany. "Let us honor the old connection with Sweden," he wrote; for he still thought of German unity in terms, not of government, but of culture. His ideal combined all Germans into a nation, placing Scandinavians, Dutch, and English in close secondary relationship. When he formulated the law of politics as applying to the situation, he made it serve the cultural end.

I am speaking of the law of politics [he wrote in 1808], which as the finest sublimation of the spirit of the age, as the highest terrestrial necessity of things carries within itself its own basis and judge. This law may not be confused with the conception of civil law and civil justice without taking from the ruler all power and boldness and all grandeur and majesty from his acts. Its sphere is far wider, for from it alone can one appeal to God, the people and posterity, who in this region condemn injustice, cruelty, and faithlessness.[45]

Politics offered a means of realizing the spiritual union of the people; it designated the highest unity possible, and sat like a crown upon the nation of brothers. This kind of politics was far removed from *Realpolitik*. Arndt was no predecessor of Bismarck.

Arndt quickly perceived that he no longer fitted into the academic and provincial environment. He found Pomerania controlled by particularists and the University full of pro-French professors and students; even his old friends had turned to Napoleon and did not wish the peaceful atmosphere disturbed. When on the birthday of the Swedish king Arndt proposed to make a speech, his colleagues, objecting to his stirring up political trouble, prevented him from doing so and kept close check on him. Arndt thought of withdrawing from the University, of buying a farm and establishing a school for boys in which he could teach his ideals unmolested, but the plan could not be executed. The last tie with this secluded existence was broken when his fiancée, Charlotte Bindemann, withdrew from their engagement. If Arndt had married, the exigencies of a family might have compelled him to stay in the safe and dignified academic circle. Instead, he could henceforth devote all his love and energy to another cause. During October, 1810, he requested his release from the University and in the course of the next year, at forty-two years of age, he began a new life of service to the German nation.

Arndt turned to active German nationalism only after all other means for living as he wished had failed. Wherever he went the shadow of Napoleon either directly or indirectly fell upon him and upset his repose. His own ideals for the individual and society contrasted sharply with those of the French ruler, and if he expected to achieve them he had first of all to overthrow the latter. His philosophy imposed the necessity for action upon him; Napoleonic domination drove home the lesson. Arndt recognized that he must find aid in this conflict and, in accordance

[45] Cited by Ruth, *op. cit.*, p. 159.

with his training as folklorist and historian, he turned to the cultural group to which he belonged, the German nation. This group, which formed the last hope for defeating the French, possessed the numbers and strength esential for doing so; and since it had produced Arndt it was competent to achieve his ideals. Arndt turned to the German nation as a group which by virtue of common cultural heritage he could lead and employ for his own purposes. Having failed to maintain pleasant relations with his professional colleagues, having failed to persuade either Swedes or Germans to accept his ideals, having failed to influence the masses by his writings or the young by his teaching, having failed to win the woman he loved, having failed to be anything more than a restless dilettante of unrealizable ideals, Arndt sought to revive his life by nationalism. The worse his material situation grew, the more exalted became his sense of his own mission. His mood changed from that of dreamer to that of doer. Events which would have crushed an ordinary person sent him back to the deep well of his mysticism. By the close of 1810 he believed that he was "the instrument of an unknown God." [46] "I often feel," he wrote in December, "that many goals lie before me." [47] He had tried enough of ordinary life to have found it bitter; henceforth he would be a "wild man" fighting for the creation of a new world. Even if he failed, he said, he would have lost nothing.

From late 1811 until the final downfall of Napoleon Arndt traveled over Central and Eastern Europe wherever he found patriotic service to perform. Whether as free-lance writer or as Baron vom Stein's secretary, this German nationalist worked and fought with all his mental and physical strength. In quantity of production and effectiveness of appeal he led the propagandists. He felt happier than ever before or after because he was unfettered, active, fighting enthusiastically for the victory of his ideals over foreign and internal enemies.

A detailed account of Arndt's life during the War of Liberation need not be given. He regarded the war as a holy one with

[46] Ruth, *op. cit.*, p. 38.
[47] Langenberg, *op. cit.*, pp. 77-78.

God on the side of the Germans and fighting against the devil and Napoleon. He advocated the use of every means for destroying Napoleon, including the *Landsturm* in its most exaggerated form. Every man, woman and child, he urged, must mobilize against Napoleon, every animal, every inanimate object must be utilized or destroyed so that the enemy could not use it. If the princes refused to lead the people, the latter must rebel. While admitting that the French Revolution had thrown up many ideas for the future, Arndt denied to the French "the virtue and insight and moderation" necessary for executing them. The Germans, he believed, possessed these characteristics. They would put through a revolution of an entirely different kind. They would break up no peoples, topple no thrones; their region was above the earth. Arndt proclaimed the presence of a new age and awaited a new glory for Germany the like of which had not been seen for centuries; but he rejected the thought that it could be achieved after the manner of the French, of Mirabeau, Danton, Robespierre and Sieyès. The German, he argued, does not turn to madness, as they had done; for such misfortune his sin was too small.

Arndt emphasized the need for a spirit of union in Germany and did not concern himself greatly with its external form. In order to defeat the French and realize their heavenly mission on earth the Germans must all, from the Baltic and North Seas to the Carpathians, from the Vistula to the Scheldt, be of "one faith, one love, one courage and enthusiasm." [48] Let no one be first and no one last, no one the commander and no one the subject. "Let us all strive and compete to see which one will be most pious, most obedient and most humble in service to the fatherland," he cried. "Then not even a devil can defeat you." [49] Nonetheless the outbreak of war in 1813 stimulated Arndt's interest in political factors, and he devoted some of his most effective writing to the question of political unity. Condemning cosmopolitanism as contrary to the divine order of nature, he proclaimed the right and the duty of all Germans to combine. Blood,

[48] *Geist der Zeit,* III, 177.
[49] *Ibid.,* p. 186.

customs, and ways, natural frontiers, and especially language held them together. Above all the Rhine must be German, for without it, he said, Germany would remain a weakling whom France could overcome at any time. Because Germany lay in the center of Europe she must be united in order to be strong. Once she was consolidated, she would use her central position to keep other countries at peace. She would exercise a benevolent influence over all nations, encouraging them to inaugurate constitutional governments and social reforms. By German unity Arndt meant during these years of war actual political unity with a central head, a constitution, an efficient government. Up to 1814 he still regarded Austria as the leader of the Germans; but disgusted by Austrian diplomatic slyness and military diffidence and thrilled by Prussian hatred of Napoleon and the vigor of the Prussian attack, Arndt transferred his loyalty to Prussia and henceforth agitated in favor of unification under her control. He demanded an emperor or king, compulsory military service, an imperial code of laws, imperial courts of justice, a Reichstag for all Germany representing aristocracy, burghers, and peasants and civil liberties for the individual. He loudly declared that he loved and revered Prussia as the savior of Germany from the French, proclaiming her the leader of a new age. In this issue, as in all others during these years, he based his argument on his heart, on his love for his fatherland and his folk, and in the second line on right, politics, honor, and loyalty to the German name.

It lies in the nature of a nationalist never to be satisfied. Even magnificent fighting, especially by the Prussians, did not wipe out Arndt's negative criticisms and doubts. While he found another reason for believing in the Germans to a larger degree than in other peoples of racial purity,[50] he chafed at the failure of all Germans to rush to the standard, reform themselves, and live according to his ideals. In 1814 he sadly concluded that the Germans still fell short of constituting a nation: they lacked

[50] He warned against permitting more Jews to come in because they formed an alien body. He had no objection to Jews born in Germany and tending to become German.

public loyalty and a common spirit and manifested slight interest in freedom and national unity. "Not for centuries," he wrote in March, 1814, "has God moved through human affairs to perform his wonders as he has through the foolishness, stupidities, even through the worthlessness of our age. It must mean something great, but I do not see how this race can bear it and carry it through."[51] Much had changed, much has improved; yet, he cried, how much remained to be done. He predicted the continuation of war during his life, war in which the race would be destroyed. He had reached the nadir of discouragement.

During this time Arndt fell back on the panacea of all intellectuals. The present generation lacked the qualities of greatness: the young must be saved by education. Arndt read Fichte's *Reden* and was deeply impressed by the wisdom and fervor of this educational program. His mind rushed to plans for schools, for a national academic society of all German patriots. Looking backward he soon reached the conviction that the revival of Germany had started in the universities, the only place of freedom left by Napoleon. The mantle of the prophets of old, Arndt thought, had descended upon the professor.

Arndt still believed in the future, declaring that "God has awakened us and turned our thoughts to something higher and for that we praise Him."[52] Divine and earthly life, political and human life (the antithesis is significant for his slight comprehension of politics) would be united some day and then for the first time the Germans would be one strong and glorious nation. That was the dream to which Arndt remained loyal throughout his life. He served a world of his own fabrication, one, however, which should be created and led by the German nation. The great revolution of humanity still lay ahead. Although Arndt lived for forty-five years more (of no significance for the purposes of this essay), he never saw the fulfillment of his hopes.

In the third part of *Geist der Zeit,* published in 1813, Arndt gave the key to his nationalistic activity.

[51] Langenberg, *op. cit.*, p. 130.
[52] Langenberg, *op. cit.*, pp. 132, 139, 142-43.

> I have seen misfortune, I have suffered, it has scarcely moved me to tears. But when I have thought of the folk and seen it and when the great feeling of it has gripped me, I have always had to weep in the depths of my soul. When a great crowd moves before me, when a band of warriors passes before me with flying banners and sounding trumpets and drums, then I feel as if my feeling and acting were not an empty illusion, I feel the indestructible life, the eternal spirit, and the eternal God. . . . I am egoistic and sinful like other men, but in this exalted human feeling I am immediately freed from all sins, I am no more a single suffering man, I am one with the folk and God. In such moments doubts about my life and occupation disappear. The compulsion of my feelings tells me that I do right; I shall use this justification by my love and my hate because I must.[53]

Public service, nationalism, compensated Arndt for psychological insecurity. He felt little concern about personal cases of misfortune, showing a singular disregard for the intimate realities of a personal situation. A public event or the hardship of a group moved him profoundly. Then his feelings grew excited and he forgot himself—his disappointment in life, his uncertainty about the choice of profession, his failure to achieve greatness and immortality. In those moments his feelings overwhelmed his doubts and he knew ecstatic happiness. He merged himself in the people and losing himself became one with the eternal spirit and the eternal God. What he loved and hated was that which God loved and hated; emotions overwhelmed reason and silenced disturbing questions. Confidence came to him by way of emotional union with something outside or above himself. The whole man drew together and acted as a unit; the mystery of nationalism occurred.

To understand this confession (it was not written as a confession) one must return to Arndt's life. At first the peasant boy absorbed the folklore of the North. He went to school, to the university, became finally a scholar. But the professions for which he was trained did not satisfy him; his emotions defied the restraint of academic objectivity. He could not return to farming

[53] *Geist der Zeit,* III, 161-62.

because he was well educated; he could not preach because he felt no calling to pursue rationalistic theology. He loved to dream, to wander, to compose poetry, to collect old tales, but these activities would not provide him with a living. Arndt was lost to the life of his fathers without feeling attached to any other life. Uprooted, uncertain, and insecure, he longed for a world according to his wants. He first created this world in his imagination upon the basis of his love for his boyhood home. But this was only a vision, an idea without reality. He could not be sure of it any more than he could of himself. No recourse was open to him, however, except that of perfecting this ideal, and he did so. He was attracted by bourgeois life, even by professorial life, but his honest peasant judgment told him that they were superficial. Repeatedly he had to fall back into dreams and vagabondage, escapes from an existence which he disliked and in which he was not at home. Discovering that he felt happiest when serving others, and wishing a full life for man, he sought to reform existing society according to his needs. In doing so he forgot his sadness; he had a purpose and he found comfort and assurance in becoming one with society.

The Napoleonic crisis turned Arndt's attention to the nation as a body of people speaking his language, understanding his culture, sharing a common history; a body of people above all sufficiently large to defeat the conqueror. If the French had won, Arndt's ideals and hopes would have been crushed. Arndt sought to destroy Napoleon to save himself. In his extremity he turned to the Swedish or the German people for aid; when the Swedes failed him, he fell back on the Germans and declared that if they would accept his ideals, they could overcome the enemy. Arndt would thereby achieve two objectives, the destruction of the French menace and the winning of the Germans to his ideals. In this work Arndt found contentment. Forgetting his troubles and guided by love and hate, he became confident, self-assured, one with God and the nation, and submerged all his problems in his nationalism. He loved the Germans because he was saving and reforming them, because he was cutting them to his pattern.

Mysticism replaced reason. Group-feeling supplanted egocentricity. Certainty threw out doubt. The dreamer had a mission, the vagabond a goal, the discontented professor a glorious occupation, the widower and jilted lover an object of affection, the full-blooded, ardent, vigorous man a magnificent task.

IV. KLEIST

HEINRICH VON KLEIST, born in 1777, came of an aristocratic Prussian family with a lineage dating back to the year 1176. The inherited traditions of six hundred years made him a historic figure at birth. The numerous branches of his family were scattered widely throughout East Elbian Prussia and were intimately bound to one another and to their caste. A Kleist was an aristocrat and a Kleist before he was an individual. His standards were set; his choice of career limited, his ways of thinking and of acting largely prescribed. A male Prussian aristocrat could follow one of three possible careers: officer in the army, official in the bureaucracy, or lord over an assemblage of land and serfs. Since the Kleists of Heinrich's branch lacked the material basis for the life of a rural lord, they had usually entered the army. The future poet was reared in the dull garrison town of Frankfort on the Oder, where his father was stationed.

The reasons for young Kleist's continuing the military tradition are less important for this study than the fact that he did so. Perhaps his youth offers a clue to his docility. When not quite fifteen years old, he went to Potsdam as a member of one of the most exclusive Prussian regiments, advancing in rank at the usual rate. His friends were aristocrats; the society in which he moved set the tone for all Prussia; and the royal family, which knew the Kleists, took notice of Heinrich and at times invited him to court. Military life for an officer entailed few hardships and offered a pleasant routine with respect from inferiors, from peers, and even from superiors. In order to rise to some significance one needed merely to have ordinary intellect and physique.

Kleist spent six years in these surroundings before he determined to resign his post, but it required an additional year for him to summon up courage for taking the necessary steps. By his resignation in 1799 he made the first break with the tradition of his family and his caste. He began modestly and uncertainly a rebellion, which in some respects was his own French Revolution. It evoked a crisis within him and between him and society, creating conflicts, agitating his beliefs and hopes, and setting him at odds with the social order to which he had been accustomed. It imposed upon him the severe task of working out a new life for himself in which he could realize his desires. In place of accepted standards he had to discover new ones; in place of a traditional profession he must find another; in place of acquiescing in a philosophy of life he must seek one to his need. In the course of his search he ultimately discovered nationalism.

Before analyzing the nature of this crisis, one must try to explain some of the forces drawing Kleist into conflict with his social environment. An early teacher described the boy as a "fiery spirit," easily aroused, exalted and unsteady, yet possessing a remarkable understanding and an ardent desire to know, "at once the most open, most diligent and most unselfish character in the world." [1] His extraordinary sensitiveness and his love of the good promised a life full of personal and social difficulties, one of unusual endeavor and, if favored by the necessary ability, of unusual achievement. When Kleist entered the army, he seems to have been a sociable person with a sense of fun, a strain of sentimentality, and a desire to perform well his duty as an officer. Shortly before his death he wrote that since his earliest youth he had "lived constantly in my thoughts and writings with beauty and morality." [2] In Potsdam he indulged his love of music and enjoyed himself; but at the same time, since military obligations left him with sufficient leisure to cultivate his mind, he availed himself of all the opportunities for doing so which the garrison town offered. As a result of his studies of the literature

[1] Wilhelm Herzog, *Heinrich von Kleist. Sein Leben und sein Werk* (Munich, 1911), p. 17. On Kleist see also the excellent articles in *Schriften der Kleistgesellschaft* and Friedrich Gundolf, *Heinrich von Kleist* (Berlin, 1932).

[2] *Heinrich von Kleists Werke.* Im Verein mit Georg Minde-Pouet und Rheinhold Steig herausgegeben von Erich Schmidt (Leipzig), V, 433.

of the Enlightenment he accepted the faith in rationalism of that movement. He believed that:

the purpose of creation is perfection . . . and that after death we shall advance from the plane of perfection which we reach on this star to another and that we can also use there the treasure of truths which we lay up here. Out of these thoughts I gradually built up a religion of my own and the effort never to stand still a moment and always to advance unceasingly toward a higher degree of culture became the only principle of my activity. Culture seemed to me the only goal worthy of effort, truth the only wealth worthy of possession.[3]

The exalted ideal which Kleist here set for himself eliminated from significance such external objects as riches or honors. Knowledge and truth became for him objects of religious reverence. He longed to perfect his education and soon perceived the restricting influence of his profession.

Equally if not even more compelling as a reason for resigning from the army was Kleist's growing aversion to military life. In a letter of 1799 he said to a friend:

Because of these considerations military life, to which I was never heartily devoted because it carries in itself something thoroughly incompatible with my whole being, became so much an object of hatred that it was gradually burdensome to have to contribute to its purpose. The greatest marvels of military discipline, which were a source of wonder to all who knew them, aroused my intense scorn; I considered the officers so many drill masters, the soldiers so many slaves, and when the whole regiment displayed its skill, it seemed to me a living monument of tyranny. Furthermore, I began to feel acutely the evil influence which my position had on my character. Often I was forced to punish when I had gladly forgiven or to forgive where I should have punished, and in both cases I felt myself the culpable one. At such moments the desire naturally arose within me to leave the position, in which from two quite opposite principles I was constantly made a martyr. I was always doubtful whether I should act as a man or an officer, since I hold it impossible in the

[3] *Ibid.*, pp. 2-4.

present state of military discipline to harmonize the duties of both.

And I considered my moral development as one of my holiest duties, because, as I have shown, it was to lay the basis for my happiness. So there was added to my natural disinclination toward the army the duty of leaving it.[4]

When Kleist reported his decision to his family, there arose the question of how he would make a living suitable to one of his station. All the means of dissuasion—sarcasm, mistrust derived from a longer and more intimate experience with life, predictions of a dreary future, amused superiority—were arrayed against him, but in his own mind Kleist had so completely rejected the military career that he remained unmoved by them. Protected against want for a time by a small property, he trusted in education to develop all the capacities with which the divine order had endowed him. As for a career, he felt no worries. He was willing to perform any kind of honorable work. "No one need hunger," he said, "who is willing to work." Perhaps in time after he had prepared himself for life, he wrote the same friend, he would seek a post in the bureaucracy or elsewhere.

But I doubt it [he continued] because I would always be shy of renouncing the golden independence of the reign of reason once I had been so fortunate as to capture it again. . . .

In this conviction I face the future certain of a joyous and happy life. Content within myself and through myself, my friend, where can the blow of fate strike me if I guard this independence fast in my innermost soul? My heart warms more and more to the decision which even for a royal reward I would never renounce, and my reason strengthens what my heart says and crowns it with the truth that it is at least wise and advisable in this changing age to tie oneself as little as possible to the order of things.[5]

In these statements there appeared the trend, noticeable at the end of the Enlightenment, especially in German idealism, of the individual to retire within himself and seek happiness in the cultivation of his own mind and soul. Withdrawal from so-

[4] *Ibid.*, pp. 31-32.
[5] *Ibid.*, pp. 37-38.

ciety enabled one to follow the course of his own ideals, mainly taken from the Enlightenment, and to build a new personality. Kleist's resignation from the army inaugurated the period of his search for those values of life congenial to his nature. After he had clarified the new standards and made firm and secure a new Kleist, he could, he thought, return into society without danger. But when he sought to rejoin the group, he found that society had not kept pace with him. He felt alien in the old order and advocated reforms which would permit him to be socially adjusted. He was so wrapped up in the task of re-creating himself, however, that he did not appreciate the need for society until he perceived his own career endangered. Then he arose against the menace of Napoleon and the French and in his search for assistance appealed to the nation. The ideals which he had developed for himself permitted him to recognize the value of a group of free individuals who would wish to see in others qualities like his and would appreciate the need of these for purposes of defense against a foreign aggressor.

It is manifest that Kleist loved freedom. He hated army life because of its combination of despotism and slavery. In defending his resignation he ignored the fact of social responsibility, basing his argument entirely upon subjective grounds. The full implications of his rebellion were not as yet clear to him. The antithesis between living according to reason, cultivating one's intelligence, devoting one's life to pure knowledge, on the one hand, and following the guidance of one's heart, developing completely one's personality, on the other, remained concealed beneath a youthful confidence in nature and the power of the human mind.

The real turning point in Kleist's life came between 1799 and 1801. Although a detailed history of these two years need not be given, the several aspects of the crisis must be explained in order to reveal the mental and physical conditions which enabled Kleist to discover the nation and which set the limits to the extent of that discovery.

Kleist wrote in 1799 that each person should work out a plan for his life.

I hear thousands speak and see them about their work without its ever occurring to me to ask, "Why?" They themselves do not know; dimly felt inclinations lead them on; the impulse of the moment determines their activities. They remain children forever and their fate is a game of chance. They feel themselves guided and drawn along by unseen forces. They follow these, feeling their own weakness, wherever these lead them, whether it be on to happiness, which they then only half enjoy, or to sorrow, which they feel doubly.

Such slavish submission to the moods of the tyrant Fate is surely most unworthy of a free and thoughtful man. A free man of thought does not stay where chance tosses him, or, if he does stay, he does so for reasons. He feels that man can rise above Fate, that in the right sense man may even direct Fate. He decides according to reason what is the greatest happiness for him, he draws up his own plans for life and strives with all his powers in accordance with certain defined principles toward his goal. Even the Bible says, if you will attain the Kingdom of Heaven, you must lend a hand toward that end.

As long as a man is not able to work out a plan of life for himself he is and remains a child; as a child, he remains under the control of his parents, as a man, under the control of Fate. The first act of a man's independence is the drawing up of such a plan of life. How necessary it is to do this as early as possible! I have learned that through the loss of seven priceless years, which I devoted to the army, seven lost years never again to be recovered, which I could have used for my plan of life if I had understood earlier the need of making one.

The man who acts according to definite principles is recognized by the effectiveness, coherence, and unity in his conduct. The high purpose for which he strives is the focus of all his thoughts, feelings, and actions. Everything which he thinks, feels, and wishes has relation to this purpose. All his spiritual and physical powers strain toward this common goal. Never will his words oppose his actions or his actions contradict his words; for each of his utterances he will have to provide reasonable grounds. When one knows his goal, it will not be difficult to discover the bases of his conduct.

A plan of life is to a man what an itinerary is to a traveler. To begin a journey without an itinerary means to expect chance to lead us to the place which we ourselves do not know. To live without a plan of life means to expect chance to give us happiness as we ourselves do not understand it.

Indeed, it is impossible for me to understand how a man can live without a plan of life and I feel in the sureness with which I make use of the present, in the calmness with which I look into the future what an inestimable joy my plan of life assures me, and to be without a plan of life, without a firm purpose, always hesitating between uncertain desires, always in contradiction with my duties, the butt of chance, a puppet on the string of Fate—this unworthy situation seems so despicable to me and would make me so unhappy that death would be by far more desirable.[6]

Reason, he maintained, afforded the means by which a plan could be worked out. But Kleist's devotion to reason, even so early in his career, depended to an extraordinary degree upon other than rational considerations. Kleist was mainly concerned with finding an absolute goal and guide for life. Since the Enlightenment offered intellectual and moral self-dependence as the goal and reason as the guide, he accepted them out of inexperience and lack of understanding of his own needs. He revealed the confusion of his thinking in the same letter of 1799 as follows:

Man must hold something sacred. To us to whom the religious ceremonials and the dictates of conventional well-being are not sacred, the laws of reason must be all the more so. The state asks of us nothing more than that we do not overstep the ten commandments. Who orders us to exercise the virtues of love of mankind, patience, modesty, gentleness, if not reason? The state assures us our property, our life, our honor; who assures us our inmost happiness, if not reason? [7]

Because he was an emotionalist seeking to follow a life of reason, Kleist had to hold something sacred; since he could not accept the three objects of customary reverence, religious ceremonies, social conventions, and the state, he staked all upon reason. He seems not to have appreciated the fundamental contradiction of this solution. His application to a life of reason suffered con-

[6] *Ibid.*, pp. 41-44.
[7] *Ibid.*, p. 44.

stantly from his inability to keep his heart from interfering. Like Faust, on occasion he fled from his studies into the realm of refreshing emotion. He employed the term *Vernunft* to signify both the rational and the emotional faculties, regarding them as means for improving his personality. Kleist, however, was temperamentally unable to permit head and heart an harmonious life. By passionately concentrating upon his studies he suppressed his emotions and strove to keep them down. A longing to possess the whole of knowledge enticed him farther and farther into the regions of erudition only to find that the revered professors afforded dull company, that they quarreled and pushed like lesser folk. The more he seemed to learn, the less he knew; the body of facts grew with every book he read; several lives seemed necessary to evolve a plan for living part of one life. Before many months had passed the young man sighed, "Alas, it is so sad to be nothing more than learned." [8]

The second revelation to the ambitious scholar came directly from his heart. This organ would not remain docile, even with an occasional outing. Kleist fell in love, although more as a scholar might than as a poet. The young lady, another aristocrat, seems to have been rather ordinary as to mind and appearance, but she afforded Kleist an object of affection and he fancied himself her slave. At first the young lady avowed her deficiencies and endeavored to avoid the wooing; but Kleist persisted until he won her consent. He immediately began to educate her, or, rather, to use her as a means of expressing and educating himself. Their letters contained more ethics and popular science than love; his, especially, were replete with himself, his problems, his beliefs, his hopes, his feelings toward her and the world. Kleist did not intend to be selfish; he merely wrote like a person who had other and, as it turned out, deeper interests than a love affair. Wilhelmine served admirably the function of assisting in Kleist's rebellion against rationalism and the pursuit of book knowledge and in his substitution of feeling for them. She helped to relax the rationalistic tension, to educate Kleist's heart, thereby releasing in him a poetic spring.

[8] *Ibid.*, p. 198.

Growing doubt in the efficacy of intellectual life to give happiness, together with longing for a wife and home, rearoused in Kleist the will to act. He began to consider action better than knowledge. Since he could neither learn everything nor decide upon a special intellectual interest, the pursuit of which would gain him a reputation, he worried about the future. What career should he follow? What plan should direct him? What should he do? At this turning point of his life Kleist wrote to Ulrica, his sister: "My head looks inside like a lottery bag where a thousand blanks lie next to one large prize. I can well be forgiven for shuffling the tickets about uncertainly with my hand. Of course it is no help but it postpones the fearful moment, which is to decide irrevocably the fate of a whole lifetime." [9]

Finally Kleist tried a position in the Prussian bureaucracy as inspector of urban factory and domestic production. A few months of routine convinced him that the difference between the position of bureaucrat and that of officer was negligible. On November 13, 1800, he described his reactions to his fiancée as follows:

> I cannot take up an interest which I am not allowed to test with my reason. I am supposed to do what the state demands of me and still I am not to investigate whether that which it demands of me is good—I cannot do it. I have my own purpose before me according to which I must act, and if the state directs otherwise, I dare not obey the state. I should seek to make good the claims of my reason against the wish of my superiors. No, Wilhelmine, it cannot be; I am not suited for any post. I am really also too clumsy to administer one. Order, precision, patience, indefatigability, those are characteristics which are indispensable in an office and I lack them entirely. I work gladly only for my education and in that I am unsurpassedly patient and untiring. But to write out lists for salary payments and to keep accounts! Ah, I should hurry, hurry to finish them and to get back to my beloved studies. I should steal the time from my post to devote it to my education. No, Wilhelmine, it will not do. I am even too stupid to acquire a post. For, content to gain knowledge for myself, I am little troubled whether others recognize

[9] *Ibid.*, pp. 199-200.

it in me. To parade it or to offer it for sale would be quite impossible for me, and would they favor one who takes pride in doing without every favor and who wants to rise by no other claim than through that of his own deserts? But the more decisive is this, that even a post, even if it were a minister's position, cannot make me happy. For, Wilhelmine, one thing is sure, I am happy at home or not at all, not at balls, not at the opera, not in society, even if it were in the company of princes, even if the society were that of our own king. And should I want to bury myself in a big city and throw myself into a chaos of complicated situations in order to live quietly with my wife? Should I earn a position of honor and be decorated to impress my wife and children? I shall not talk about freedom because you have already scolded me once for doing so, although you really, like all women, cannot understand it rightly; but love and education are two indispensable conditions of my future happiness and what could I have of them in a post unless at most a poor, mean part of each? If I wanted to study, a secretary would bring me a box of documents; if I wanted to follow a great thought, a servant would come to tell me that the waiting room was full of strangers. If I wanted to spend the evening with my wife, the king would have me called to him, and to rob me of my nights, I should have to journey to the provinces to count the factories. How I should want to curse the orders and the riches and the whole beggary of the great world! How bitterly I should weep for having failed to fulfill my mission in life! How I should long for dry bread and love with it, for culture and freedom. No, Wilhelmine, I must not choose a post; I despise the kind of happiness which it would bring.[10]

The most significant remark in this apology is one which was made almost incidentally, "I shall not talk about freedom because you have already scolded me once for doing so." Kleist's problem was ultimately that of achieving freedom to be himself, to live according to nature's plan for him, to become and remain, not an aristocrat, officer, or official of the Kleist family, but to become and remain that unique personality, Heinrich von Kleist.

At court [he wrote in 1800] men are divided as once the chemists divided metals, namely, into those which let themselves be stretched and pulled and those which will not allow this. The first

[10] *Ibid.*, pp. 151-52.

are then diligently struck with the hammer of arbitrariness, but the others, like alloys, are thrown away as unusable.

The best kings gladly develop slumbering genius but then suppress it. They are like lightning which sets inflammable things on fire but beats out the flames.[11]

Shyly, but with the premonition of the powers which lay dormant within him, Kleist added: "I feel somewhat embarrassed to say this myself, but I cannot deny that the thought has flitted through my soul that this might happen to me."[12] He wished to escape this fate.

The short experience in the Prussian bureaucracy not only convinced Kleist of his unsuitability for that kind of work but likewise left a definite impression upon his social thinking. The contrast between the freedom which he wished and the mercantilist domination by the administration over the subjects of the state turned this egocentric young man unknowingly into an apostle of Adam Smith. Love of freedom, fundamentally personal and in the main defensive, began to condition Kleist's views regarding governmental policy toward society.

So far as I can see [he wrote] the whole Prussian commercial system is very military and I doubt whether it would find me a very eager supporter. Industry is a lady and one should politely but cordially invite her to bless the poor country with her entrance. But they [the bureaucrats] want to drag her in by the hair. Is it any wonder that she sulks? The arts cannot be forced like military handgrips. But they think they have done well when they destroy fairs, build factories, erect workshops by the dozens. Is he to whom an harmonica has been given an artist? If only he understood music, he would fashion himself an instrument. Arts and sciences, if they do not help themselves, are not helped by the king. They merely ask of the king to be let alone to pursue their way.[13]

The moment had not yet arrived when Kleist was primarily concerned with the troubles of society. His own difficulties monopolized his thoughts. Slowly and cautiously ambition was ripen-

[11] *Ibid.*, p. 168.

[12] *Loc. cit.*

[13] *Ibid.*, p. 169.

ing in him to become a writer; but two obstacles stood in the way: first, he was a Kleist; second, he had almost no income but wanted to marry. The combined pressure of family, love, and economic need threatened to block the realization of his personality. The conflict of every age of transition, that of society versus the individual, was once again being fought out with Kleist as the battlefield. He denied any concern with worldly goods; his wishes were, he said in 1800, a cottage, a wife, and knowledge. He declared his independence of the aristocracy, denouncing pride of birth and of class as prejudices which he would not accept. Wilhelmine, however, did not share this degree of emancipation. Kleist faced the dilemma of persuading her to forsake the scale of living to which she was accustomed or of violating his own soul.

The difficulty of his love affair does not seem to have affected Kleist so much as other uncertainties in which he found himself. He was uncertain as to the possibility of discovering a plan of life, the merits of reason as against feeling, the choice of a career, the relative value of knowledge and of action. These affected deeply his relation to the society with which he came in contact. At first dissatisfaction with himself found vent in dislike of the artificiality and triviality of society, and he became a shy, silent creature avoiding society.

Ah, my dear Ulrica [he wrote], I am not at home among people; it is a sad fact but the truth. And if I am to give the reason without beating about the bush, it is this: they do not please me. I well know that it is with men as with a mirror, a question of the individual nature of each as to how outside objects work upon them. Many a man would stop scolding over the corruption of manners if it once occurred to him that perhaps the glass on which the picture of the world falls might be dirty and crooked. If I am not comfortable in company, that is less because other people than because I myself do not appear as I should like. The need of playing a role and an inner dislike of it make all society burdensome to me and I can only be happy in my own company, because then I can be my true self. One cannot be that among people and no one is. Alas, there is a sad clarity which nature has happily spared many men who see only the superficial in things. This tells me the thought behind every expression, the meaning behind each word, the motive of every action; it shows me everything about me and even myself in my whole pitiful nakedness and my heart is disgusted before this nakedness. Then there comes over me an inexplicable embarrassment which I cannot overcome, apparently because it has a purely physical source. With the greatest difficulty I can only hide it so that it does not become striking. Oh, how painful it is to be outwardly quite strong and free while, like a child, one is quite weak within, quite crippled as if all one's limbs were bound, when one can never show them as one would like to, never act freely and must even forego that which is great, because one feels beforehand that one will not hold fast, because one is dependent on every outward impression and the simplest maiden or the worst blackguard can destroy him by the most feeble persiflage.[14]

Kleist's unhappiness and bewilderment appeared in every line of his letter to Ulrica. The complications of life were piling high. In this distressing mood he reread Kant. The hard assertions of the Königsberg philosopher confirmed his suspicion that the search for absolute truth, for objective knowledge, for a definite plan of life was futile.

The thought [Kleist wrote] that here below we know nothing, absolutely nothing of Truth, that that which we call Truth here is something quite different after death and that consequently the effort to gain possessions which will follow us into the grave is quite fruitless and vain—this thought has shaken me in my inmost soul. My only and highest purpose has sunk; I have no other.[15]

He no longer knew what he should do, what task in the divine order of things he should set his hand to. He feared that if he seized upon a plan, it might be a false one and ruin his life.

Since this has happened, I am disgusted with books. I lay my hands in my lap and seek a new goal toward which my spirit could happily strive anew. But I do not find it and an inner disquiet drives

[14] *Ibid.*, pp. 197-98.
[15] *Ibid.*, p. 207.

me hither and thither. I go to coffee houses and smoking rooms, concerts and plays. I run about in order to distract, to numb myself, I commit follies of which I am ashamed to write. And the only thought which, amid this outer tumult, busies my soul unceasingly and with growing anxiety is this: your only and highest purpose is gone. I have wanted to force myself to work but I am disgusted with everything which smacks of knowledge. I cannot take a step without knowing clearly whither I want to go.[16]

Kleist, the aristocrat, the Prussian army officer, the Faustian student, stood bare, stripped of contact with society, nature, and God. He called himself "another sacrifice to the madness of which the Kantian philosophy has so many on its conscience." [17]

During the rest of his life Kleist attempted to reëstablish these contacts. He had to find his own objective and to weave it into the pattern of existence; he had to discover some means of fitting himself again into the group. Out of his endeavors to do so there arose potentialities which circumstances molded into nationalism.

Following the collapse of his ideals Kleist fled from himself, his family and friends, and his fiancée. With his sister, who attached herself to him, he went to Paris and then alone to Switzerland. He doubted whether he would ever return to Prussia, where he felt that in the eyes of his relatives and friends he was a failure. "It is so disgusting to live," he wrote.[18] He begged his fiancée to join him in Switzerland and live on a peasant holding, hoping that manual work would quiet his thoughts and provide him with a worthy occupation. When Wilhelmine refused to leave her home for this mad venture, Kleist eliminated her from his life, thereby breaking almost the last connection with his homeland. One tie alone, the feeling that he was a Kleist, remained; for travel, as well as the collapse of his exalted ambitions, left him acutely aware of family. He felt too proud to return home before he had accomplished something which would restore to him the respect of society. This something must with one stroke lift him high

[16] *Loc. cit.*
[17] *Loc. cit.*
[18] *Ibid.*, p. 228.

into the company of the great; otherwise he vowed to continue his self-imposed exile.

During this chaotic period in Kleist's life two points of anchorage began to appear. One was that he definitely wished to write. In Switzerland he found happiness again in literary composition. "I have no other wish than to die," he said in 1802, "after I achieve three things, a child, a beautiful poem, and a great deed."[19] It will be recalled that a few years previously his trinity of desires had been a wife, a child, and knowledge. (An intermediate combination had been a wife, a home, and freedom.)[20] The contrast between the two lists reveals the shift of objectives. Kleist was maturing; he was finding his vocation; in setting out to accomplish a great deed he was establishing a new standard of success. In the next few years he concentrated upon his writings.

The second point to which he made fast was feeling as a directing force. In spite of Kant, Kleist refused to believe that absolute assurance was unattainable, preferring death to uncertainty. Even during his period of chaos he clung to phrases like "my inner urge," and soon after he had fled from Berlin in 1801, he believed that he had found the solution. "Every goal is false," he wrote, "which is not set for man by pure nature."[21] While retaining the idea of an absolute, he substituted for the implementation of reason that of pure nature. Nature, however, acquired a somewhat different meaning from the usual one. As a result of his reading, general experience, and psychological necessity he came to interpret the purposes of nature by way of feeling. The writings of Rousseau and his followers substantiated the validity of this medium, which his love affair and the manner of finding his vocation had disclosed to him. He had loved in spite of his reason; he wished to become a poet for no other cause than that he felt an urge in this direction; he had rebelled against his profession and society because his nature forced him to do so. Hating

[19] *Ibid.*, p. 287.
[20] *Ibid.*, p. 217.
[21] *Ibid.*, p. 226.

the artificiality of urban life, he longed for the solace and inspiration of the country, of organic, emotional, subjective nature. Instinct had decided him in every crisis. The conception of nature presented by the Enlightenment gave place to one of romanticism and transformed a scholar into a poet. From the extreme of faith in rationalism Kleist went to the extreme of faith in feeling, the ultimate defense of a poet in a hostile world; without eliminating entirely the influence of reason, he placed feeling in dominion over it.

The full significance of feeling to Kleist can be grasped only in connection with his conception of the Ego. It has already been shown how Kleist struggled with the problem of finding the kind of life suited to his capacities. The severity of his combat with this problem clearly manifested itself in the fact that, because he took everything personally, he went to pieces when he read Kant. A German critic has said that for Kleist the Ego assumed religious proportions, expressing the divine; it was an original thing, "the basis of human existence, an indestructible, eternal, clear and steadfast (*unverwirrbar*) source of absolute certainty of the eternal in the midst of the transient and the finite."[22] The relation of feeling to Kleist's Ego may be summed up by the same critic:

Feeling is the image of this holy self-certainty of the Ego with respect to its destiny; it is the direct, momentary unity of the immediate psychological consciousness of the Ego with its meta-psychological eternal basis of existence; it is the "conscience" of the Ego, if Kleist had not avoided this juxtaposition taken from the world of reason and substance. Feeling is analogous to the idea of idealism, an absolute imperative; its violation is the greatest sin, only it is not an unending abstraction devoid of content, but an unendingly concrete, absolutely determined, entirely individual imperative. The direct "demoniacal" certainty of the Ego about its own eternal law expressed itself most purely as momentary feeling, since indeed the relation to the world which constitutes the psychological existence can be interrupted only for the moment. The more the

[22] Gerhard Fricke, *Gefühl und Schicksal bei Heinrich von Kleist* (Berlin, 1929), p. 63.

directness of thought—which exists only in relation to "object" without overcoming the gulf between itself and the object—is eliminated, the more ineffective the relativity of a reality controlled by chance is, the more purely can the power of feeling come to the fore. Thus the "momentary" scales of intuition, thus the meaning of "first" feeling. . . . Since the meaning of feeling, this divine fire in the soul of the individual . . . cannot be known through thinking of its nature, but only by seeing and experiencing its power and effect.[23]

The question of what to do with one's life could not relate to the inner person alone; it involved also the relation of the self to other individuals. Kleist did not become the psychopathic individualist which some writers have tried to make of him,[24] for he never ceased to be aware of his responsibilities as a social person. The tragedy of his life lay mainly in that he could not reconcile and harmonize obligations to himself with those to family and society. He realized that the Ego and the group complemented each other; but he pondered how he could bring them together. What he had written in 1799 still held true: "A thousand bonds hold men together, similar opinions, similar interests, similar desires, hopes and expectations;—all these ties do not bind me to them, and this may be a main reason why we do not understand each other."[25] Kleist had grown away from his own people, becoming, as he said, a new person with different ideals, interests, and hopes; yet he longed to return and suffered intensely from isolation. Thoughts of death came repeatedly to his mind.

23 *Ibid.*, pp. 75-76.

24 Kleist did often act eccentrically in society. The stories told about him are many. Perhaps the most understanding picture is that given by Wieland. Kleist, he said, was a lonely and silent young man. In conversation he would suddenly follow a train of thought of his own and forget his interlocutor. Often at the dining table he would murmur to himself as if he thought he were alone and occupied with some other object. "He finally had to admit to me," said Wieland, "that in these moments he was occupied with the composition of his dramas." When Wieland thought of the unhappy career of this young and gifted aristocrat, he felt great pity for him (Herzog, *op. cit.*, pp. 4, 256-57). Unfortunately, few people had the sympathetic understanding of this fellow writer.

25 Kleist, *Werke, op. cit.*, V, 49.

The conflict between Kleist and society undoubtedly accounted in part for his urge to write and afforded him the materials for many of his works. As he grew older the problem increasingly occupied his interest. His early works dealt more with difficulties of individuals as such, while his later ones treated those arising between individuals as members of society. When taken together they pose the two problems of Kleist's life: how he should become himself, and how he could do so while remaining a happy member of a group. The attempt to answer these questions led to his nationalism.

Since Kleist believed that feeling must guide the action of the individual, he immediately confronted the difficulty of establishing social relations upon some kind of objective and permanent basis. He, whose love affair had failed, appreciated from his own experience the tenuousness of the thread of understanding between individuals. He soon perceived that if he, a seeker and a sensitive rebel scarcely understanding himself or knowing where he was headed, were to preserve intimacy with society, he could do so only through absolute and mutual trust. Without such trust the social group becomes the plaything of accident, as does the Ego when it is not guided by feeling. Trust is created and preserved by love; the more trust between man and wife, as between burgher and burgher, the greater the love. Thus Kleist reduced social relations to the most subjective terms. He was seeking a kind of society in which he would be content, in which he could live and work according to his desires, in which he would be trusted and loved and could trust and love. Thereby he conceived social relationships in terms which would mean nationalism when applied to the proper group.

The external course of Kleist's life never ran smoothly. He seemed temperamentally unfit for routine. One day he found ecstasy; on the next he wished for death. After he had determined upon his career as author, the state of his feeling depended upon the success or failure of his work. In January, 1803, when he thought that he was succeeding in the construction of his drama, he wrote from Switzerland, "I am approaching complete terrestrial happiness."[26] In October he wrote his sister from Paris that he had burned all his manuscripts and would join the French army at Boulogne in the hope of attaining death. He was next heard from as he lay ill and penniless in Frankfort on the Main, whence he returned to Prussia. After first trying to enter again the Prussian army, he obtained in 1804 a position in the bureaucracy. Sent to Königsberg for training, he recovered his mental equipoise but suffered from repeated illness. Although his pride seems to have been broken and his ambition dulled, in Königsberg he wrote some of his finest works and was able to earn a scanty living. He described his state of mind to Altenstein, the future Prussian minister, in June, 1806, as follows: "I sit here as if on the edge of an abyss, my soul fixedly bowed over the deep in which the hope of my life has disappeared, now animated by the desire to draw it up by the hair, now depressed by the feeling of hopeless inability."[27] He endured the restraint of bureaucratic life only a few months. While journeying to Berlin after the French conquest of Prussia, he was taken prisoner and sent to France for internment.

The lines of Kleist's development into nationalism during this period must be traced in some detail. In that period of his life which was dominated by the philosophy of the Enlightenment he conformed to the prevailing mode of cosmopolitanism. He felt no special pride in being a Prussian or a German, no particular obligation to the Prussian king and once wrote defiantly that he could easily find another ruler, whereas the king of Prussia might encounter difficulty in obtaining other subjects. He even thought in 1799 of migrating to Southern France, at least for a period of years, and in 1801 he wished to leave Germany forever and become a Swiss burgher. He used the word fatherland as loosely as any free citizen of the world. First as a young man trying to find himself and then as a writer engrossed in his craft, he frankly took no interest in politics or other group affairs. Napoleon and the French provided the occasion for the flowering of Kleist's na-

[26] *Ibid.*, p. 292.

[27] "Neue Briefe Heinrich von Kleists. Mitgeteilt von Georg Minde-Pouet," *Deutsche Rundschau,* CLXI (1914), 115.

tionalism. The development of his life and ideals had prepared him for reacting in this manner; but the elements out of which his nationalism was to grow lay quiet until the foreign enemy vitally affected his existence. To excite Kleist to nationalism a more directly personal endangerment was required than merely the French defeat of Prussia or Austria.

Kleist disliked the French intensely from the time of his first contact with them in 1801. He had come to France at a most unpropitious moment. Having lost faith in knowledge, he was scarcely more than a mass of raw feelings. Without doubt he would then have hated any strange people. Paris and the Parisians horrified him; Paris because it was filthy and unsafe, Parisians because he thought them cold, artificial, and cynical. Rousseau, he wrote, would be ashamed of the French for desecrating nature and for seeking to conceal the fact of their loss of freedom by celebrating with excessive display the anniversary of the fall of the Bastille. In addition, his aversion to urban sophistication and triviality strengthened his initial antagonism to a people whom he knew best from his residence in Paris, the largest city on the Continent. Kleist had regarded the French as possessing the finest knowledge of the eighteenth century. Yet when he contrasted Parisian libraries, full of the greatest books of the world, and French excellence in science with the repulsive conditions in French society, he found confirmation of his belief that knowledge and science availed merely to amass luxuries. Repugnance to knowledge and reason deepened his antipathy to the nation which had stood most conspicuously for them, and he considered the French civilization riper for decay than any other.

At practically every crucial point in Kleist's career Napoleon and the French interfered. In 1801 their part had little significance; their example merely proved conclusively to Kleist that his revulsion against the faith of the Enlightenment in knowledge was justified. In Switzerland, where he moved, he soon suffered a rude interruption of his writing by the French invasion. He had intended to buy a Swiss home, but fearing that thereby he might become a French citizen, he again became a wanderer. His next contact with the French, apart from the interlude in 1803 when he sought death by proposing to join the French expedition against England, took place in the period of Austerlitz and Jena. The French invasion of Austria evoked from Kleist a letter to a friend in which he expressed practically his entire nationalistic program of a few years later. Advising a war of destruction against Napoleon, in this letter he proposed a means of arousing the "national spirit"—a popular assembly, sacrifice of one's wealth—and he wondered why someone, a French emigrant perhaps, did not assassinate the tyrant. He predicted that Napoleon would not leave Austria soon and that the German constitution would be radically changed with Napoleon's chief satellite, the king of Bavaria, becoming the new king of Germany.

Although Kleist showed in this letter a keen understanding of the French threat to Germany and of the means necessary for meeting it, he preserved a generally cool and disinterested tone. While following events attentively, he did not feel as yet personally affected. Nor did his attitude change when in the next year Prussia collapsed at Jena. "It would be horrible," he wrote his sister, "if this tyrant should establish his empire. Very few people comprehend how ruinous his rule would be. We are the subject peoples of the Romans. The aim is to plunder Europe in order to enrich France." [28] He felt the general misery of the time and longed to weep in his sister's arms. But, unless his trip to Berlin in the next year concealed some patriotic design, he responded like an ordinary timid subject and did nothing. In fact his thoughts, according to his own words in the following year, were occupied with entirely other things. When early in 1807 the French seized him and two companions and sent them to prison in France, Kleist wrote that "perhaps there were not three persons in the world of less concern to them [the French] at the time than we were." [29] Since the arrest of the three seems to have been a mistake, one would expect Kleist to have roared with double fury at the French. Little of the sort occurred. He stood his imprisonment more calmly than did the other two men. Shutting himself off from the French entirely and from his fellow

[28] Kleist, *Werke, op. cit.*, V, 330.
[29] *Ibid.*, p. 335.

prisoners, he continued his literary work, and his letters during these days rarely revealed anger, although he longed to be back in his own country and out of a "most disagreeable situation." [30] He wrote at the time, "You have always thought me isolated from the world; nonetheless, no one is perhaps more intimately connected with it than I am." [31]

Whether Kleist was really so acutely aware of world happenings as he claimed remains uncertain. For a disciple of freedom he adjusted himself quickly to physical incarceration. His remark referred at the time more to a literary awareness than to a political or patriotic one. Kleist was accumulating experiences and data to be utilized in his works; he was not consciously storing up wrath to be poured at some more opportune time on the enemies of his country. And yet the patriot was maturing as the writer assimilated his materials. The feeling of nationalism waited for conditions to become more propitious before it should burst forth. Not until 1808 did they evoke this response in Kleist.

After his release by the French in 1807 Kleist settled in Dresden, where he spent the happiest months of his life. Together with Adam Müller and two other friends he founded and edited the magazine *Phöbus,* which ignored political subjects and devoted itself to literature and art. He was writing and publishing with recognition, and even expected some of his dramas to be produced. He associated with congenial and stimulating friends, who introduced him into the highest society. At last he was earning a living and, so he dreamed, had prospects of becoming famous as a writer and financially independent as a successful publisher and bookseller. The ministers of France, Austria, and Russia in Dresden helped him and his colleagues to obtain subscriptions to *Phöbus;* and the French minister even aided them in their effort to obtain the privilege of publishing the Napoleonic Code and other official French materials in Germany. This right, Kleist informed his sister, would firmly establish the business; but he cautioned her to draw no political conclusions from the connection.

[30] *Ibid.,* p. 339.
[31] *Ibid.,* p. 341.

"Everything without exception which I had hoped for," he wrote his sister in October, 1807, "is being fulfilled." [32]

In voicing his happiness Kleist forgot that he lived in a troublous time, when ventures were far from being certainties. Through pressure applied on the government by already established competitors, he and his friends failed to receive permission to establish their bookstore. Their plan to enter the publishing business also failed to materialize, and with it the hope of spreading, at great profit to themselves, official French publications. Last, in the late spring of 1808, even *Phöbus* declined.

Kleist had suffered from straitened circumstances practically ever since resigning from the army. His own property had barely sufficed to maintain him for a time; and as the expenses of traveling and illness were not covered by any additional revenue, he turned frequently to his sister for aid. After he began to write, he was able to sell his work for small sums and he believed, probably with justice, that if the age were not so unsettled, he could live from his publications. In December, 1805, he wrote to a friend: "For the arts [he meant writing as well as the fine arts] the times have perhaps never been favorable. It has always been said that they must go begging. But the present age lets them starve. Where shall the openness of soul, which is necessary for their enjoyment, come from in times when misery . . . strikes everyone?" [33] After the defeat of Jena in 1806 his difficulties increased, but he still hoped that with the establishment of peace he could support himself by his pen. In Dresden he seemed to be realizing his desire, when again circumstances beyond his control interfered. In August, 1808, he wrote to his sister as follows:

> In spite of the complete failure of the project for a bookstore, up to now *Phöbus* has been able to maintain itself. I do not know what will happen to it if war breaks out. I could easily convince you how good my situation is and how full of hope my prospects for the future are if this ruinous age did not defeat our efforts. At the same time, the conditions under which I live here are bearable and I fear greatly that they are not much better for all of you. Through

[32] *Ibid.*, p. 353.
[33] *Ibid.*, p. 324.

the Master of Ceremonies, Count Vizthum, I have sold another play to the Saxon theater and plan to do this in Vienna, if the war does not prevent me. I cannot hope to succeed in Berlin, because there they produce only translations of small French pieces and in Cassel the German theater is abolished and a French one put in its place. If God does not come to the rescue, it will be the same way everywhere. Who knows whether in a hundred years anyone in this locality will any longer speak German.[34]

A more direct statement of the external reasons why a person should turn nationalist can scarcely be found. If Kleist had been successful in his writing and publishing in Dresden, he probably would never have embraced nationalism, for he felt little concern about political conditions until his own career was directly endangered. His case illustrates that of an egocentric writer forced back into the group, showing how the fate of one became identified with that of the other. Once more Napoleon and the French interfered in Kleist's life; their imperialism accounted for the uncertainty of the age, which prevented literature from receiving popular support. They were ultimately responsible for Kleist's inability to find a stage for his dramas and even threatened to destroy the German language, vehicle of his thought. His previous political indifference to the French invasions of Germany disappeared. In its place there sprang up a hatred so great that Kleist identified himself with the nation-group suffering likewise from the invasion. In the last half of 1808, during the time of the decline of *Phöbus* and his other hopes, he composed the first of his nationalistic dramas, *Die Hermannsschlacht*.

Two questions demand consideration: What enabled Kleist to become a nationalist? Why did he choose the nation rather than a state like Prussia or Austria as the social unit for opposing the French?

An answer to the first question must begin with reviewing the traits of Kleist's character—originality, egocentricity, pride, ambition and emotionalism. Kleist once wrote, "There is a sad clarity which nature has fortunately spared many men who see only the

[34] *Ibid.*, pp. 377-78.

surface of things. . . ." [35] One might dismiss these words as another example of poetic fancy if evidence in Kleist's life of there being something more were not so overwhelming. From childhood his acute sensitiveness had been a determinative force in his life. He was endowed with a gift of direct penetration to the soul of things, which in turn led to or enhanced his loneliness and social maladjustment. Kleist's egocentricity, and connected intimately with this his pride, his emotional instability, and his love of freedom, arose out of a combination of profound insight and social sensitiveness. Although this is too simple an analysis of Kleist's complex psychology, nonetheless, his nature contained an inner unity which revealed itself in his actions.

In his search for individual and social values Kleist first tried knowledge and then turned to the most elemental forms of human existence, a home, manual and finally literary work and freedom in which to cultivate both. Concentrating his entire energy upon the acquisition of these basic things, he appreciated deeply the need of all three because he had to fight so long to gain two of them and failed completely to win a home. The effects seem to have been threefold. First, in learning to treasure the elemental forms of life Kleist schooled his vision for ultimately discovering another basic form, the nation. Second, rebelling against the social order in which his family lived, he created in his relations with society a tension which made him acutely aware of the group and led him to try to restore perfect harmony between his life and group life. In the effort to do so he sought to discover some means by which each would feel an organic relationship with the other. This search ended in nationalism. Third, because of the tension between himself and society, he evolved the ideals of a society in which he would be happy, and he strove to realize them by his work as a nationalist. To him as to others nationalism meant the fulfillment of a vision of a model society suited to his peculiar personality; but, as will be shown, Kleist's picture remained a sketch.

When viewed from another angle, Kleist's character appears

[35] *Ibid.*, pp. 197-98.

to have manifested pride and ambition, both spurs to action. Since he had an enormous physical as well as mental and emotional energy, he escaped the pitfalls which prevented the aesthetically minded romanticists and the mediocre and normally lazy mass of mankind from becoming pioneers of nationalism. He never shared the romanticists' easy contentment with dreams. The scope of his ambition attained the dimensions proper to one who was to rise so high above the level of humanity as to become a nationalist. At the age of twenty-two (1799) he aimed to acquire the whole of knowledge; four years later he was struggling with the composition of a tragedy which should combine the qualities of Aeschylus and Shakespeare; after another seven years he assumed the role of prophet, who should arouse the German people to a sense of their nationhood. One might add that his death marked the crowning deed of ambition of his life; for by taking his own life, he expected in the next and more perfect world to reach ideal union with the woman who died with him.

The main problem which troubled Kleist from his boyhood had to do with living as nature intended him to do. Throughout his life he struggled to find an absolute which fitted him and no one else. Unfortunately, since he could rarely be certain that he was fulfilling the intentions of nature, he suffered constantly from doubt, especially as to his proper role in society and his relations with the group. The search for that role kept him alert and opened his mind to the possibilities of nationalism as a way of uniting himself and society. By confiding the direction of his life to feeling he strengthened a thousandfold his egocentricity and increased enormously the assurance with which he acted. He easily developed a sense of mission and believed that as a prophet he could aid the German nation. Having taken this step, he readily conceived of the German nation as having its own destiny, and this idea led him to regard the nation as an organic unit. Belief in a personal absolute, moreover, compelled him to respect other personal absolutes in society and to demand that each trust the other unconditionally. In order to trust, one must love. Kleist's philosophy of life inclined him to accept the social qualities which, when transferred to the nation, constituted the basic elements of nationalism.

The acceptance of feeling as the guide to one's life brings with it an intense awareness of each immediate moment. Each act or each thought has its concomitant feeling which makes it significant. Kleist differed from the romanticists in being so literal in the use of details. In his writings as in his conduct he preferred the concrete. He filled his works with particulars in order to bring the actual completely before the reader, and he never avoided items which offended morals if their inclusion served his purpose. The same intense response to the immediate colored his life. When Kant destroyed his waning belief in reason, Kleist did not philosophically meditate the quandary in which he was left; he rushed away from his family and fiancée to Paris. The failure to combine the excellencies of Aeschylus and Shakespeare in a drama entailed immediate destruction of the manuscript and search for death. His biography teems with illustrations of this impetuous literalness.

The particular connection in Kleist between devotion to the concrete and his becoming a nationalist must be analyzed. He became a nationalist suddenly. In 1807 he felt indifferent, so far as one can judge, toward politics and the fate of Germany. No doubt his mind contained the seeds of nationalism in his aversion to Napoleon and the French and in his premonition or even fear of the effects of the Napoleonic domination; but the student of his career is scarcely prepared for the outburst of nationalistic feeling in *Die Hermannsschlacht*. The explanation lies in Kleist's literal concentration upon the moment; he regarded each moment or each action as a concrete absolute in itself and therefore vitally important. When he perceived the collapse of his hopes in Dresden, he squeezed the complete meaning out of that event as an absolute thing. That this misfortune was a personal one caused Kleist, not to belittle it as a sad yet inconsequential event, but to become aware for the first time of the menace to the German people of the French domination. The momentary feeling aroused by the incident became the expression of an absolute need and offered the way for satisfying that need. The similarity to Fichte's conception of God's revealing himself is apparent. In the minds of both men an event assumed the proportions of an absolute, requiring the use of every means to meet the danger. Both were emotionally unstable and thought or felt in extremes. They loved and hated and hence came to demand that the members of the German nation love each other and hate the enemy.

Because Kleist had accepted feeling as a guide for living, he was prepared for nationalism. In one as intelligent as he, trust in the guidance of feeling requires the cultivation of the imagination as an aid to intense feeling, or, more accurately, intense feeling and a vivid imagination go hand in hand. Kleist possessed both, as one would expect in the case of a writer. Since at least 1800 he had consciously stimulated his imagination, at first by devoting some time each day to meditation and then by writing. As a dramatist he learned to portray action directly, to feel himself completely into the plot. His short stories reveal the same capacity. By this training Kleist enhanced his sensitiveness to a social situation and was able to orient himself into the plight of Germany in 1808. The composition of dramas taught him to comprehend a tragic situation in actual life, thereby fitting him to become a nationalist. Furthermore, to create a new scene or action a writer must use the materials which he knows. Although Kleist's figures and situations never lacked actuality, they arose, not from his external observations, but from his inner being. They were not imitations; they were his own creations, however real they might also be. The significance of this manner of working lay in the author's ability to portray something which had not actually existed. More easily than ordinary men, Kleist could envisage broken, defeated, humiliated Germany transformed into a nation able to drive out the French and to live in the idealistic manner which he dreamed for her. His work cultivated his sense of the value of social action and prepared him better for imagining a nation in arms moved by a common spirit. Since in his dramas he could impart to social groups the qualities and ideals which he desired, he persuaded himself that an entire nation could also be unified by common ideals. He learned to conceive in the large and came in time to see the nation as a whole and to plan for it. "It is my sadly overstrained soul which can never enjoy what is but only what is not," he wrote in 1801.[36] His works arose in part out of this preference for that which did not exist, as did his nationalism. In both he portrayed his ideas and ideals. Perhaps one may also add that by his writing Kleist stimulated his emotions. He resembled Fichte in his susceptibility to the powerful influence of words. As writers both constantly excited their feelings and imaginations, thus enabling themselves, more easily than persons who lacked these spurs, to discover the nation and to try to arouse a new feeling toward it.

The influence which Adam Müller exerted in transforming Kleist into a nationalist cannot be precisely estimated. The two authors associated intimately in Dresden and read each other's works. Müller had already formulated his theory of the social function of literature. The literary man, he believed, must be sensitive to political and social conditions and must seek in turn to affect them. External affairs forced the truth of this assertion upon Kleist's attention. Henceforth he never ceased to follow this standard in his writing. An egoist like him whom destiny intended to be a writer was undoubtedly encouraged to follow the bent of his inclinations toward the nation and toward nationalistic endeavors so that he could fulfill this destiny. Kleist's interest remained literary and prevented him from deteriorating into a mere polemist; but the contrast between the policy of *Phöbus* in 1807-8 and the *Berliner Abendblätter* of 1810-11 revealed the transformation of a poet into a poet-patriot. By adding the social and political materials of nationalism Kleist enriched his repertory as a writer concerned with the literary quality of his work. One may say that the poet and the patriot blended, not because of Müller's influence but with the aid of it.

Analysis of the factors and forces which enabled Kleist to become a nationalist does not explain why he selected the nation as the object of his devotion. Potentiality is not always synonymous with realization. The question of why he turned to nationalism and not to state-ism or some other loyalty can be answered

[36] Kleist, *Werke,* V, 271-72.

only in general terms. Kleist, like Fichte, began as a cosmopolitan. This had the negative effect of preventing him from being so devoted to any one state or province of Germany that he could not develop a love of entire Germany; he did not first have to overcome a Prussian patriotism, which might have made him object to transforming Prussia and incorporating her into the nation. Nationalism signified the creation of a new society imbued with the feelings of fraternal love.

In formulating the positive explanations for Kleist's turn to the nation one can eliminate at the start the influence of printed matter. While Kleist read some of the nationalistic literature of the period and used a long quotation from Arndt's *Geist der Zeit* as the basis of a short article, he seems not to have been greatly impressed by this literature. He responded to events so personally that reading affected him ony in proportion to the intensity of his need for the ideas which books offered. He did not propagate secondhand and undigested proposals borrowed for the sake of making a name. His fear that the French would destroy the German language and culture directed Kleist's attention to the nation. His instrument of work was the German language; his objective lay in creating German culture; his public included all those who used his language. As an author he was one of the first to appreciate how much French domination menaced the independent culture of all Germany. He was not Prussian, not Austrian, but German. Personal interest induced him to see a national interest; to defend himself he had to defend the nation.

Of almost equal importance in focusing Kleist's attention upon the nation was the belief that only the combined power of the entire nation could defeat the French. Experience had proved that neither Prussia nor Austria alone could eliminate the enemy. The recognition of a common fate, of a common task against a common opponent, created in time of crisis the inclusive and elemental form of sociopolitical life, the nation. An agglomeration of disparate individuals and states, each with its own interests, each with its antagonisms against others, each pursuing a selfish end irrespective of the whole, became ennobled in Kleist's mind by adversity into a brotherhood, a folk, a nation. The enemy was a nation, he thought; Germany must also be in order to preserve herself. Values were reduced to the basic ones, the defense of that which made one German.

In a short article written in 1809 and entitled "Über die Rettung von Österreich," Kleist wrote:

> Every great, general danger, if it is squarely faced, gives the state for the moment a democratic appearance. To allow the blaze which threatens a town to spread without hindrance for fear that the crowd of men necessary for fighting it might get beyond the control of the police would be madness and might occur to a despot but never to an honest and conscientious ruler.[37]

The statement explains why nationalism flames up in times of danger. Misfortune leads to a simplification of social relations and of the problems of life, to intimacy and a feeling of love between the sufferers. This simplification and the accompanying concentration upon essentials enable all individuals and all classes to draw together in unity of mind, soul, and purpose. Danger makes everyone brothers. Since almost everyone can understand the issue, everyone can comprehend the necessary solution and act to effect it. Each person must be free to take the initiative. Docility and fear of breaking a law or custom bring defeat or destruction. A common danger may be met by a blind outburst of wrath aimed solely at defense; but in so far as everyone needs the help of everyone else and people feel and act as one, they partake of the social spirit of nationalism.

Kleist did not come to nationalism by way of the history of the German people. He lacked the historical-mindedness of the romanticists, even though he used historical incidents in his plots. One institution of a famous past, however, remained alive until 1806—the Holy Roman Empire. When Napoleon abolished it and split the German area into parts under separate rule, he could not obliterate the vivid memory of the old Empire. It had stood for a degree of German unity, however slight, and for Kleist it pointed toward the body which must be preserved and which must realize its oneness in order to exist—the German nation.

[37] *Ibid.*, IV, 119.

Back of the basic facts lay the less clear effect of other influences usually associated with the rise of nationalism. In traveling through Germany Kleist found some parts beautiful and others ugly. Although he shared the romanticist's love of the rural landscape, had a deep respect for the common people and longed for a home, he never grew devoted to a particular country or population as Arndt did. Undoubtedly, the love of them enhanced his appreciation of that which he must protect against the French and gave him some feeling of a nationalist; but as objects for arousing his sense of the nation they played a minor role. Neither was Kleist influenced by a comparison of his nation with others. He was almost devoid of philosophic interest in matters of this sort, reacting directly and personally without much reflection. While he recognized differences between the French and the German peoples and despised the former, he never pursued the contrast between them beyond superficialities. Unlike Fichte, he did not consider the Germans a chosen nation or strengthen his love of his own nation by belittling and hating another. His dislike of the French stopped short of leading him to the Germans as Germans. Kleist grew exalted about the German nation and its mission only once, at the height of his nationalistic feeling. At all other times he preserved his regard for all nations. Although his aversion to the French may have inclined him to think of the Germans as a unit, one cannot venture to say more.

Nationalism offered a solution to almost all the problems which beset Kleist's life. The defeat and elimination of the French and the conclusion of peace would restore conditions in which he could earn a satisfactory living from his writing and thereby fulfill his destiny. Nationalism provided him with the opportunity and the incentive for achieving a great deed. It would enable him to recover his prestige with his family, to reëstablish and maintain intimacy with society. It would reconcile his German feeling with whatever loyalty he still felt toward Prussia, since he would be struggling for the sake of both. Nationalism would permit him to work toward the formation of a society in which he would fit, a society which would be imbued with the spirit of freedom, would be prepared to slough off restrictions upon individuals, and would allow their relations to rest on trust and love. Above all, nationalism gave Kleist absolute assurance as to what he should do. During his life he had sought blindly the work which destiny intended for him. The crisis of 1808 revealed to him with perfect clarity his mission to save the nation. More than on any previous occasion he recognized his task and for the first time could concentrate all his efforts upon it. His writing became an heroic deed; it served his country; by writing he could be patriotic, win fame, and return to the group. The only change he need make was to charge the content of his works with nationalism. Since nationalism commanded as complete realization as possible of oneself in order to increase for the nation the wealth of human resources, the problem of the individual versus the group was solved for him. Through nationalism freedom was likewise reconciled with family and caste tradition. It satisfied Kleist's longing for something to love. Having no wife or family of his own, he lavished his affections upon the nation. Nationalism brought together the scattered strands of his existence and gave him happiness.

The immediate occasion for the outburst of nationalism in Kleist called for simple and direct recourse to action. Napoleon must be defeated, driven out, and crushed by fair means or foul. He had attacked the Germans without cause and invaded and despoiled their land while they were living in peace. He personified the forces of evil. Napoleon reminded Kleist of those things which he hated, military affairs, from which he had withdrawn; war and conquest, against which he had bitterly inveighed as early as 1792; despotism, which in various forms he had fought during all his mature years; and lack of respect for other nations than the French, which violated his devotion to freedom and fraternity. "How unhappy I would be if I could no longer be proud," Kleist had written in 1804.[38] Napoleon threatened to destroy this feeling by obstructing the fulfillment of his destiny or, to be more specific, by preventing him from earning a living. But Kleist's pride was hurt in a more elementary way; the French, he thought,

[38] *Ibid.*, V, 308.

regarded and handled the Germans as beasts, worth only a shot for the sake of their fur. The war against Napoleon was a holy war, Kleist declared, and Germany's soil was sacred. He besought the Germans to fight for house and home, the entirety of that which once was theirs, for God, fatherland, and emperor; for freedom, law, and morality, love and loyalty; for beauty, knowledge, and art; for the resurrection of a "greatly sunken and decadent generation, in short, for goods whose value cannot be estimated, which must be defended against an enemy at any cost." [39]

In the Catechism for Germans composed in 1809 Kleist explained why Providence had permitted Napoleon to scourge the Germans. The Germans, he wrote, had overexpanded their reasoning power; "they reflected when they should have felt and acted; they believed that they could accomplish all by their wits and paid no heed to the secret forces of the heart. . . . They sought money and possessions with immoderate and ignoble lust for them. They carried on trade and commerce so zealously that the sweat poured from their brows, believing that a peaceful, comfortable and carefree life was all that could be gained in this world." [40] This statement reads like a portrayal of the standards and objectives against which Kleist had rebelled. He urged the Germans not to waste their energies in evolving the model solution to their danger, telling them not to wait, as Fichte prescribed, for educational reform to create another and a different generation, but to act now. The crisis was acute, he said, and the times out of joint, unusual danger demanding unusual defense.

The methods by which Kleist hoped the Germans could crush the French resembled closely those which the most ardent of the Prussian reformers tried to persuade the government to use. Whether Kleist borrowed his ideas from them or whether both he and they worked them out independently and simultaneously cannot be determined, although the latter case seems more likely. The methods proposed included firing the entire nation with hatred of the French, utilizing the power of men, women, and children in the war of liberation, employing every means for de-

[39] *Ibid.*, IV, 107, 120.
[40] *Ibid.*, p. 107.

stroying the enemy—devastating the German territory in front of it, killing the opponents in any manner and wherever found, refusing to associate with them in any way, even to the point of preserving complete silence toward them, destroying the good as well as the bad. "Hate is my office and revenge my virtue. . . . Do not leave one alive," said Hermann in *Die Hermannsschlacht*.[41] If this generation cannot perform the deed, he declared, the next one must. Kleist wrote the following words in the form of a dialogue:

> Q. If everything should be destroyed and neither man, woman nor child should remain, would you still think the struggle justified?
>
> A. Of course, father.
>
> Q. Why?
>
> A. Because it is pleasing to God when men die in the cause of freedom.
>
> Q. What is then anathema to him?
>
> A. If they live as slaves.[42]

The measures proposed by Kleist resembled closely those prescribed by the advocates of the *Landsturm*. The nation was to become a camp of armed men assisted by the women and children, the children growing up with the objective of destroying the enemy.

In the light of his own experience Kleist knew that only through the emotions could the German nation be aroused to the necessary point for fighting the French. He kept his nationalistic appeal as simple and elementary as possible. Why should a German love his fatherland, he asked? Not because it is rich or famous, but because it is his fatherland. Why should a German try to restore his fatherland? The reason was self-evident, Kleist said. In his two nationalist dramas, *Die Hermannsschlacht* and *Der Prinz von Homburg*, however, he described those social and political relations most conducive to arousing nationalistic feeling. The ideas contained in them also occur in his few political

[41] *Ibid.*, II, 407, 405.
[42] *Ibid.*, IV, 112.

writings. They suffice to show that Kleist held true to the social ideals which he had worked out for his own life. In becoming a nationalist he merely extended these to the social group.

The history of Kleist's life can be summarized in the statement that it portrayed the struggle for freedom to be himself. At first he had had to rebel against the shackles of a military career and the standards of his family, then against the domination of knowledge, and in the last years of his life against the crushing power of Napoleon. Up to his nationalistic period he had to defend his liberty as an individual without regard to social consequences. After 1808 he had to unite his powers with those of the nation lest both the nation and he lose their individualities. Naturally he believed that the nation would defend itself most actively if it possessed the characteristics which he admired. Therefore he endeavored to persuade it to accept his ideals. What did this mean?

If all members of the nation were as proud and individualistic as he, Kleist argued, the nation would be composed of ardent, active citizens, each more eager than the other to aid the common good. Each would demand or be given freedom to cultivate the best qualities within himself in order to fulfill his destiny. Each would have a mission to perform which would endow him with an absolute quality. What he said or did must be considered because it reflected the workings of Providence. The nation must not merely permit but must encourage the free and full development of each member; it must welcome the active participation of each member in the affairs of the whole. The members, equals each in his own sphere of ability and activity, would be brothers. The lives of all would be sacred because they belonged to the nation. The rulers must respect the subjects and consult them; the subjects must advise the rulers freely and frankly. The nation must consist of free men, devoted to the whole and therefore devoted each to himself and proud of his own powers.

Kleist had evolved for himself a conception of freedom similar to that of Fichte and Hegel. In the 1790's he had believed in the contract theory of the state and society and had been indifferent to the social group or the state, except in so far as it was of value to the individual. He had emphasized his rights, not his duties, and had based the contract upon reason. By the time Kleist wrote *Der Prinz von Homburg* he had come to other conclusions. During the interval the Napoleonic invasion had developed his political and social views. He preserved the ideal of individual freedom but he deepened it and lent to it a new meaning. He had learned that society, something more than a mass of individuals, was an organic unity with its own destiny and superior to king and to subjects, in other words, a nation. Nationalism makes ruler and subject equals in that both must serve the nation. If either does not, the other must try to persuade him to do so and not arbitrarily break away to join some other society. The moral decision in this case rests on general rather than on individual grounds; but these general grounds are no longer rationalistic, being instead historical, organic, social ones. In the theory of the social contract the individual can break the contract in order to live rationally and freely; in the nationalistic theory he must work within the nation to improve it. His destiny is bound up with the nation. Kleist's deep sense of personal destiny enriched his sense of national destiny and made him wish to transform the nation into an organic union of individualities. Freedom to Kleist meant, not individual license, but the will to subordinate oneself to a nobler social good.

One should not forget that Kleist accepted feeling as an infallible guide. Therefore he did not desire nationalism to interfere with the freedom of feeling. In *Der Prinz von Homburg,* the ruler, at the beginning of the play a strict enforcer of the law, comes to recognize the fruitful power of feeling in organized society. He conforms to Kleist's own ideal. But the Prince of Homburg, the emotional hero, learns that feeling must direct action which benefits both the individual and society. Feeling, law, government must all contribute to the welfare of the group; but Kleist continued to believe that among them feeling was the most powerful and most trustworthy guide to action. Nationalism was an emotional ideal.

In *Der Prinz von Homburg* Kleist showed how a nationalalistic society could be held together and brought to coöperate.

He transferred to nationalism the means, absolute trust and love, which he had worked out previously for reconciling the individual with the group. Both *Penthesilea* and *Kätchen von Heilbron* are plays of unconditioned love. Significantly, they immediately preceded *Die Hermannsschlacht,* in which Kleist transferred this unconditioned love from individuals to the nation. Trust and love formed the foundation of nationalism. An idealist who seeks to create a new society must think it possible for ordinary human beings to trust and love each other. To be powerful in war against the French or to be potentially strong a nation must be composed of individuals who love each other so completely that they will sacrifice everything for the nation. They must have entire faith in others before they will take this risk. The history of the German wars against Napoleon showed the futility of one state's fighting alone in the hope that some others would assist. It revealed the futility of a war of the kind that the eighteenth century waged for glory, self-aggrandizement, or dynastic purposes.

It has often been argued that, under the influence of Adam Müller and the aristocratic circles in Berlin, Kleist returned to the tradition of social and political reaction. Kleist's entire life furnished evidence to the contrary. Kleist had loved freedom from his early years, had repudiated the aristocratic standards as prejudices and had fought a long and fairly successful personal war against them. In Switzerland he had come in contact with young men of democratic sentiments; in Prussia he associated closely with two of the leading reformers, Altenstein and Stägemann; and in the few months before his death he became an enthusiastic admirer of Gneisenau, a third. He had studied Adam Smith and twice (1800 and 1806) in his correspondence had advocated freedom of economic enterprise. In examining his relations with Adam Müller one is impressed with the fact that Müller influenced him only along certain lines, particularly in respect to the relation of literature to society and the organic nature of society. Even in these matters Kleist preserved a strong element of Rousseau-ism. In 1809 he pressed Altenstein to employ Müller in Prussia; in his letter he revealed his own hopes and Müller's part in realizing them. In the same year Kleist spoke of Prussia, not as a political integer in itself, but as a support for the German nation. He wished the Prussian government to collect all the forces possible around it for the defense of Germany and he recommended Müller to Altenstein as one of them. He himself came to Berlin a year later in order to offer his services for the fatherland in the one state relatively free of French control. In this letter to Altenstein he praised Müller for his farseeing way of thinking, for the practical turn of his mind, for his deep concern with the rebirth of the fatherland and the practical manifestation of his patriotism in newspaper articles. In other words, Kleist praised Müller for those attributes which accorded with his own nationalistic ideals. Kleist and Müller coöperated in 1810-11 on the *Berliner Abendblätter,* but evidence is again lacking that Kleist accepted his friend's reactionary views. As editor Kleist set a policy of using articles on both sides of a controversy and he adhered to it. Furthermore, the two political essays which he wrote for the *Abendblätter* contained strong denunciations of the particularistic and selfish policies of the Prussian aristocrats and defended Hardenberg's reforms. Kleist approved entirely of changes in the constitution of Prussia (he was referring to a breach of aristocratic privilege which Hardenberg was making) if thereby the state would profit, and he thought that it would in this case. There is no reason to doubt Kleist's honesty in expressing these views, even though at the time he wrote them he was trying to gain favor with Hardenberg. Kleist's life attested to the integrity of his assertions and intentions. Reactionary Prussia represented that against which he had revolted. Reaction in Prussia in 1810-11 closed the Berlin State Theater to his dramas. A new Prussia and a new Germany would both accept these with enthusiasm and realize his other hopes. He had every reason to remain true to his love of freedom and his nationalism.

At the time of the Franco-Austrian War of 1809 Kleist wrote a short essay in which he summed up the issues at stake in the conflict. The essay contained the most complete picture of the ideal nation which Kleist ever made and can be used as a summary of that which lay nearer his heart than the political aspects of nationalism.

It is a question of a community whose thousandfold roots [he wrote], like those of an oak, grip the soil of our time; whose top, shadowing virtue and morality, touches the silver seam of the clouds; whose existence has been hallowed through a third of the life of the earth. It is a community unacquainted with the spirit of power and conquest, which is worthy of life and understanding as is no other, which cannot think of its glory without at the same time thinking of the glory of all who dwell on the earth; whose freest and greatest thought, achieved by poets and soothsayers on wings of imagination, is subjection to a world government which would be set up by the free choice of all brother nations. It is a question of a community whose truthfulness and openheartedness are exercised alike toward friend and foe and have become known among the neighbors as a byword; which, risen above all doubt, like the possessor of that famous ring, is one which others love most; whose innocence, even at the moment when the stranger smiles at or even mocks it, still arouses his secret respect; one whose name a member only needs to mention in order to arouse confidence in the furthest corner of the earth. A community which far from bearing in its bosom a sign of superiority, rather, like one of modest disposition, has not believed up to the present day in its own majesty; which like the bees has flown about untiringly sucking up everything which it found good, just as if nothing good were originally within it; in whose lap the gods have preserved the original of humanity in purer form than in any other place. A community which in the exchange of services has remained debtor to no one, which gave back to the peoples, its brothers and neighbors, something for everything which it received. A community which, on the obelisks of the age has always been among the bravest and most ready, which has, indeed, laid the cornerstone itself and perhaps was set apart to put the copestone in place. It is a question of a community which has given birth to Leibnitz and Gutenberg, in which a Guericke weighed the atmosphere, Tschirnhausen bent the rays of the sun and Kepler demonstrated the path of the planets; a community which can show great names as spring can flowers; which had Hutten and Sickingen, Luther and Melanchthon, Joseph and Frederick, in which have lived Dürer and Cranach, the glorifiers of temples, and Klopstock has sung the triumph of the Savior. A community which belongs to the whole of mankind, which even the South Sea islanders would rush to defend if they knew it, a community whose death no German shall survive and which shall be brought to a bloody grave before which the sun darkens.[43]

This passage described a dream which Kleist hoped that the German nation and the world would one day fulfill. The plea (for that was its true nature) to the Germans revealed even in its proportions the real Kleist. Politics and political figures were scarcely mentioned. The social organization was built on the ideals of freedom, absolute loyalty and trust, innocence, modesty, devotion to the common good by realizing one's individuality. In this society the guidance of feeling could be confidently followed. The attributes which Kleist assigned to his society would enable the individual members of the nation to perfect culture as far as humanly possible. Kleist sought a nation in which he could achieve his exalted hopes as a writer, in which everyone else would have the same opportunity to be stirred to cultural creativeness and to stimulate and encourage others. In this society great persons would receive recognition, and Kleist would be able to take his place alongside Kepler, Luther, and others. It was a poet's dream.

Nationalism lifted Kleist into a realm of exaltation and imparted to him the function of prophet. The German nation, he wrote in the essay quoted above, should be the model for humanity. Contrary to his usual sense of reality, Kleist in this essay tended to elevate his own nation above the rest; it had laid the foundation of the obelisk of history and perhaps it should set the copestone. Elsewhere in his writings he was more modest, but for once he grew almost Fichtean. In the next year he assumed the guise of Zoroaster to announce his role as editor of the *Berliner Abendblätter*.

God, my Father in Heaven, Thou hast set for man a free, beautiful, rich life. Human and animal forces of endless variety animating him make him monarch of the earth. Yet, strange to say, he lies bound by chains, overwhelmed by unseen spirits; dazzled by error, he disregards the highest things and wanders blindly about

[43] Kleist, *Werke,* IV, 115-16.

among sorrow and nothingness. Alas, he is even pleased with his situation; and if there were no past and no heavenly hymns to give knowledge of it, we should have no inkling of the heights, O Lord, whence man can look about him. But from time to time Thou lettest it fall like scales from the eyes of one of Thy servants, whom Thou choosest, that he may see the stupidities and errors of his kind; Thou callest him with the quiver of speech that he, unafraid and loving, may walk among them and with arrows now sharper, now gentler, wake them from the strange sleep in which they lie bound. Me also, although unworthy, O Lord, hast Thou in Thy wisdom chosen for this task, and I gird myself for my work. Fill me completely from head to foot with a feeling of the suffering which this age endures and with insight into the misery, the half-truths, the lies, the hypocrisy, from which it results. Steel me with the strength to bend the bow of judgment and in the choice of arrows to strike wisely each man for what he lacks, to fell the ruinous and those who cannot be saved to Thy glory, to afright the vicious, to warn the erring, to stir the foolish with the gentle sound of the arrow tip about his head. And teach me to plait the garland that I may crown in my way him who is pleasing to Thee. Above all, may love for Thee, O Lord, awake, without which nothing, not even the least, succeeds; that Thy Kingdom may be glorified and may flourish through all space and all time. Amen! [44]

The tone of godly authority which Kleist used in this prayer reflected the height to which he had soared in his search for the absolute. The once-frustrated author was to guide mankind into a golden age, where amid the abundance of freedom and creative action, frustrations would disappear. One would expect Kleist to attempt this role; his whole life had been a search for the divine. Since he failed to find it in the existing order, he easily followed the inspiration of his desires and sought to create a society in which the absolute would be revealed directly and freely. Nationalism expressed the ideals by which and in accordance with which this new society was to be created.

When one leaves the realm of Kleist's ideas in order to study his proposals concerning the future political organization of the German nation, one is impressed by the meagerness of these. Both

[44] *Ibid.*, pp. 127-28.

Austria and Prussia, he thought, should be included in the new Germany; the Hapsburgs should be restored to the imperial seat; the powers of the separate states should be curbed for the sake of the needs of common rule. But on the whole Kleist left the question of future organization to a "general Reichstag" of the "imperial estates," by which he meant the rulers of the separate states. Since he thought always in personal terms of relations between ruler and subject, he took monarchism for granted. As stated above, he believed that the monarch should consult his subjects, just as he should consult his fellow rulers; and Kleist held that rulers and subjects would coöperate for the good of the whole.

Kleist's picture of the future social structure exhibited similar incompleteness. His reliance upon the guidance of feeling and his love of immediate action were not conducive to clarity of thinking and limited his understanding of the institutional and social implications of nationalism. He believed that if the feeling of nationalism was present the rest would follow.

Kleist was imaginative about real problems of the present and lacked the philosophic-social imagination for carrying his mind into the future by way of a concept like freedom, as Fichte did. As a dramatist, he put existing beings into pictures of action; his vision of an ideal nationalistic social order focused upon the individual members rather than the social whole. In his writings Kleist handled mainly personal problems; he was intensive, not extensive. The nation consisted of individuals; it was not a transcendental ideal. It must be filled with certain moral qualities for the sake of these individuals. Even *Der Prinz von Homburg* was not altogether a patriotic drama; its nationalism was tempered by Kleist's interest in the plot as such and by his concern with the characters as individuals.

Social status restricted similarly the scope of Kleist's thinking about the social content of nationalism. Unlike Fichte, Kleist never had to fight his way up the ladder. He had only to defend himself and his ideals against his own social group and had no need to envisage a society in which caste had been abolished. He was not a thoroughgoing social reformer, wishing merely to loosen existing bonds so that men could act with freedom. His criticisms of existing society extended only so far as was necessary to obtain freedom for himself. Later, in order to preserve this freedom against the French, he had to arouse society. Otherwise, he wanted to create, to write, to live as he pleased. His nationalism was more negatively defensive than positively reforming. He did not believe in social equality; it is doubtful whether he ever thought much about it. The future society in which he would be adjusted and happy was one in which classes might continue to exist. High birth and egocentricity limited his appreciation of what the realization of the ideals of freedom and trust and love would mean to the lower classes, of how it would transform specifically the order of society. Fichte's comprehension in these respects extended much further.

As a writer of dramas Kleist dealt with specific situations and actions. In these plays he created his own world and realized his desires. Fichte, the philosopher, formulated his conception of a nationalistic Germany in general outlines which could not be filled out within his own lifetime. Fichte was kept loyal to his nationalism because of the enticing nature of this general picture. Kleist, the dramatist, burned with nationalism while his emotions were aroused, but his devotion diminished in the same way as his concern with a plot once the play was completed. Tragedy, wrote Aristotle, purges the emotion. Kleist could relieve his feelings by making nationalism victorious in drama.

Nationalism never became the ultimate good to Kleist. In enumerating the objects which must be defended against the French, Kleist included many which lay beyond the nation. The fatherland occupied a modest place alongside law, morality, freedom, and beauty. Kleist dreamed of the ultimate establishment of a world kingdom which would include all nations. Except during one interval of exaltation nationalism played the part for Kleist of an instrument for the realization of cultural and political cosmopolitanism.

The analysis of the limitations of Kleist's nationalism helps to explain why in 1811 he took his own life. An ardent, complete nationalist would not have despaired and violated his obligations to the nation by so selfish an act. He would have suffered adversity for the sake of the group in the hope that he could aid it in the future. Kleist at the time of his death seems not to have considered his national duty at all but to have thought only of himself. Since 1808 he suffered constantly from lack of funds. He could find no position which would provide him with a living and he earned almost nothing from his writing. Want stirred his nationalism again to action. He wrote in April 1809 from Dresden to a friend as follows:

> I find that one must throw himself into the scales of the age with one's entire weight, whether it be heavy or light. You will find enclosed my small contribution thereto [his poems]. . . . I wish that I had a voice of iron and could sing them to the Germans from the top of the Harz.[45]

Shortly after this letter he left Dresden for Austria, where he hoped to edit a nationalistic journal, *Germania,* which would especially arouse North Germany. The Austrian government and the outcome of the war of 1809 ruined the project and left him in great financial distress. "Woe to you, my fatherland," he wrote in a poem. "Your faithful poet is prevented from singing your fame!"[46] Then he turned to Prussia and for some months edited the *Berliner Abendblätter* in the hope of making a living while again serving patriotic purposes. But in this paper he permitted Adam Müller too free a scope for criticizing Hardenberg's measures of reform and aroused the antagonism of the government. His efforts to transform the journal into a semi-official organ failed. His money was about gone; he could not persuade any theater to stage his dramas; he failed to obtain a post in the Prussian army; and when he visited his sister in Frankfort on the Oder in 1811, he was received with anger and abuse for being a failure and a financial burden.

> Our relations here [he wrote just before his death] . . . are worse than ever. They expect the Emperor Napoleon on a visit, and if this happens, it may be that a few words lightly and cleverly

[45] *Ibid.,* V, 385-86.
[46] *Ibid.,* IV, 38.

spoken will solve all the problems over which our politicians are breaking their heads. You can easily imagine how this prospect affects me; . . . there is not a spark of light in the future toward which I can look with pleasure and hope. A few days ago I was with Gneisenau and gave him a few things which I had worked out. But this all seems, as the French say, so much mustard after dinner. It is really strange how everything which I undertake comes to ruin, how every time that I decide to take a step, I find the ground sink under my feet.[47]

Shortly afterward he shot himself.

Kleist had become aware of the nation when the French threatened to prevent him from continuing his career as a writer. He had realized that only with the nation's aid could he maintain himself and preserve his pride. Between 1808 and 1811 he discovered that his own nation was either unable or unwilling to help him; its political leaders rejected his proffers of aid and threatened his material independence. Life on earth seemed hopeless. Kleist the nationalist was forced back into Kleist the individualist. His egocentricity reappeared as the basic thing in his life and the group connections of nationalism receded from importance as their usefulness diminished. Nationalism had accomplished nothing for Kleist; it had earned him no bread; it had brought him no fame; it had not restored intimacy with his family and class; it had not enabled him to act heroically; it had not assisted him in realizing his own destiny; it had not furthered his literary production. Unlike Fichte, he had no philosophic vision of a future nation to comfort and revive him. He lived in the moment, not in the future; he loved the details of the present and assigned to them absolute significance. When his nationalism failed to realize any of his hopes, he returned to his ego and concluded that death alone remained. Knowledge, feeling, nationalism, and death—these sum up the means by which he had endeavored to solve his problems. Three of them failed him; the last one was definitive. It was a personal, egocentric act which could be achieved independently of any outside aid; it was Kleist's own deed and satisfied conditions of abso-

[47] *Ibid.*, V, 428-29.

luteness as nothing else had done. In this moment nationalism assumed a minor place in the history of an egoist who had not found a social order appropriate to his genius. A few days before his death he wrote that his life had been "the most anguished that ever a man lived." [48]

[48] *Ibid.*, V, 435.

V. GNEISENAU

THE course of Gneisenau's evolution into a nationalist can be followed only in broad outlines; for this army officer, who spent most of his life in Prussian service, left behind few data about himself, particularly for the period prior to 1806. The details of his boyhood and young manhood are so obscure that even legends about him have been few. Like Napoleon, he held an inconspicuous military post until war—in his case the Battle of Jena—released and revealed his genius. In addition, he practiced the Stoic virtues, disclosing few of the secrets of his soul and preserving no evidence of them. He left the historian, curious about the development of his nationalism, no other recourse than that of interpreting the known facts with considerable latitude.

It is almost as difficult to fix the limits of Gneisenau's nationalism as to determine how he became a nationalist. Combining the two problems, one may ask how Gneisenau became a nationalist to the extent that he did. Emphasis should be put on the limits to his nationalism; for in his thinking he neither went beyond the cosmopolitan ideal of freedom nor conceived of the necessary institutional basis for nationalism, confining himself to proposals for a few practical reforms. Although Gneisenau manifested many traits of a nationalist, he never deserted the solid structure of the politico-territorial *status quo*. His evangelism remained confined to the simpler lines of nationalism, freedom, and revenge, and, except briefly during the years of acute crisis in Prussia, he did not aspire to create a new man, a new society, and a new world order.

Gneisenau came of a Swabian family, which had emigrated to Austria before the reign of Charles V and, having turned Protestant, had been driven in poverty from the country. At the time of the Seven Years' War Gneisenau the elder served as a lieutenant in the Austrian artillery. While stationed at Würzburg, he gained the affection of the daughter of a Catholic artillery officer. Since he was a Protestant, without estate or income except his salary and forced to live as a mercenary officer, the young lady's family, which was of wealthy and proud burgher stock, protested strongly. In spite of this, he married and took his bride off to the war. On October 27, 1760, the Gneisenau of this essay was born at Schilda in Saxony. His mother happened to be accompanying a part of the Austrian army temporarily in occupation of the area. She immediately had her son baptized, asking to serve as godparents a major, a watchmaker's wife, an imperial lieutenant, the youngest daughter of the town clerk, and a petty state official. At the time of the birth of the son the husband and father was retreating hurriedly with the army and a few days later, because of the approach of Frederick the Great, mother and son had to follow even more hurriedly. During their flight in the night the wagon carrying the weak convalescent and her child broke down and they were transferred to a peasant's cart. Upon the continuation of the journey the mother lost consciousness, and the baby slipped from her arms, to be found lying in the road by a soldier in the escort. The mother did not recover from the horrors of the ride and died shortly afterwards.

Gneisenau came into the world outside of a fixed orbit. He was half-burgher, half-aristocrat, without the traditions or material basis of either class. He could become Protestant or Catholic; he could imitate his father and enter military service or choose another profession; he could become a subject of any ruler. He seems to have had no relations with his father's family and, due to his mother's death, no contact for some years with his other grandparents. His father, roving the German realm in search of a living, left his son with a poor family which reared him like a wretched peasant. He spent the first years of his life under the raw treatment of persons devoid of personal interest in him. He had bread enough, but with it plenty of abuse. Having come casually into the world, he had been casually left to his fate. In fact, as he said later, he was uncertain whether he was he; on the night in which as a babe he had fallen from his mother's arms he might have been exchanged for someone else. The story goes that out of pity for the boy the village tailor wrote his grandparents in Würzburg and one day a coach appeared and took away young Gneisenau, then nine years of age. When for the first time in his life he entered the elegant, brilliantly illuminated home of his grandparents and saw gathered there officers in their gorgeous uniforms, it seemed like magic to him. He had moved overnight from poverty to comfort and, without troubling for a reason, he accepted the change as another inexplicable event.

Gneisenau often felt uncomfortable in the environment of Würzburg. He received as much education as this center of Catholicism offered, acquiring a taste for reading and studying that never left him. But he complained later that his Jesuit and Franciscan teachers had known little and had imparted less to him, and felt especially indebted for his education to a friend residing in his grandfather's house who lent him books, a rarity in any Würzburg home at that time. Having been drilled in Luther's Catechism he likewise disliked the Catholic religion. Although he would not anger his grandparents by officially becoming a Protestant, he continued to worship in Lutheran churches, for which he frequently received the unpleasant epithet of "Lutheran dog."

The significance of these Würzburg experiences may be regarded as threefold. First, Gneisenau early became conscious of fundamental religious differences and received a personal lesson in rationalism. That he ended as a Kantian will surprise no one. Second, he did not enjoy a normal growing period, free of cares and sweetened by understanding and sympathetic parents. As he wrote later: "The stormy course of my life and my wavering from the path of right and goodness resulted solely from my poor bringing up. I have experienced little that was good or praiseworthy, and when the child's heart is not warmed by fine examples, it remains cold forever, unless some other guardian angel takes care of it."[1] Since he did not find other guardian angels, he cultivated the virtues of a Stoic and began to practice that self-control which later distinguished him. The "Lutheran dog," son of a disobedient daughter, continued to receive practical training in the art of holding his tongue and guarding his actions. Third, and in connection herewith, he was unable fully to feel that Würzburg was his home. He remained a stray and, like young Fichte, was in a sense a misfit.

Gneisenau's life from the death of his grandfather (1772) to his entrance into the University of Erfurt (1777) remains as obscure as his early years. The reliable facts can be reduced to the following: His father married again, settled in Erfurt as a building inspector, lived unhappily with his wife, acquired five more children and brought his eldest son to live with him. Gneisenau continued to see "little that was good or praiseworthy" in this new home or to find affection. His financial status seems to have been characteristically uncertain. He remained at the University of Erfurt somewhat over a year, residing with one of the professors. He learned some mathematics, engineering, history, literature and music. The story is told that he fell in love with his host's daughter, became involved in a duel, and wasted in a short time the sum of money inherited from his grandfather. In spite of his enjoyment of study, perhaps for financial reasons, he left the University in the winter of 1778-79 and joined an Austrian regiment stationed at Erfurt. After eighteen years of rapidly shifting fortune he followed the example of his father and of many other impecunious aristocrats in turning soldier of fortune. Living in a century of enlightened cosmopolitanism, like his father he entered the service of the monarchy which in the Counter Reformation had forced his ancestors to flee from its land.

It is indicative of his character that Gneisenau joined the Austrian army when the war of the Bavarian Succession was in progress. When after a few months peace was established, he transferred to the service of Ansbach-Bayreuth. Legend holds

[1] Hans Delbrück, *Das Leben des Feldmarschalls Grafen Neithardt von Gneisenau* (Berlin, 1920, 4th ed.), I, 18.

that a duel and an overstayed leave shared in causing the move. In any case, Gneisenau now entered the forces of a prince who hired his soldiers out to England and in 1782 he was shipped with his battalion to America. He remained in Canada for a year and a half without even approaching the sites of the war, returning at the close of 1783 to garrison duty in the sleepy town of Bayreuth. Within two years he sought service in the more active army of Frederick the Great. As a young officer with American experience, he had hoped to enter Frederick's own suite of officers; instead, he received the post of first lieutenant in the small garrison town of Löwenberg in Silesia. After twenty-six years of good and bad fortune, he resigned himself to the fate of drilling raw troops at a salary barely sufficient to maintain him in an area devoid of almost every attraction. For the next twenty years until the Battle of Jena he endured this existence.

One biographer has said of Gneisenau that upon entering Prussian service he seemed to bury his ambition.[2] The assertion is true only in part and needs to be elucidated. Stoicism was strongly developed in Gneisenau as a protection against a fickle fortune which otherwise might have destroyed his independent spirit. He had tried to combat the handicap of impecuniosity only to witness a mounting burden of debt, an affliction from which he constantly suffered. It is reported that two-thirds of his salary went to pay off debts, and from this fact one realizes how necessary a modest and retiring existence was to him; but he preferred it in order to regain his independence of spirit. The state of his finances remained critical until after the overthrow of Napoleon, when the Prussian government took care of him as a hero. The need of frugality helped to hold him to his studies and prevented him from conforming to the pattern of an officer. To rise in his profession he had to employ other means than those of social connections and wealth, and, since his inclination lay in the direction of study, he took the slow road of preparing himself quietly for the moment when his opportunity might come.

Gneisenau could have ignored his debts, choosing an easy

[2] *Ibid.*, I, 40.

but dependent existence. Poverty afforded him inducements toward either an easy existence of sycophancy or the more difficult one of independence. In a letter to his half brother in 1788 he described the lessons of his own experience:

> You are now at the point of entering into the world without those supports which often make failures endurable to people of your age and position, namely, worldly possessions. Remember that your honor is your one treasure, that the loss of it is seldom to be replaced, and that we have a strict judge within us who never forgives us for any offense to him. Remember that a courtly manner and courtesy toward others are means necessary to offset a lack of worldly goods.[3]

The circumstances of his birth had forced Gneisenau to shift for himself. The instability of his social position accentuated his concern with his own conduct as an individual and his relations with society. He became more conscious of social problems than an aristocrat of assured position and income might have done. He was unable to take society as a matter of course or to wait until its problems were forced upon him. Standing somewhat outside existing society while personally dependent upon it, he might have become a timid apologist for the *status quo* rather than an objective critic of it; but he had to take a conscious position.

The sensitiveness of Gneisenau's conscience and the strength of his will account for his choosing the hard road of personal independence. Without these a career like his would have been unthinkable. He practiced the categorical imperative before, so far as is known, he had ever heard of Kant. In a period of social transition like that in which Gneisenau lived the man of action conforms to the ideal which the astute philosopher only later formulates into theory.

In two letters to his father, one in 1788 and another in 1796, Gneisenau expressed his formula of success. The passages are so revealing that they deserve to be quoted in full. In 1788 he chided his father as follows:

[3] G. H. Pertz, *Das Leben des Feldmarschalls Grafen Neithardt von Gneisenau* (Berlin, 1864), I, 37.

I like to look into the future and for that reason I wish to induce you to recommend emphatically to my brothers to learn what they still do not know. They do not seem to be convinced of the necessity to do so and cite the example of L. and N. I assure you that because of this very ignorance these two persons will not maintain themselves long and will certainly not rise to higher military rank. How many officers who already have higher rank are now being suddenly dismissed, oftentimes with apparent injustice; but the injustice disappears when one investigates matters more closely and finds that they lacked something fundamental. You certainly do not wish the same fate for your sons. And since in this connection I am familiar with the orders given to the chiefs and commanders, I prophesy for them such a future unless they take their career more seriously.[4]

In the second letter he wrote to his father:

For my advancement [he had just been promoted to a captaincy] I have avoided every path except the straight one. In my simplicity I have believed that perhaps punctuality and zeal in service, pleasure and ardor in drilling and a broadening of my limited knowledge, together with attentiveness to appearance, would interest my superiors in me and would in the end bring me success. These qualities have been counted to my credit and my bad habits forgotten. Therefore my advice to young people is service and more service and the cultivation of everything remotely connected with it.[5]

The contrast revealed in these letters between father and son offers a picture in miniature of the difference between the kind of officer that lost the Battle of Jena and the kind that revived the Prussian army after the collapse. Gneisenau knew that some leaders of the Prussian army were seeking intelligent officers and he mapped out what he thought the most secure and the most direct path to promotion. Throughout his mature years he possessed the ability to make a careful decision and to adhere to it and to strike straight toward the heart of an issue without being confused by details. He was developing the quali-

[4] *Ibid.*, I, 38.
[5] *Ibid.*, p. 50.

ties of an excellent commander. But his interests were wider still. He was learning to look behind the soldier to the man and society, thus laying the bases of his success later as a military and social reformer.

Gneisenau's ambition did not assume an exaggerated form like that of Fichte or Napoleon. By being modest in his demands on life he avoided exposing himself to intense disappointment. In his young manhood he wrote a poem entitled "Happiness," in which he scorned the dependence necessary for worldly success and extolled the diadem of freedom. In a poem of 1792 he declared, "The wise man who is able to control himself is free even where despots rage." [6] Although later he discovered that this statement was untrue, at the time he asserted his independence of an unpleasant world—a course similar to that of the leaders of the French Revolution. Gneisenau had as yet taken only the step of making his own happiness as independent as possible of the general fate of mankind; he did not endeavor actively to reorganize the world according to his ideals until forced by Napoleon to do so. The history of his nationalism consists in his gradual recognition that he could not entirely divorce his fate from that of society, whereas the limits of his nationalism were partly set by his constant desire to separate them as far as possible. Shifts of fortune struck him so hard that he always reserved the right, subject to his strong sense of duty, to defend his peace of mind by sacrificing his ambition.

In 1809 Gneisenau wrote to his wife, "Health gives the soul strength, and far more is achieved with this than with learning. A sound mind and a pure soul are the chief requirements for a happy life." [7] He disliked professors and never acquired a thorough theoretical training in any subject, not even in those branches connected with military science. In later years after he became famous he could not defend his views in a sharp debate which involved theory. He deplored his ineptitude as a dialectician and blamed it upon his haphazard education. Thus

[6] *Ibid.*, I, 650.
[7] *Ibid.*, I, 523.

the general purpose and the extent of his knowledge were circumscribed. Knowledge, he thought, must serve sound understanding and strengthen soul and will; it must be complementary to a sound body. This view might be expected of an officer, an aristocrat, and reader of the classics. Gneisenau kept his studies in more intimate contact with his practical work than a man of his profession was accustomed to do, so that it is impossible to separate that which he learned through experience from that which he derived from books. He used the Pestalozzian method of learning long before he had ever heard of its formulator.

When Gneisenau went to America, he was merely an alert, rather studious, young officer, whose immediate past caused him embarrassment and sorrow. Youthful carefreeness had led to duels, debts, and other misfortune which he wished to forget. While stationed in Halifax and Quebec, he seized the occasion for learning all that he could about the country and its methods of fighting. He had an inclination, not often found in military men, to reason about things and seek new conclusions. He wished particularly to discover how relatively untrained troops could defeat a standing army and found the answer in the fact that the colonists were citizens fighting on their own soil for independence. He also perceived the appropriateness of their method of fighting, learned in Indian warfare, to democracy: in battle they used the scatter formation, availing themselves of the protection offered by the terrain and fighting not as a mass but as an army of adaptive individuals. Gneisenau also discovered that, instead of relying on a train of provision wagons, the colonial army lived off the territory, thereby gaining mobility. He received his first lesson in the methods of warfare appropriate to nationalism, a lesson which the tactics of the armies of the French Revolution and of Napoleon confirmed and which the Prussian reformers later endeavored likewise to put into practice. Military organization and methods, he saw, must harmonize with political and social organization; one must change with the other.

The philosophic observer of history must marvel at the extent to which this dweller on the periphery of caste security evolved qualities and ideals different from those of most of his contemporaries. By virtue of his birth, early hardships, and character Gneisenau was receptive to the lessons of later events. He seems to have developed in such a way as to make the most of these experiences. On the basis of them he formed a new ideal for man and society, one to which he was to give at least partial institutional reality. His social and military experiences, his reading and study fitted into a pattern of thought which led him to desire reform in the direction of the liberalism and nationalism of the nineteenth century. Just as the pursuit of his studies was evolving in him a conception of man as a rational being, so his military experiences were teaching him the need of a new type of soldier. The one provided the intellectual basis of liberalism, the other the military; but whereas the one led toward individualism, the other carried the potentiality of group action or nationalism.

Gneisenau did not perceive immediately the relations between the several aspects of life. As an officer his first thoughts were of the military significance of the American example. His political sense seems scarcely to have been awakened, and his role in America, that of a mercenary hired to crush freedom, was not immediately conducive to an appreciation of the ideals for which the colonists were fighting. As in the case of other figures already discussed, Gneisenau's political views changed last. His military ones were the first to be consciously transformed, while his ideas concerning social relations, since these relations touched his person, were affected next in order. The changes in them assisted him in bringing his political ideals into line with his military views. When this occurred, Gneisenau was prepared to stand alongside the great reformers, Stein and Hardenberg.

At Löwenberg Gneisenau trained the raw troops as far as he could in the American method of fighting. He wished them in battle to be individually resourceful. While he succeeded remarkably well in molding peasants and non-Prussian mercenaries into efficient troops, he learned from hours of drilling how difficult it was to transform stupid and indifferent humanity into good soldiers. The connection between social and political organization and military efficiency became anew strikingly clear to him, and the successive defeats of the old-style armies at the hands of the French revolutionary armies confirmed the view.

The extent to which the French achievements impressed Gneisenau before 1806 cannot be gauged with certainty. He did not express his views before the Battle of Jena; but his remarks afterward disclose the fact that he had already grasped the differences between the French public morale and that of the Prussians and the reasons therefor. Gneisenau followed carefully the course of events in France, even writing an essay about some military aspects of the campaign of 1792. Three years later he transferred to a regiment which had just returned from the French war and he must have taken the occasion for widening his knowledge. Many years after the War of Liberation he said that in military and political affairs Napoleon had been his teacher. He was one of the few Prussian officers who followed carefully the course of their future conqueror, for he was among the few who could understand the nature and import of the changes made by the revolutionists and Napoleon in military techniques. The nation in arms, scatter fighting, rapid marches and the persistent pursuit of the defeated enemy until it was completely crushed, and patriotic enthusiasm—these innovations by the French held his attention, and, as nearly as one can determine on the basis of little information, stimulated his deep interest in the political and social changes in France which had helped to make her military success possible.

In tracing the evolution of an officer into a nationalist, the development of his social relations and understanding demands more attention than that of his military success. One must continually recall, however, that Gneisenau need not have developed as he did. He might as easily, for example, have treated his soldiers as a hardened officer would have done. The Prussian army afforded the opportunity to be of this type or to learn and practice humanity, and Gneisenau chose the latter course. The vicissitudes of life had already taught him to judge a person by character and actions, not by caste. As an officer he came into intimate contact with all classes and kinds of people and was able to learn their problems and to appreciate their longings. Like Luther he summed up in himself the experiences of the nation. The Prussian officer, no matter how poor, occupied a secure position in the highest society and probably most of Gneisenau's friends were aristocrats; but Gneisenau was also acquainted with the life of the burghers, handworkers, and peasants. He usually quartered with a burgher family while stationed with his regiment and, particularly after his promotion to a captaincy, transacted business with merchants through his management of the company's finances and economy. His soldiers revealed to him the world of peasant and handworker and the discontent over serfdom and other restrictions on personal freedom. Through these contacts he also acquired before Jena an insight into the reforms which would be needed to revive the state and nation. He learned first through poverty, then through debts and low income, then through management of the company's finances something about financial questions, thus preparing himself to appreciate later the value of the Prussian financial reforms. Through his work as head of a company of soldiers, he deepened his understanding of administrative and social problems, which Stein and the other reformers had to handle. He proved that in this period of transition ability and bourgeois traits of industry and honesty could advance him in the world without much aid from caste. He exemplified what freedom and nationalism could accomplish on a larger scale in developing members of society.

Within the limits of his power Gneisenau was already practicing the ideals of the Prussian era of reform even before Napoleon compelled at Jena the introduction of changes. The evidence available tends to show that he felt deeply his obligation toward society, at first, toward particular members of society, then in time toward the whole. One sees this social sense in his relations with his father and his half brothers and sisters. Although he had slight personal contact with them, he followed their lives with affectionate concern and assisted them as much as he could. He aided his father to find a position with sufficient salary to maintain himself and his family and at times reduced his expenditure even more than usual in order to give money to his father and half brothers. Partly through his influence several of his half brothers obtained places in military service and, even when they proved to be untrustworthy, he continued to help them with money and by influential contacts and advice. His social sense did not stop with his family. As an officer, he felt responsible for his soldiers and treated them as persons worthy of respect. He disapproved of the cruel and humiliating punishment imposed upon them and long before reform of the military code controlled his men by other means. His relations with his fellow officers were on an equally high plane. On one occasion a shiftless officer insulted Gneisenau, who immediately challenged him. In the duel the opponent fired first and missed. Gneisenau could easily have killed him, but when the officer pleaded for his life, Gneisenau granted it for the sake of the man's six young children. He compelled the offender to promise that he would avoid endangering their welfare by another escapade of this sort. The incident revealed Gneisenau as a deliberate defender of his honor, a considerate judge, and a serious reformer. His turn of mind was positive. He constantly endeavored to reduce the excessive drinking and gambling among his officers and to instill in them the ideal of a responsible leader, as did the Prussian reforms after 1806. Nor did he restrict his efforts to the field of morality. He lectured to his colleagues in Löwenberg on military science and mathematics. Every great military leader, he said, had carefully studied mathematics. In this work he was taking the same line forward as a few of his contemporaries in the same field, among them Scharnhorst and Clausewitz. In a sense, he was by nature a pedagogue, even a reformer. He did not shrug his shoulders at the problems of the world, but attacked them; he did not merely condemn the evils around him but strove to correct them. By this trait he expanded his interests and activity, widened his understanding and appreciation and prepared himself for becoming a nationalist reformer.

Gneisenau's regiment contained in itself a cross section of life which sufficed to manifest to a sensitive person the social evils of the period. But his military duties offered Gneisenau even more opportunities for learning along the same line. In 1798 he was twice sent with troops to suppress a peasant uprising in

Upper Silesia, an experience which, much to his distaste, he had to repeat some years later. He must have observed the bad side of serfdom, and since he followed the course of the French Revolution carefully, one may surmise that he contrasted the effects of serfdom in Prussia with those of freedom in France. As an officer, he felt doubly the value of freedom for elevating the morale of the peasant or peasant-soldier. Possessing no serfs of his own until 1804, he had acquired no enduring sense of superiority over them and no ingrained prejudices on the question of emancipation. Unlike most of his better-situated colleagues, he could regard his soldiers in a professional and a human capacity rather than as serfs temporarily removed from manorial jurisdiction. He was interested professionally in improving the quality of the troops and was learning before 1806 that peasant emancipation would serve that end.

Few great men have been so considerate of others as was Gneisenau. The humanitarianism of the century shone forth in him. He disliked intensely the swashbuckling officers who violated the dignity of the burghers and considered themselves enough superior to these moneygrubbers to use the sword on them. He admired the burghers for their qualities of caution, precision, and industry, for army administration had taught him the value of these traits. He often preferred their company to that of his more ignorant and uncivil colleagues. Numerous stories of his acts of kindness toward members of the lower classes long before 1806 attest to his humanity. One must suffice. While quartered in the home of a peasant family, he learned one day that the parents intended to remain away from a festival because they had no one to watch their children. Gneisenau insisted that they leave the children in his care. That an aristocratic Prussian officer would be so considerate, that he would take charge for a day of a numerous low-class progeny was a revolutionary act in itself. It prepares one for Gneisenau's ardent support of the abolition of caste distinction. He possessed the social imagination for understanding how people outside his caste felt. In 1806 he wrote that he judged people according to their merit rather than according to their caste, and his action corroborated the assertion.

Similar experiences and a similar intellectual atmosphere were transforming men of diverse birth and occupation into a group united by common ideals and objectives. One would expect a philosopher, poet, or historian-publicist to be influenced by ideas; but to find a Prussian army officer affected in the same way presents a rare phenomenon in history. When Napoleon's defeat of Prussia opened the way for reform, men interested in reform throughout Germany found each other, discovered that they thought alike and joined forces to remake Prussia, Germany, and even the world.

Having noted that experience had advanced Gneisenau beyond the accepted standards of social organization, one must investigate his relation to the cultural life of his period. Since a change in ideas preceded both the French Revolution and the era of Prussian reform, one may expect Gneisenau to have been deeply affected by the new thought. It must be remembered once more, however, that in his case the influence of thought and of practical experience cannot be separated. Both contributed to his nationalism. Furthermore nothing is known about the influence of a particular author or work upon him. General conclusions alone may be drawn from the kind of books he read. As a child he loved Homer and as a man clung to the Latin authors, wishing his son to be thoroughly trained in them. "The old writers mould the spirit for serious things and prepare it for difficult times," he stated in 1810 with respect to the Romans.[8] Throughout his life he read history. "Whoever draws his conclusions from the lessons of history and from human passions," he wrote in 1809, "will seldom err." [9] The purpose of his readings in these fields seems to have been primarily pragmatic. He shared the taste of the Enlightenment in preferring the classics, especially Tacitus, for their portrayal of cool, rational, and human figures. So far as one can judge, he never regarded the past with romantic eyes or sought to escape from the present into it; he remained the rationalist who found encouragement and example

[8] Pertz, *op. cit.*, I, 585.
[9] Delbrück, *op. cit.*, I, 173.

in history for orienting himself in his own age. It necessarily follows that the rationalistic, pragmatic, simple character of his historical sense limited his understanding of nationalism.

The list of Gneisenau's cultural interests is extraordinary for its breadth. He always loved music and regretted that through lack of instruction he was restricted to the use of an untrained voice. Likewise he studied architecture and designed a monument which was actually erected. As a student of languages during the first half of his life, he became proficient in speaking English and French and learned some Italian and Polish. Wherever he was stationed, he became acquainted with the possessors of libraries in the vicinity and borrowed their books. Among his papers were found copies in his own hand of many poems from French and English literature, and the history of literature seems to have attracted him as much as the literature itself. Of works in his own language he admired especially those by Lessing and Schiller, and, since he was closely acquainted with the Radziwill family, he must have read Goethe. He apparently selected many of his friends and acquaintances partly because of their cultural interests. Nor did he stop merely with reading; he wrote much poetry himself. Pegasus did not fly very high with him or very far; nonetheless when one discovers a poem dated as early as 1781 and another of 1801, one may assume that he wrote habitually. In Löwenberg he directed an amateur theater and wrote prologues to the performances. He was definitely in touch with the literary revival of Germany and derived from it encouragement for his own work in the military and political phases of national awakening.

Once the field of literature is dismissed, the historian is even less informed concerning Gneisenau's relations with contemporary culture. Philosophy ranked with literature as the two most creative branches of intellectual activity in Germany at the time. But in view of Gneisenau's haphazard education, one can well doubt whether he read much of this. In a poem of 1801 he mentioned the names of Fichte and Schlegel, though somewhat sarcastically. But among his papers was found in his own hand an extract from a pamphlet of 1799 by Fichte entitled "An Appeal to the

Public against the Accusation of Atheism." Although the date of his copying it is unknown, the passage deserves to be quoted extensively, for it reveals a connection between the military and the philosophic world of the period.

> Very often in the affairs and friendships of life [Gneisenau quoted from Fichte's pamphlet] the breast heaves with the sigh, "It is impossible that such a life should be my true destiny; there must be, oh, there must be some other condition for me." Dissatisfaction with the past, longing for something higher, better and eternal lie indestructible within the soul of man. Just as persistently the voice resounds within him that there are a duty and a responsibility which must be fulfilled because it is a responsibility. . . . Only because this is so will mankind endure the effort of striving, which has become so repulsive to him. . . . This eternal longing demands complete freedom in all our relationships. . . . A whole new world is opened to us through this condition of our being. By means of this we realize a higher existence independent of nature and springing from within; by means of this we achieve a position which is very properly called transcendental. There becomes attached to this consciousness of having done our duty for its own sake a new consciousness: the unshakable confidence that . . . after having done that which we ought to have done, those tasks beyond our power will eventually be possible. . . . It is the never-to-be-achieved yet ever-to-be-striven-for goal of our whole existence that this fundamental reason (*Vernunft*) should be absolutely and completely free, separate and independent of everything which is not itself reason. . . . It is our conscience which, when asked in any given situation, decisively says to us what our duty is in that particular situation and what we must do in order to further this goal of reason. . . . There is a law and an established order according to which the pure, moral form of thought necessarily creates happiness, just as the material and carnal destroys all happiness; an order wherein all rational beings are included and from which the morality of everyone is calculated and all happiness derived; an order of which I am myself a part, and as a result of which I am standing in exactly this place in the system of the whole and that I am in this particular situation wherein it is my duty to act in this or that manner without complaint about the results. . . . Morality and religion are absolutely one. . . . Even when one doubts God and immortality, one must still do

his duty. . . . Show only within yourself this dutiful belief and you will know God.[10]

The excerpt from Fichte contained in abstruse terms the counsel which in 1796 Gneisenau wrote his father, "My advice to young people is service and more service and the cultivation of everything remotely connected with it." [11] Fichte's assertions supported the wisdom which Gneisenau had derived from Latin writers and confirmed through experience—to do one's duty at any cost, to follow the dictates of conscience, to develop reason, to demand and defend freedom. They consoled him for acquiescing in his lot and taught him to scorn material things and to strive toward transcendental ideals, which, seemingly unattainable, would ultimately be reached with the help of Providence. As a Prussian officer, Gneisenau had learned to be guided by the categorical imperative which he found formulated in Fichte's pamphlet and, as many men in practical life do, he copied the passage because it expressed so well his own thoughts and met his needs. Whether he understood the metaphysical parts is doubtful: the moral thought attracted him. The search for transcendental goals might have inspired Gneisenau to seek a golden age of nationalism, while the necessity for performing his duty in his own station of life restricted him to the sphere which he already occupied.

The extent of Gneisenau's reading and understanding will never be known. He left in his papers long lists of books without noting which ones he had read. The fact that he drew up the lists speaks for itself. One of his biographers has aptly remarked that "his mind always stood above the common," [12] and in 1814 a professor's wife who became well acquainted with him at a watering place wrote: "There is nothing fine or good in the world of science and art in which he did not take the liveliest interest; I cannot understand how he should have had the time to read so much which was not even in his field." [13] His friend

[10] *Ibid.*, II, 335-37.
[11] Pertz, *op. cit.*, I, 50.
[12] *Ibid.*, I, 41.
[13] Delbrück, *op. cit.*, II, 132-33.

did not know of the many evenings spent in small garrison towns which he had made endurable if not pleasant by reading. She saw the final result, and it drew from her a compliment rarely paid to a military figure.

Appreciation of things cultural raised Gneisenau above the ordinary level and assisted him to view society as a whole. Unlike the circumscribed militarists, he denied that the welfare of the army always took precedence over that of the rest of society. While he did not consider the army lacking in intrinsic value and intended merely to preserve something of importance, yet his cultural interests aided him in perceiving the limited functions of the army, in placing the military within the broad framework of society. Because he understood the power of the spirit as well as of the body he was capable of becoming a social reformer as well as a military one. He could think and feel idealistically and envisage society as it might be. In one of his poems he extolled Lessing for striving toward "a higher end, toward clearer light," [14] praise which Gneisenau equally deserved. His reading, study, and constant striving toward a "higher end, a clearer light" enabled him to write in 1807: "Man must be inspired by an idea if he is to do something great." [15] This faith in idealism explains his development into a nationalist. Gneisenau was capable of conceiving something which did not exist, of imagining a new society, a brotherhood, a nation. Experience had taught him practicality, a sense of detail and devotion to duty; but the books which he read stirred in him the idealism needed to quicken these other qualities with fervor and imagination and to utilize them for a magnificent end. Without idealism the other qualities would scarcely have raised him above the ordinary; with it they made him great. When a social ideal guides the categorical imperative, a sense of individualism profoundly affected by social responsibility will arise, and if it grips a person so admirably trained as Gneisenau in administrative detail, it will make of him an inspiring figure in history.

In 1796 Gneisenau married the daughter of a Silesian aristo-

[14] Pertz, *op. cit.*, I, 637.
[15] *Ibid.*, p. 295.

crat. He had just been promoted to a captaincy at the age of thirty-six and for the first time in his life was receiving sufficient income to support a family. The circumstances leading to the marriage were somewhat unusual. Gneisenau became acquainted with his future wife by bringing her the news of her fiancé's death in a duel. When she later married him, she said that she honored him and loved the dead man. One cannot say whether the inequality of affection in this marriage influenced Gneisenau or not. Certainly he was ardently devoted to his wife and their growing family; but it is also true that their relations lacked the complete understanding which distinguished the marriage, for example, of his friend Clausewitz. That Gneisenau felt an added incentive to achieve greatness in order to gain his wife's love cannot be claimed, but it may be said that more frequently than before he became dissatisfied with himself and gloomy about his advancement.

Marriage increased Gneisenau's responsibilities and broadened his material and spiritual interests. He became more dependent upon the Prussian state by having something definite and personal in it to defend against Napoleon. As his children grew, he investigated the most modern and best methods of education. The Prussian officer read and admired the works of Pestalozzi, and with modifications used Pestalozzian method in training his own children. Thus he became acquainted with another field of reform and aligned himself with Fichte and Arndt in the matter of pedagogical views. (Gneisenau differed decidedly from Fichte and Arndt in the practical turn which he wished to give education.[16]) Marriage opened still another field of interest. In the winter of 1803-4 his wife bought an estate. Immediately Gneisenau began to study agriculture and read Thaer's writings with the same enthusiasm with which he had explored Pestalozzi's. Since Thaer defended in Prussia English agricultural methods and wished to transform agriculture from an easy way of maintaining a vestigial feudal life into a capitalistic, bookkeeping enterprise, he represented in his field that which Pesta-

[16] *Ibid.*, I, 585.

lozzi did in his and Kant and Fichte in theirs and, one may add, Scharnhorst and Gneisenau in theirs—a break with tradition in favor of reforms. Agriculture should be made self-sustaining even if custom must be violated, argued Thaer. The turn of Gneisenau's mind away from tradition, the main support of feudal-agrarian life, toward experimentation and innovation was evident from his hearty approval of Thaer's proposals. In this respect as well he was growing out of the *ancien régime* into the nineteenth century.

Although the development of Gneisenau's political philosophy lagged behind that of his social and cultural ideals, from the earliest evidence available on this subject one can perceive a germ out of which nationalism might arise. In a poem of 1786, that is, immediately after his entry into Prussian service, he wrote: "But you who have come from afar to see what Frederick's people could achieve through him, tell me, which one among all peoples imitates this wonderful drama?" [17] Manifestly at this time Gneisenau accepted the great-man theory of history; he gave Frederick the Great credit for the achievements of the Prussian people. Yet Gneisenau likewise recognized that Frederick could not dispense with his people. The key words are: "What Frederick's people could achieve through him." Gneisenau emphasized not merely the leader but the leader and his people; if the quality of leadership declined, as it did under Frederick William III, and proved unfit in a crisis, one might infer from the above statement that Gneisenau would advocate the transference of actual power to new leaders and the arousing of the people. If he did so with respect to the German people, it would mean nationalism. He would balance the hero explanation of history by a social one. Without diminishing the share of the leader, he would increase that of the people, drawing them into closer, more equal spiritual union.

The counterpart of the heroic interpretation of history consists generally in a conception of a negative relation between the state and its subjects. In 1795 Gneisenau wrote, "The sole task

[17] *Ibid.*, p. 639.

of the state is to utilize the capacities of its subjects without inquiring closely into their moral character; and it only demands of them the performance of their duty within their particular occupations."[18] A few years before in a poem on the death of Louis XVI he had written:

> As long as passions seethe within men, law and enforced order cannot be dispensed with. Woe be to him, who with rebellious hand wishes to sunder the strict bonds of order. The greater the power, the greater the wisdom demanded in the control of this power. The unguarded flame rages destructively and the stream overflows if it is not dammed with care. The wise man who knows how to control himself is free where despots rage. . . . O moderation, thou virtue of true wisdom.[19]

At this time Gneisenau proposed to restrict the functions of the state to the preservation of order and the curbing of the forces within its limits. It should use the capacities of its subjects without, except in so far as the general welfare demanded, interfering in their morals. The state, he thought, demanded of its subjects only the performance of their duties in their particular occupations. That is, he still divided society into castes, where social status and occupation were united. In several respects, however, his views on the state were capable of rapid expansion. The clause "to utilize the capacities of its subjects" might grow into a demand to reorganize the state and reform society so that these capacities could be utilized. It might expand into a conception of positive intimacy between the state and its subjects, that is, into nationalism. Likewise, the lines, "The greater the power, the greater the wisdom demanded in the control of this power," scarcely blended with the negativism of the rest of the thought. It promised an acceptance of these stronger forces and imposed an obligation of greater wisdom upon the leader. As yet Gneisenau mistrusted these powers and inclined toward the maintenance of the *status quo;* but he might some day need to use them and thus turn toward nationalism.

[18] *Ibid.,* I, 49.
[19] *Ibid.,* pp. 649-50.

In the passages which refer to the functions of the individual Gneisenau manifested another inclination which might lead to nationalism. Advising patience and moderation, he moralized about the way of preserving one's freedom even under tyranny and stressed the fulfillment of duty to one's special calling. In these respects he defended political docility and was still a Stoic. By restricting the authority of the state in the sphere of morality and culture, he allowed the individual some freedom. His nationalism would grow out of the recognition of the difficulty or, under the circumstances, the impossibility of maintaining moral and cultural liberty without political and legal liberty. One significant bent of mind was to assist him in making this discovery. Nowhere in these quotations did he stress the rights of the individual as over against the state; on the contrary, he spoke of duties. By expanding the scope of these, Gneisenau ultimately concluded that caste distinctions must be abolished so that the individual might better perform the duties required by the state. The concept of duty showed that, far from being a social atomist, he thought in terms of the group.

Gneisenau never was and never became thoroughly a laissez-faire liberal. His Stoicism and training as a Prussian army officer prevented him from ever demanding the extreme individualism of Fichte or Wilhelm von Humboldt in the early 1790's. The army had instilled in him the value of duty and strong leadership, the need and ways of group action, the dependence of the leader upon the followers, and vice versa. It had taught him the importance of individual intelligence, spirit, and enterprise, that is, the qualities necessary for evoking the maximum strength in a group. He had not as yet given the concept of individual freedom and of social duty a rich content and he had not as yet brought them into organic unity. He was still a self-dependent individual, shocked by the excesses of the French Revolution. But when he enriched and united them, he became a nationalist. In place of a mechanistic, rationalistic view of the state, he put one of an organic unity; instead of dividing the functions of burgher and state, instead of regarding the state as an indifferent utilitarian unit and the burgher as another, he was to merge them by means of public feeling.

The story of Gneisenau's development into a nationalist is rather complicated. It has to do with his relations to the French Revolution and with his marriage, although the second also nearly caused the conclusion of his public career. Each of these experiences matured his thought and understanding, in some respects along similar lines, in other along different ones. In 1795 Gneisenau wrote: "One must accept men as they are and not as they should be." If he had continued to believe this, he would never have become a nationalist, for the essence of the realistic view of mankind is a strong mistrust of enthusiasm and passion, whereas that of nationalism consists in the hope of changing men into something unselfish and fine. As has been seen, Gneisenau was horrified over the excesses of the revolutionists in France, and as a staunch monarchist he solemnly denounced the beheading of Louis XVI. He was still an intellectual aristocrat. But how could one be a nationalist without exalting enthusiasm and passion? Between 1795 and 1806 Gneisenau changed his views. From an idealist merely with respect to things cultural, he became one with respect to men in action; from a Prussian army officer with Roman calm, he became an inspired defender of German liberty.

Undoubtedly the most direct influence in releasing Gneisenau's emotions was his marriage. While the published letters to his wife maintain a natural reserve, occasionally they reveal a rich and powerful capacity for loving, which contrasts sharply with the dull, rationalistic poetry of his earlier period. In these poems he had often tried to express a mood, but an ordinary mood and in an ordinary manner. In his letters to his wife he even at times became romantic. In fact, his Stoicism seems to have been a safeguard against the power of his feelings. A letter to his wife in 1810 lends credence to this belief:

If I understand myself rightly, I have always been more adapted to solitude and literary pursuits than to association with such circles as those into which I have been thrown in recent years. I need far more a soothing environment which softens my passions and the quietness of nature and of rural life than those occupations which by their very nature arouse my passions. Likewise, in the past few years I have already begun to feel the detrimental effects of my activities. I am quickly irritated and strongly moved. Even the mere recounting of those things which I have seen and experienced agitates me profoundly and nearly stifles me. Whether it be as a consequence of the meanness of mankind or because of the noble virtues of some of them, I feel more strongly moved than is proper and I can no longer control my feelings. The object for which I am striving is, of course, of a high nature. Oftentimes I sweep persons along with me by my manner and frequently I have thereby aroused a spark of enthusiasm. You know to what I am referring. Through this frame of mind, however, I give advantages to my colder, more calculating enemies; and thus I do not fail to become a sacrifice of this ruling and overpowering feeling. I long, therefore, for solitude and separation from worldly affairs.[20]

Gneisenau possessed the rare combination of keen intelligence and rich emotionalism. Until his marriage he had been unable to combine them, especially to release the latter without endangering his peace of mind. The relaxing effect of matrimony permitted a more balanced union and a more confident exercise of these two qualities. When the time came after Jena, he could put his complete equipment of reason and emotion at the service of nationalism.

Gneisenau began early to prophesy that Napoleon would attempt to take North Germany, including Prussia. Disgusted with his king's policy of peace, early in 1803 he saw the connection between Prussia's fate and that of the rest of Europe. "The interrelationship of politics," he wrote, "is so manifold that no shot can be fired in the Mediterranean without resounding in Germany." [21] In the winter of 1805 he wished Prussia to ally with Austria and even without Russian aid to strike Napoleon; but, he added sadly, the two powers would not ally until they had both suffered the greatest humiliation.

[20] *Ibid.*, I, 586-87.
[21] *Ibid.*, p. 85.

The recognition of the Napoleonic menace to Prussia did not necessarily bring with it recognition of the need for reforms to combat it. Hans Delbrück, Gneisenau's ablest biographer, maintains that before Jena Gneisenau shared with the other reformers the feeling of a vague need for reform, but that the disaster first revealed to him the urgency of thorough change.[22] In the main Delbrück's view is correct. Yet Gneisenau's immediate recognition of the causes of Prussia's collapse and of the measures which should be taken leads one to believe that he was not caught unawares. The Battle of Jena may have confirmed his thought or it may have caused him to combine ideas worked out beforehand into a coherent program. He was left uncertain before Jena about the value of these ideas because he did not know what would be the outcome of a pitched battle between Napoleon's French patriots and the army inherited from Frederick the Great. His eager interest in foreign affairs during the decade or so before Jena could hardly have been divorced from a concern about internal affairs. A satirical poem of 1801 gives a hint of his thoughts, permitting one to see that this inference, which is supported by Gneisenau's entire experience and by his interest in cultural and social life, was correct. The poem was a rebuke to an author for not courting favor, for not praising the powerful, for not avoiding strife, advising him to eschew politics and to treat inconsequential topics. It concluded by saying:

> The individual must live and let live,
> And his first duty is to help himself.[23]

Since this advice was the opposite of that which Gneisenau had practiced, one must conclude that even at this time he was troubled by political issues. Having grown out of the cultural and social traditions of the eighteenth century, he was beginning to cast off the political tradition.

Lack of sufficiently engrossing activity made Gneisenau moody, while the care of a steadily increasing family strained

[22] Delbrück, *op. cit.*, I, 42, 114-15.
[23] Pertz, *op. cit.*, I, 52.

his finances and kept him restless. Forced to be separated from his family, in 1801 he wrote his wife as follows:

> I am suffering from a disease to which very few mortals are probably subjected. It is that of dissatisfaction with myself. Indeed, you always raise my spirits again with your loving letters, which makes them for this reason alone so very welcome to me, and yet these tormenting thoughts continually recur. I look with sadness into the future and curse the follies of the past. Farewell, my love; I embrace you with the tenderest love of a husband and father. If I were only worthy to possess you! My eyes fill with tears at this thought.[24]

Whatever the "follies of the past," the main theme of his complaint was that he saw a sad and uncertain future for himself and his family. He advanced slowly in his profession; his salary did not adequately meet demands; and he was kept at the constant drudgery of drilling troops.

Within a year after his wife purchased an estate he wished to leave the army and devote his entire energy to agriculture. The Prussian army and public questions, including reform, fought for a place beside the more immediate interests of managing an estate, educating children, and caring for a recurrently pregnant wife. Two reasons alone persuaded Gneisenau to remain in the army, the need of his salary, and the political insecurity of Europe, especially Prussia. If Napoleon attacked Prussia, Gneisenau might not be able to carry out the improvements necessary to make his estate pay. As war became menacing he followed public affairs with increasing interest. Napoleon's acts forced him in 1805 to leave his wife alone with four sick children, the difficulties connected with technical improvements on the estate, and a poor crop. During November he wrote his wife these words:

> As a soldier, I see nothing but disorder about me and, as a landowner and father of a family, I am afraid of being ruined. As a subject of the state, I visualize the possible approach of disaster, due to delayed preparation and the lack of forceful countermeasures. Only luck, prudence, and firmness can save us. And yet I still look

[24] *Ibid.*, p. 75.

trustfully to Him who governs everything for the best and I strengthen my heart with confidence in Him.[25]

A man could not have had more personal cause to detest Napoleon. A few weeks later he wrote a friend: "What do you think about the present situation? Is not the world mad? What extraordinary physical and moral phenomena!"[26] In spite of his fears, Gneisenau still thought that if Prussia would join Austria, Napoleon might find his Pultawa in Silesia.

In July, 1806, Gneisenau again grew worried and uncertain. "Great discontent," he said, "prevails among us about the peace; whether with reason is still a great question. Since who is able to decide what would have been the result in case of a contrary course . . . I strive to forget public affairs by devoting myself zealously to personal affairs and I have had some success in agriculture."[27] Immediately before the Battle of Jena, when Gneisenau heard that the enemy was advancing up the valley of the Saale, he hurriedly put down his fears as follows:

As a patriot I sigh. They have neglected much in the time of peace, have wasted themselves on trifles, have indulged the public's lust for display and have neglected war matters, a very serious affair. The spirit of the officers is excellent and because of this I have great hopes; but, but . . .

I know what the French will do next; what we shall do, I do not know. I predicted long ago the attack along the Saale. Alas, I sigh in the lower ranks and my advice is of no consequence. My heart is depressed when I consider the probable outcome. O, fatherland, self-elected fatherland! I am forgotten in my small garrison and can only fight, not advise.[28]

If Gneisenau was unnoticed in Prussia before Jena, the collapse of the state permitted him to become great. He was already forty-six years of age and had served as an officer for over a quarter of a century without ever having engaged in battle. Being one of the few officers who conducted himself with bravery and intelligence during the disastrous days, he was soon consulted by

[25] *Ibid.*, pp. 96-97.
[26] *Ibid.*, p. 98.
[27] *Ibid.*, pp. 108-9.
[28] *Ibid.*, p. 113.

authority and, as he stood admirably each test of responsibility, rose within nine years from captain to general. In March, 1807, he portrayed his experiences during the Prussian disaster of 1806:

> Near Saalfeld I received a shot in the leg which made me jump into the air. I made my retreat limping. Near Jena I fought on horseback and posted the last troops, but in the end I ran from the field with the others, in good company with nobles and princes. I fought again near Nordhausen and at the end crept through the Harz Mountains, cut off from the rest, but finally came upon them also running. That was terrible. Rather die a thousand times than to have an experience like that again. But our generals and governors! Those will be wonderful lines in history. The famed Prussian army out of practice and domesticated by long years of peace! If a state wants to be military, it must carry on war. War is an art and every art must be practiced. My fine establishment in Silesia is destroyed. I was on the road toward being a well-to-do person, but am now a beggar. The difference is not great when one compares this short space of time with eternity, and this is the only true point of view.
>
> Lieutenant, pull your tail in. . . . Yes, like fugitive dogs we pulled in our tails, but we shall once again show our teeth.[29]

The war caught Gneisenau at the most unpropitious moment. He was, of course, heavily in debt. The introduction of modern methods of agriculture upon his estate had just begun. His wife, already with five children and pregnant again, had to manage the estate alone without the necessary energy and ability. The disorder of defeat and flight was so complete in Prussia that for eight months in 1806-7 Gneisenau received no word from his wife and did not know whether his sixth child was a girl or a boy. He consoled himself with the thought that he had been a soldier before he became a husband and father; but he was haunted by the fear that through the war with Napoleon he and his family might become beggars.

> The most severe misery is everywhere about us [he wrote]. . . . The possessor of property will probably be ruined; new people, new

[29] Delbrück, *op. cit.*, I, 54.

circumstances will arise and those returning will no longer find things as in 1806.

No one will be able to return to his former conditions and everyone will have to adjust himself to a toilsome, tumultuous and uncertain life. Our long sojourn in the garrisons has spoiled us and effeminacy, love of pleasure and enjoyment have weakened the military virtues. The whole nation must go through the school of misfortune; and we shall either die in this crisis or, after having experienced this bitter misery and when our bones are no longer here, we shall develop into something better.[30]

A person as vigorous and active as Gneisenau could not reconcile himself to fate. He had too much at stake. An open mind and an honorable heart, he often said, would bring one through the world. Without believing in progress or working out any philosophy of history to bolster up his morale, he continued as an officer to perform his duty. But he did more. He assumed the aggressive against Napoleon. By December, 1806, he was urging the continuation of the war in coöperation with England, Russia, and Sweden. When the Prussian government rejected this proposal, he was eager to rouse the people to war against France. By way of reply, the government sent him to drill recruits in a village on the northeastern border of Prussia. The state was so stripped of power and resources that, as Gneisenau said, "the circumstances are enough to drive mad anyone wishing to go forward." [31]

After being isolated in this village on the Russian frontier for some months, Gneisenau was recalled to Königsberg and, partly by accident, so the story goes, was selected as commander of Colberg, one of the few fortified towns holding out against the French attack. In this post he established his reputation; henceforth he could not be ignored by the government. In striking contrast to the immediate surrender by their commanders of almost all the other fortified towns of Prussia, Gneisenau defended Colberg against superior forces until the Peace of Tilsit stopped the combat. Conditions which he met in Colberg were typical. The previous commander, an aristocrat of the old order, believed in the

[30] Pertz, *op. cit.*, I, 389-90.
[31] *Ibid.*, I, 156.

strict preservation of caste. He would not associate with the burghers, refused their coöperation in the defense, and disliked the volunteer corps organized by Schill. The townspeople suspected that he was willing to surrender to the enemy. Again, characteristically enough, he was a dull fellow without a plan for defense and devoid of initiative. In every respect he differed from Gneisenau, who immediately associated the burghers in the defense, treated them as social equals, and roused a common feeling of patriotism in them and the soldiers. He put a tempestuous old man named Nettelbeck in charge of extinguishing fires caused by the bombardment, a revolutionary act before Stein restored self-government to the towns, and used Nettelbeck's knowledge and influence, praising him publicly as a model burgher. In him he saw the kind of patriot that must be created in order to save Prussia and Germany from the French. He employed a new type of defense which he had learned during his military studies, borrowed money from the burghers with which to continue the defense, bought arms, advanced burgher soldiers to officers' positions and rewarded merit and bravery among the soldiers irrespective of caste. They were all fighting for a single end, he said. Many of his troops were recent recruits and all of them belonged to companies which had not been considered competent to take the field. The courage which they displayed proved to their leader what power lay in a soldiery inspired with an ideal and free to realize it. In Colberg Gneisenau achieved in miniature that which he desired for all Germany, when its spirit should become the spirit of German nationalism and its measures of defense identical with those used by the Prussian state at large. He set there the pattern for the Stein-Hardenberg-Scharnhorst reforms.

Gneisenau had hoped that the defense of Colberg would inaugurate active German coöperation with England and Sweden against Napoleon, but he was disappointed; peace came, and with it the task of Prussian reform. He was called to assist as a member of the military commission.

Fundamentally Gneisenau believed that stupidity and weakness of spirit were responsible for the collapse of Germany before Napoleon. By throwing the blame upon moral debility, he encouraged himself to hope for regeneration. But he knew that the defeat of a state like Prussia could not be explained so simply and that he must know particulars before he could recommend reforms. In making his reports this Prussian officer did not stop at criticism of the military; he diagnosed all the evils of the Prussian state and society. He condemned the government for not taking the lead and for not having instituted reforms long before the catastrophe. With respect to the army, he found everything wrong, the system of recruiting soldiers and of selecting and advancing officers, the relations between officers and privates, the methods of punishment, the administration of the quartermaster's department, the organization of the army, the method of fighting. He was disgusted with the failure to bring the army to parity with that of Napoleon and to reorganize the state and society so that the military improvement could be made. He damned the aristocrats as having utterly forgotten "their original destination," as having "sunk into effeminacy, imbecility, and passiveness. From this class, generally speaking, no voluntary efforts can be expected. Overanxious about its little property, it pays homage to every conqueror." [32] When later the aristocrats fought reforms and associated on pleasant terms with the French invaders, he despised them even more intensely. He missed among the Prussians or the Germans, disunified geographically and socially, a "common spirit." But he believed that this common spirit could be aroused and advocated reforms for that purpose.

Since Gneisenau counted out most of the aristocracy, he directed his efforts toward the middle and lower classes. He wished to employ all possible means to defeat the French, even if it entailed a revolution in the organization of state and society. On the question of reform the officer proved of one mind with the philosopher, the poet, and the historian-publicist. They all focused their endeavors on the lower classes, whose ranks were capable of furnishing soldiers and were still capable of enthusiasm. If the upper classes gave out, leadership and power must be sought in the masses, they argued, in this search discovering the nation.

[32] *Historische Zeitschrift*, LXXXV, 37.

Gneisenau had learned from the French Revolution the power to be gained through reform.

> The Revolution [he wrote in 1807] has awakened all forces and given to each force an appropriate sphere of activity. In this way heroes rose to the head of the army, statesmen acquired the chief administrative posts and, finally, from their midst came the greatest man of them all to the leadership of a great people.
>
> What infinite power lies sleeping undeveloped and unused within the womb of the nation. Within the breasts of thousands and thousands of persons there lives a great genius, but their lowly condition prevents its flowering. While the kingdom falls in all its feebleness and disgrace, perhaps somewhere in its most miserable village a Caesar follows the plow and an Epaminondas lives from the scanty produce of the labor of his hands. Why did not the courts make use of the simplest and surest means, that of providing a career for this genius, wherever it may be, and of encouraging these talents and virtues, no matter from what class or rank they might come? Why did they not choose this means of strengthening themselves a thousand times over and of opening to the common citizens those triumphal gates through which now only noblemen may pass? These new times need more than just old names, titles, and diplomas; they require fresh action and strength. But they say, "It is better—our glory will remain—to die on our ancestral bed of state unbesmirched by any subordinate alliance with genius of common origin than to preserve oneself through a union with it."
>
> The Revolution has set in action the national energy of the entire French people, thereby putting the different classes on an equal social and fiscal basis, thereby transforming the vital strength of the people and their resources into interest-bearing capital, thereby abolishing the former relationship of the states to one another and the balance of power. If the other states wish to reëstablish this balance, they must open and use these same resources. They must take over the results of the Revolution and so gain the double advantage of being able to place their entire national energies in opposition to the enemy and of escaping from the dangers of a revolution, dangers which are not altogether over for them because they did not prefer a voluntary change to a violent one.[33]

[33] Pertz, *op. cit.*, I, 301-2.

The quotation indicates what reforms Gneisenau advocated and how completely he wished to transform the Prussian state. It is not necessary to describe all these measures, an enumeration of which will suffice. Gneisenau supported the abolition of serfdom and the establishment of self-government in the towns. He defended the proposal to create a Prussian central representative assembly with wide advisory powers and complete control over finances. He approved the destruction of caste privileges in both civil society and the army. The position of officer should, he thought, be open to members of any class. Cruel and humiliating forms of punishment for officers and privates should cease. The standing army should be abolished as a costly, snobbish, egocentric and inefficient burden, as an instrument which divided the civil and military and deprived the civil population of the right and duty to fight for the country; universal military service should be introduced. The officers should be trained in military science, the soldiers in the methods of scatter fighting. Both should be allowed more initiative in battle. Since he believed that no one class had a monopoly of talent and that education alone accounted for the difference in ability between classes, he wished everyone to be taught, and he advocated the Pestalozzian method with a military turn. If one wishes to provide a people with a powerful incentive to fight, he said, one must identify it with the country. "A good constitution, which proceeds from the throne and which is the envy of other nations," he asserted, "will increase attachment to the regent, and neither ambition nor egoism is in a position to combat a government which sets as its goal the prosperity, enlightenment, morality and civil freedom of the nation." [34] Gneisenau wrote these lines in order to win over the king to his ideas. When he used the words "regent" and "government," he implied the state, and he desired the state to be so organized that the people would have every inducement to feel itself a part of it and to defend it. He wished the people to fight, so he indicated in the same memorandum, out of bitterness against its oppressor, attachment to its monarch strengthened through his

[34] Wilhelm Capelle, *Gneisenau* (Leipzig and Berlin, 1911), p. 77.

beneficent state reforms, respect for its constitution, love for the fatherland and revenge. A few lines later he added "honor."[35] There should be revolution from above. The reforms should enable the nation to feel a fraternal spirit of love.

It must not be thought that because Gneisenau advocated the same ideas of reform as other nationalists he also shared the high degree of their comprehension of the nation. The one was far easier than the other, and Gneisenau never quite clarified his vision of a German nation. He sometimes referred to the Prussian nation, sometimes to the German nation. From his use of the term one must conclude that by nation he meant any group of people united by common traditions into a political (Prussia, Bavaria, Hesse) or semipolitical (Germany) body capable of some or all of the actions characteristic of a state. He never defined the term nation or gave it a special significance as a concept designating an ideal condition of the future. He never built a philosophy of history around it, dividing the nationalistic from the prenationalistic era. He associated with it the idea of fraternal devotion to a common end but he did not make this a distinguishing factor. He continued to use the word in the loose and casual manner of the eighteenth century, failing to conceive clearly the nationalism of the nineteenth. Reform was within his vision, nationalism but partly so. He was at most a situation-nationalist.

An explanation of Gneisenau's inability to conceive reforms fully within the framework of nationalism becomes complicated. He did not have the great capacity of a philosopher or poet to think in terms of abstractions. Although possessed of enthusiasm and imagination, he had not cultivated them in the field of social philosophy; instead he had been drilled in a careful regard for details. Among the fields of knowledge he had gone most deeply into mathematics, geography, and engineering, but he had never pursued these into the realms of pure theory. As an army officer, he had performed the task in hand or had let his mind work around this task. He had learned practical application. The Prussian state existed; a German one did not. He could try to reform

[35] *Ibid.*, p. 76.

Prussia, he could not put his hands on Germany. An organization for Germany would first have to be created; a German spirit must first be aroused; something tangible must exist before one could work with it. Gneisenau's literal, practical mind wasted little effort on such a Germany. He could not wait for a new society to be created but wished to act now. Furthermore, Gneisenau was a Prussian officer. His first loyalty was to his state. Duty called forth Prussianism, not Germanism. His profession as soldier deprived him of a path which might have led him into German nationalism. He did not seek a German public, for he sought no public. He did not intoxicate himself by words, for he was a fighter. He did not try to create something entirely new, but strove to improve the instrument of which he formed a part. Fundamentally he was a defender rather than a creator. In time he might take the step into German nationalism; but before conditions justified or demanded it, he concentrated his attention upon the task in hand in Prussia. While he appreciated entirely the value of a common spirit in uniting for common action all classes and elements in the state, as a Prussian officer he believed in first stirring up this spirit in Prussia. Once this was achieved, it might be practicable and advisable to arouse a common German feeling, but he did not set his mind to this future possibility.

Notwithstanding the fact that Gneisenau had traveled in Germany, America, Poland, and, after 1809, in England, Sweden, and Russia, he had had no cause to become deeply interested in national differences. He knew that peoples varied, as did classes and individuals within a nation; but he was neither a folklorist nor a romantic historian eager to note these distinguishing features between nations. He was a Prussian aristocratic officer conversant in French, English, and Polish and willing to accept a man of competence and good conduct of any nationality. He did not consider the Germans unique. On the contrary, he found that some Germans stood for one set of principles and others for another set, as was the case with English and French. He lacked the capacity for identifying the Germans in particular with an absolute ideal; in fact, he knew too much about them to do so. In 1812 he wrote: "The world is divided into those who fight, whether through coercion or voluntarily, for Bonaparte's ambition and those who fight against it. It is less a question of country than of principle." [36]

The above statement manifests another limitation to Gneisenau's German nationalism. His principles still remained those of eighteenth-century cosmopolitanism. He loved freedom and the benefits of self-respect, public and private morality, and cultural improvement which it would bring. Reforms in Prussia should achieve a twofold aim, first, they should realize the ideal of social freedom within the state and, second, they should thereby create a common spirit for the defense of freedom. In his writings Gneisenau never used as an argument for resisting Napoleon the establishment of a greater German nation. He rarely pleaded for the defense of Germany or Prussia, always advocating the preservation of freedom and humanity. Prussia and Germany should serve that end. Fortunately he did not need to choose between Prussia or Germany and freedom, for the interest of one coincided with the interest of the other. It is significant that Gneisenau exalted freedom rather than group feeling or nationalism. In a sense, one may say that the first move toward German nationalism was made by a cosmopolitan, who discovered the importance of the nation as a means of defending cosmopolitan ideals. As a defender, he had to look abroad for allies. So cosmopolitanism assisted nationalism and vice versa. Gneisenau took only this first step. He kept to simple, real things like liberty and protection, which seemed menaced, and, since he saw no close, direct, and practical value to be expected from German nationalism, he became only partially a German nationalist. His idealism helped to bring him as far along the road to nationalism as he traveled, while the nature of these ideals either prevented him from advancing farther or manifested his inability to do so.

Although by birth Gneisenau belonged to no particular state and might have felt himself a German, by material interest he was bound to Prussia rather than to Germany. His wife, his position, and his property were all of this state. Nonetheless, he never

[36] Friedrich Meinecke, *Weltbürgertum und Nationalstaat* (Munich and Berlin, 1919), citing Pertz, *op. cit.*, II, 369.

became a staunch Prussian. He owed military allegiance to the king rather than to the country. He received slow and grudging recognition, so he thought, in Prussian service, and knew that the king disliked him. He was even less satisfied with the conflict among the Prussians themselves. The opponents of the reforms indifferently or passively accepted the French restriction on freedom; they blocked the work of reconstruction which would realize the ideal of freedom within Prussia; and they were his personal enemies, obstructing his advancement. If the situation of his family had permitted him, he doubtless would have quit Prussian service in disgust at the King's pusillanimity, and he did take leave in order to seek more active employment elsewhere. On several occasions he proposed that Prussian territory be transferred to another state. Prussia remained an object of his devotion only in so far as she fought or by reforms prepared to fight Napoleon; when she was active, he was loyal; when not, he wished service elsewhere. Prussia, like Germany, England, Sweden, Austria, or Russia, was a means to Napoleon's defeat. He felt anxiety about Prussia and Germany only because he was a Prussian-German. Prior to 1806 he had served against the American colonies in their war of independence, had helped to destroy Poland, and had advised his brothers to find service in the Danish or Dutch army. After 1806 he developed some appreciation of German nationalism; but his feeling for the national group remained secondary to the devotion to liberty. He remained an arrested nationalist, restrained by his ideal of freedom and his sense of the actual and possible.

Gneisenau's nationalism was likewise essentially limited by his profession. To be an efficient army officer, Gneisenau had to serve a cause larger than himself and adjust himself to the needs of the army. He had learned to subordinate himself to the army, at least to that purpose which the army served. He was schooled in objective duty, which fortunately furthered personal advancement. The better one ministered to the group, in this case to the army, the more recognition one received. The profession of poet or philosopher inclined toward egocentricity. Gneisenau was no egoist, intent on reforming an institution or a society to his wishes or creating a new nation to his needs. He had the actual and practical goal in mind of improving the fighting power of the Prussian army in order to defeat the French, thus, as he thought, preserving freedom.

The proposals which Gneisenau made for Prussia's reform resolved themselves into two kinds, those pertaining to domestic action and those pertaining to international action. The first type had to do with methods of fighting, the second with the manipulation of the balance of power. Under the first head Gneisenau advocated popular insurrection like that in Spain against Napoleon; under the second he projected changes in the international state system and in political frontiers to strengthen the anti-French forces. The two lines supplemented each other, and ultimately Gneisenau chose to preserve Germany by means of the balance of power rather than by political unification.

Gneisenau believed that only the complete destruction of Napoleon would secure peace. He saw Prussia's fate dependent upon that of the rest of Europe. As soon as Spain and Austria were ruined, Prussia's turn would come, he said, and he besought the Prussian king to reject Napoleon's conditions for peace in 1808 and join Spain in war. In 1809 he pleaded for Prussia to align herself actively with Austria against Napoleon and again in 1811 he begged the king to act. Although he preferred Prussia's entering the war on the side of one or more other Powers, he was not particularly concerned about the year or the date. He agitated for war at any time. But he thought that it must be a popular war, whether or not foreign assistance were forthcoming. He wished Prussia through reform to win the wholehearted support of her own population and by becoming a model state to gain the affection of non-Prussian Germans. "It is just and at the same time politically wise," he wrote the king in 1808, "that the people should be given a fatherland if they are vigorously to defend a fatherland. This is particularly necessary because of those other German-speaking peoples who did not formerly live under the Prussian scepter, but desire now to join us for freeing our common German fatherland." [37] He then continued at some length:

[37] Capelle, *op. cit.*, pp. 73-74.

When once the German nation through proclamation and deed has been given the happy hope of beneficent state reform, there is no doubt that a large part of the nation will rise to defend our cause against our oppressor. . . . One will then see fifteen or more million men fighting for one national goal, that is, for independence. The interest which the royal family will arouse throughout the whole of Germany because of their misfortune will become even greater when the House of Brandenburg, to the head of which they are indebted for such liberal principles, assumes leadership over the union for German independence and German freedom. . . .

After that let us begin the glorious struggle with courageous hearts and a confidence in Almighty God, Who will not forsake a just cause unless He has already decided upon our downfall for higher purposes and has let us fall so low in order to allow that Germany where freedom of religion first flourished to give birth to political freedom as well, together with the ennoblement of the people, which can only flourish through mutual independence. Never before has a more wonderful cause been fought for, since it is a matter both of the independence and ennoblement of the people. Perhaps within only a short time the rejuvenated state will appear, more beautiful, more flourishing, more powerful than ever, internally happy, respected and feared abroad and with the Prussian Regent as restorer of German freedom at its head. Whose heart does not beat with happy hopes! [38]

On several occasions later Gneisenau lamented over the "poor German nation" and extolled the "great German cause"; [39] but he never again went so far toward German nationalism as in 1808. Here he spoke of a "common German fatherland"; he subordinated Prussia's interest to that of the German people, even hesitatingly suggesting another historical mission for the Germans to fulfill in the establishment of political freedom coupled with the "ennoblement of the people." But it is manifest that he was not thinking of German political unity. It was freedom of which he was dreaming. He accepted the existing state system. In wishing to see the Hohenzollern king at the head of the "union for German independence and German freedom," [40] he meant merely that

[38] *Ibid.*, pp. 74, 77.
[39] *Ibid.*, pp. 78-80.
[40] *Ibid.*, p. 74.

Prussia should exercise a moral power over the Germans through the excellence of her ways. He desired most eagerly spiritual unity for purposes of defense. The positive idealism of a Fichte or Arndt for a nation of the future was largely lacking in his nationalism.

In the same year Gneisenau composed his proposals for a popular military organization and technique of fighting. Believing that the old methods would not suffice to defeat Napoleon, he laid down the revolutionary rule that "whoever is not with us is against us," even within Germany. In addition to compulsory military service for all males above the age of seventeen, he demanded that the economic resources of the state be mobilized for war, that all incompetent or uncoöperative officials be supplanted by able ones, and that the clergy be intimately associated with the work of defense. He introduced a democratic element by proposing that each battalion elect its own officers and underofficers, and for greater efficiency wished the civil power throughout the country, even in decisions of life and death, to be put in the hands of the military authorities. The memorandum manifested the most violent nationalism. In it Gneisenau advocated the absolute organization of the state for war, the incitement of the entire population against the enemy, and the employment of public education and of religion for this end. Every possible means of fighting should be used.

All supplies of grain will be removed before the advance of the enemy and the region before it will be laid waste, the mills will be stripped of their essential parts, and women and children will take refuge in districts of which there are so many in the North and which can be made inaccessible with little effort. Suitable cities will be surrounded with palisades, provided with block houses and prepared for defense. Whatever is destroyed will be a common burden on the nation.

Signals will be placed on landmarks and heights, so that it will be possible to know of the approach of the enemy. All men able to bear arms will then advance against it. Decisive battles will, however, be avoided whenever success is not absolutely assured; petty warfare will be carried on, the columns held back, the enemy tired out and an attempt made to come to decisive hand-to-hand fighting in night encounters. Where the enemy advances with superior strength, there will be retreat, followed by attacks on their flanks and rear. Strong passes are to be tenaciously defended.[41]

By imposing upon the state the economic burden of restoring property destroyed in war, he formulated a nationalistic ideal which was not realized until France did so during the World War. Even the social structure should be rearranged in accordance with the conduct of individuals during the war.

Any peasant who owns land on which services are due will free his land of encumberment by fighting to the last for the cause of independence.

The goods and wealth of all those who show themselves lax or inclined toward the cause of the enemy will be confiscated and distributed among those severely injured in the war and among the children of those fallen in the service of the fatherland.

Every title of nobility which is not renewed by wounds received in the war of independence, by bravery, by great sacrifices made for the fatherland or by valuable counsel will cease to exist and from this time on only titles of nobility newly won in this manner will be recognized by us.[42]

"We recognize all Germans as our brothers," he wrote, thereby binding them together by a special blood relationship. Nonetheless, he immediately denied any intention of forcible annexation of territory to Prussia, and in declaring that Prussia must proclaim a free constitution he held out the attraction of liberty to

[41] "All the campaigns of the Emperor Napoleon [Gneisenau wrote in 1812] have been calculated on the basis of short duration. Move quickly, surround the enemy by maneuvers, fight him in separate groups, weaken him through fear and end a short war by a quick peace, which assures the French soldier the pride of victory and turns over to his caprice the lands he has overrun—that is the kind of war upon which the French Emperor relies. But, as soon as he is forced to wage a long war, as soon as the French soldier is deprived of the possibility of living at the expense of an oppressed population and as soon as there is prospect of a long, hard fight, then one may flatter oneself that one has already won a psychological victory; and then perhaps even victorious battles may force him to retreat. Let everyone remember the Battle of Eylau—and at that time there was as yet no Spain" (*ibid.*, pp. 120-21).

[42] *Ibid.*, pp. 79, 80.

those Germans desiring to unite with her. In case any German princes should lead troops against Prussia on the side of the French their thrones should be forfeited and their subjects should elect "more worthy regents" in their stead. "Their ministers will be declared outlaw if they do not at once coöperate with our plans." But the memorandum reveals nonetheless definite limitations to Gneisenau's nationalism. Gneisenau did not perceive that the realization of his plans for military defense would necessitate the unification of all Germans, even by compulsion; he stopped short of discussing the relationship between nationalism and freedom. The proposals for a future Germany receded almost into obscurity before the immediate duty of destroying the enemy. Such was the nationalism of an army officer.

The weakness of Gneisenau's nationalism is best seen in the fact that shortly after his proposals of 1808 to the Prussian king he supported the idea of establishing, under British control, a North German kingdom to include part of former Prussian territory. As late as January, 1813, on the eve of the Prussian War of Liberation, he advocated this measure. He wished definitely to interest England in the defense of Germany and the complete overthrow of Napoleon, although the two objectives did not necessarily coincide. No doubt he was driven to this project by his bitter disappointment in Prussia and by the precariousness of his position. The Prussian king let pass without action every opportunity for revolt and when Austria was defeated again in 1809, Gneisenau blamed the German misfortune on the cowardice and incompetence of the rulers. Even at the risk of complete impoverishment he took leave of Prussian service in 1809 in order to find action elsewhere against Napoleon. In spite of trips to England, Sweden, and Russia in the succeeding years, he made no headway.

Sometimes in and sometimes out of active Prussian service, Gneisenau was neither superfluous nor indispensable. Hardenberg rebuked him gently for overhaste, and when Gneisenau in 1811 repeated his hot plea for a national uprising, the king remarked about part of it, "as poetry, good." Gneisenau knew that the king meant to damn his entire proposal and in the bitterness of his discouragement replied:

. . . Religion, prayer, love for the ruler, for the Fatherland, for virtue are nothing else than poetry; without them there is no uplifting of the heart. Whoever regulates his acts by cold calculation will be an inflexible egoist. The security of the Throne is founded on poetry. Many of us anxiously watching a tottering throne would be able to find a peaceful, happy place in quiet retreat, many might expect even a splendid one if instead of feeling we coldly calculated our own advantage. We should be indifferent toward every ruler. But the ties of birth, of affection or of gratitude bind us to our accustomed liege lord; the hardships which our Sovereign must endure only hold us the more securely; with him we shall live and die; for him we shall forego the joys of family; for him we shall sacrifice life and goods to an uncertain future. This is poetry—poetry of the noblest kind; for this I would strive my life long. I count it an honor to belong to that band of zealots who risk all to save all for Your Majesty; for truly, to make such a decision requires an enthusiasm above all selfish reckoning. There are many who are so inclined, and I am far behind them in nobility of spirit; I shall try to become like them.[43]

If this feeling had been turned in the direction of the nation it would have become true nationalism. All that Gneisenau achieved by his sacrifices was to establish firmly his position in history as an unselfish idealist and to strain relations between himself and his king and himself and his wife even more than he had done by his activity in the matter of reform.

During this period Gneisenau's material situation was desperate. He shunned Berlin, where the French might seize him, and feared that even his family might be taken as hostages. He thought that he was ruined financially. Estates and their owners were being traded by princes like cattle, he said, and he considered his own estate as an "inn where he was lodged for as long as it pleased God, his creditors and Napoleon." [44] He was thinking of emigrating, but he did not dare because his family and

[43] Capelle, *op. cit.*, pp. 117-18.
[44] Delbrück, *op. cit.*, I, 210.

property tied him closely to Prussia. He declared that he was a sacrifice to his own idealism, that he had not taken into account the egoism and cowardice of men. He was undermining his health, he lamented, by sorrow and anxiety, and came to believe that only with the aid of a Higher Power could the world be saved. During these three years of searching in and outside of Germany for aid against the French, he called himself an "apostle of a holy Evangelism." [45] By 1812 he became so discouraged that he wanted to retire to his estate. "France has won," he said, "not because of her talents, since we compare well with these Gallics, but because of the weakness of her opponents. . . . I shall no longer try in vain, like a second Sisyphus, to roll the rock uphill, but shall watch the storm from under shelter." [46]

In spite of his threats to retire, Gneisenau was planning in 1812 to arouse the German people and to combat Napoleon by organizing a German legion. Then the War of Liberation began. For years he had avowed that the only choice for Prussia was between political destruction and war. Now the hour had come. When he read the king's proclamation, *To My People,* he wished that it might say "that revenging Providence had at last taken the cause of the people under its care; that it would be unworthy of divine beneficence not to seize the opportunity; that independence was the greatest good in life and without it the other goods of life would have no value." [47] Like all typical nationalists, he thought that God fought on his side. But to him the highest good in life was independence; not an ideal nation of brothers but freedom constituted the goal of the military man.

Gneisenau served as chief of staff for Blücher during the entire war and was primarily responsible for the magnificent victories of that leader. He proved to be as ruthless and untiring a fighter in war as he had been a proponent of reform during peace, upon one campaign enduring, so it is said, for five nights without sleep. When victory came, he enjoyed it like a gourmand. Drunk with enthusiasm over the outcome of the Battle of Leipzig, he

[45] *Loc. cit.*
[46] *Ibid.*, I, 271; Pertz, *op. cit.*, I, 464.
[47] Delbrück, *op. cit.*, I, 291.

wrote on October 22, 1813: "The greatest happiness in life is the satisfaction of revenge against an insolent enemy. . . . The state is saved. The Throne is secure. True, we are impoverished; but we are now rich in military glory and proud of our newly regained national independence." [48] He was referring to Prussia, not to the German nation. "We have quaffed long draughts of our national revenge," he wrote later in the same year,[49] and it is uncertain whether he meant revenge for Prussia or Germany. Early in the next year he credited Providence with having led the army up to the present and after Waterloo he was determined that Napoleon should be destroyed. England, he said in his quarrel with Wellington over this issue, had grown rich during the wars, but Prussia had become impoverished. "Our nobility will never be able to regain its place." The revenge of the peoples, he declared, demanded Napoleon's death.

Victory brought with it the problem of the fate of the German states. A few reformers like Stein and Hardenberg desired the political unification of Germany in some form, but not so Gneisenau. His biographer Delbrück has written:

> . . . While Stein and Hardenberg were still trying to make the impossible come true, Gneisenau wrote to them as early as 1814 that he considered it impossible to draft a good German constitution; Bavaria and Württemberg would not conform. For this reason one should confine one's efforts to the needs of Prussia, which was the first concern. But Prussia, which by its prowess in war was already winning fame in entire Germany, must in the future be so constituted that the other Germans would of themselves desire to join with this state. The best means to that end would be a good constitution. Furthermore, Prussia should make itself the protector of the arts and sciences in Germany so that in this way it might win public opinion still more to its side. Thus the war would be opened for new gains to be made in the future, "less by the force of arms than by the liberality of its principles," and Prussia would stand glorious for what alone can bring distinction to a people, namely, "fame in war, constitution, and laws and cultivation of the arts and sciences." [50]

[48] Capelle, *op. cit.*, pp. 133-34.
[49] Delbrück, *op. cit.*, I, 406.
[50] *Ibid.*, II, 31.

For Germany as a whole Gneisenau wished only military security, and to achieve it he returned to his former proposal concerning the principle of the balance of power. Since Prussia had recovered so magnificently from her defeat of 1806 and other German states had aided her, he no longer thought of defending Germany against Napoleon by interesting England territorially in North Germany. Judging from a letter to Hardenberg of June, 1815, he was not thinking merely of the Germans. "The world demands," he wrote, "that they be made safe against the restless spirit of a bad but capable and courageous people, and with justice. Woe to them and shame upon them if they do not seize upon this unique opportunity to secure forever Belgium, Prussia and Germany." [51] Although Gneisenau seemed to place the world, Belgium, Prussia, and Germany on a parity, undoubtedly he felt most concern about Germany, and for the sake of her protection wished Prussia to be strengthened by territorial gains. In 1814 he urged Hardenberg to acquire Alsace; in the same year he was eager for war in order to destroy the dualism of Prussia and Austria in Germany and to place Prussia on top. In the next year he proposed to Hardenberg other territorial changes without ever expressing a wish for the political unification of Germany. The work of the Congress of Vienna disappointed him greatly. "My dear Arndt," he wrote in August, 1815, "Put on mourning. Everything indicates that a second Peace of Utrecht is being concluded. Germany's misfortunes are to be perpetuated." [52]

After the war against Napoleon Gneisenau soon retired from active service. He was disgusted and embittered by the struggle of the reactionaries against the reformers and felt deeply the king's antagonism to himself. The fact that Blücher had become famous through military successes which Gneisenau had made possible rankled in the latter's mind, and since the time of activity was past, Gneisenau sought to live more freely than military duties permitted. Until his death in 1831 he kept aloof from public affairs except when especially consulted; he was content to

[51] Capelle, *op. cit.*, p. 154.
[52] Delbrück, *op. cit.*, II, 287-88.

manage his estate, to read, and to enjoy leisure; his ambition slowly faded.

Gneisenau had never harbored the desire to make over society. "A man must be fired with enthusiasm for an idea," he wrote in 1807, "if he is to accomplish anything great." [53] But the dominant idea in his case was that of liberty rather than nationalism, and when he found that resistance to Napoleon could be aroused and sustained without thorough social and military reforms, his devotion to reform diminished and after Waterloo almost vanished. He had wanted action, and reform had been a means of bringing it about. In religion he scorned mysticism; in politics, except during the years of inactivity against Napoleon, he did likewise. This exception brought him as near to nationalism as he ever came. Possessing a strong sense of historical continuity, Gneisenau appreciated the value of using existing forces and building on existing loyalties. He was much more ready to break with the past in internal reforms than in interstate organization, since internal reform might be a necessary prerequisite for military defense. The army officer served a definite state in a concrete way and disliked tampering with its external shape; his profession had so conditioned his thinking as to curb sharply his political imagination. His sense of social reform was too restricted to the existing political structure to admit of his conceiving of a loyalty to a new nation or nation-state. He stopped in the region between liberty and nationalism, between practical detail and idealism, between the sense of duty to Prussia and that to Germany. He possessed some of the qualities of a nationalist and lacked others. He never focused his enthusiasm, his imagination, his vigor, and his passion upon the nation or understood the nature of the nation; he failed to buttress liberty with fraternity and to associate them with the nation.

[53] Pertz, *op. cit.*, I, 295.

VI. NATHUSIUS

THE biography of Johann Gottlob Nathusius reveals a figure who neither approved nor opposed nationalism but remained indifferent to it. He never grew alarmed about the Napoleonic domination over Germany, the political disunity of the German people, or the future of the nation, for the trend of his development lay toward liberalism. The study of his life in relation to nationalism poses two problems, that of the extent to which he approached this new feeling, and the explanation of his failure to achieve it.

Nathusius, who was born in 1760, belonged to the same generation as Fichte and Gneisenau. His father held a minor position in the Saxon bureaucracy and in times of high prices his scanty stipend failed to provide enough food for the family. Nathusius, writing later in his own life, described his father as follows:

My father was a serious, honest, and righteous man, extremely prudent, but also frank. He would publicly censure bad people, even though they were distinguished, faithfully carrying out his official duty, to which he was bound by oath, without regard for personalities and thereby making enemies of Count von Solms and other so-called notabilities of the locality. He likewise maintained the dignity of his official post. Indeed, though he received a salary of only five taler and twenty groschen a month, he knew how to uphold his position. As an official of Saxony, he preceded all others in the district who were only officials of the Count, and also took precedence over them when they marched to the Holy Communion, even though they were far better paid than he. That angered them, causing them always to inquire of the pastor before going to Holy Communion whether, by chance, my father was also going. If so, they would not go. He was so far from being a hypocrite that he could never be polite to or say a pleasant word to any person who he was convinced was not deserving thereof. If an injustice happened to anyone, even though of no concern to him, he would take up his case with zeal. He respected his superiors when they merited it, but when they did not, he let them know of his contempt, thereby incurring occasional displeasure. He helped everyone with advice and action according to his ability, but whoever treated him unjustly by obstructing his path or by offending his good name, him would he hate to the point of persecution until the day of reckoning. He put little stock in outward religious worship and went seldom, therefore, to church and then only after much pleading on the part of my mother. He did, however, have an inward religion. He venerated God, and I have often seen him in silent prayer. He admonished us children daily with the words: "You should pray diligently and then," he would add, "everything will always come out well for you. I also pray for you that everything will work out for you." In short, my father was a man of character and original in his own way.[1]

It is evident from this description that Nathusius was impressed by the qualities in his father which resembled those of a liberal—self-esteem, individuality, independence of thought, speech, and action, religious unorthodoxy, disregard of caste, absolute integrity—and he strove to perfect these traits in himself. Although he softened the edges by cultivating ease and poise in social intercourse and developed another basis for his liberalism than that of pride and security in government service, he learned from his father the essential value of liberty and equality and saw the possibility of practicing these ideals. His father lacked a spirit of fraternity, the basis of nationalism, and Nathusius likewise failed to develop it. He became an individualist rather than a group-thinker and actor, that is to say, a liberal rather than a nationalist.

As a boy Nathusius loved to study and wished to prepare himself for a profession, preferably the theological one, and to enter state service. His natural inclination, his imaginative power, and his subsequent success show that he would have made an excellent student. His active interest in theological and philosophical problems and his enjoyment of the study of science con-

[1] Elsbeth von Nathusius, *Johann Gottlob Nathusius. Ein Pioneer deutscher Industrie* (Stuttgart, 1915), pp. 16-17.

tinued to the end of his life. If he had been able to pursue an academic career, he might have followed a course into nationalism similar to that of Fichte or Arndt. His love of theology indicates the capacity in him for abstract thinking, for appreciating ethical and cultural ideals, possibly for looking to the German nation as an instrument capable of saving and reviving the world. His imaginative ability would have assisted him to conceive of a nation which did not exist, while intimate connection as a bureaucrat with the state might have taught him its importance and have introduced him to the subject of politics. He might have come to envisage a society in which his father's poverty and his own hardships would not obtain and, like certain of his contemporaries, have called for thorough economic and social reform. He might have learned to think in terms of the group and to wish to spread these goods to the entire nation. In short, he might have been led to regard the new era in the history of mankind as that of nationalism. Unfortunately, he never had the chance to test and develop his imagination academically on any question of politics or of social ethics. His father was unable to assist any of his children in obtaining an education, and when Nathusius himself tried to earn or borrow the money, he failed completely. To his abiding regret, he had to renounce his hopes and become an apprentice to a merchant in Berlin. Henceforth, except for such interest in religious and philosophical problems as an amateur might sustain, he concentrated upon the practical problems of business life.

There is no reason to believe that Nathusius suffered any permanently bad effects from his compulsory change of occupation. Although his apprenticeship was long and severe, he became neither psychopathic nor even unhappy, accepting his lot and proving as successful in it as he doubtless would have been in the field of theology.

In Berlin [he wrote later in his autobiography] I began my duties as youngest apprentice, which included going for the mail and to other places and, like a day laborer, carrying from the cellar and attic the syrup, blubber, olive oil and everything that was sold during the day. In the evening I had to make and paste paper bags and grind coffee until ten o'clock. On Saturday I had to scrub all the store counters and clean the blubber and oil containers. I had to sweep the store daily, to shine the shoes of my employer and the clerks. Meals were very poor—among other things spoiled dried cod, which the worms had already begun to nibble at and which no one would buy any more. The portion which one received had to be eaten. Frequently when I had eaten about half of my portion of codfish, I lost it by vomiting. We also looked for the chance when possible to throw it secretly into the fire. This brings to my mind the bacon rind, which I frequently had to eat cooked in beer-vinegar, flour, and syrup. In short, I believe that a negro boy would have been treated better than I was. Nor did a day pass without boxes on the ear from the clerks. I was very often teased by my comrades because of my poverty and my poor clothes. . . .

All of this so depressed me that I was constantly serious and pensive. I was, however, willing and diligent and I noticed that my employer meant well by me. Then came the winter, which was very severe, and since I always had to live in the cold and did not have anything warm to wear, my hands and feet froze. Even now my fingers are not perfectly straight. The cook first took me in charge and bandaged me. But since it was so very bad that I could not walk any more, an army surgeon was called in. It was even suggested that I be sent back home again and this suggestion was only given up through the influence of the cook, an aged person who had been in the house for many years and who also succeeded in having me treated better henceforth. She could not, however, altogether protect me from the abuse of the two clerks and my comrades, the two apprentices. They were to a certain extent in conspiracy with one another; and the reason for the clerks' mistreatment of me was that, remembering the admonition of my father, I did not want to be led into disloyalty. They wished me to bring coffee, sugar, Provençal oil and other goods to a house where they foregathered on Sundays with other clerks. I refused, and they made me atone for it. Since I could no longer stand the abuse, I complained about it to my employer, or rather I went to the old cook who had always protected me, to have her ask Mr. Herr if these things were going on with his knowledge and consent. He investigated the case very thoroughly and upon convincing himself of their conspiracy and dishonesty dismissed them all. . . . Those who served after them were for the most part good people. I was then the oldest apprentice and was not only respected by my employer but also by the new clerks.

Because of the bad food and the strenuous work during my years of apprenticeship, I have always been small and weak, whereas my brothers were all unusually large men.[2]

In spite of the severe treatment Nathusius did not lose his ambition or his sunny disposition. Poverty turned Fichte to protest against the present organization of society and started him on the way toward nationalism as a means of correcting these conditions; but it incited Nathusius to overcome his handicaps and to develop his abilities along the lines required for success in the existing society. Fichte rebelled, whereas Nathusius adjusted himself. From the time of his arrival in Berlin he had determined to become a "school-trained merchant."

There was lacking, however, all means for this [he wrote in his autobiography]. The store in which I was employed was almost solely a retail store for groceries. I was merely employed to make and paste paper bags and to take care of sales. A special skill was needed in the making of paper bags; they had to be so pointed at the bottom that very little could go in. For that reason, too, one had to fill them very gently and with little shaking. There is a special knack to everything. This was part of the merchants' code, for it was thought that the merchant could not exist if he conformed to the usual moral standard. When the raisins were spoiled they would be sprayed with a little syrup, thus making them look very bright and fresh again, and so on. This and other things like it were what I learned in those six years.

Making paper bags did, however, help me a great deal. The bags were, for the most part, made of waste paper from the book printing shops and the bookstores; there were especially many fragments of the *Allgemeine Deutsche Bibliotek* from the Nicolai Publishers. I read these with avidity as well as was possible with a small oil lamp and in the secrecy in which I had to do it. In this way I learned almost all the branches of knowledge by name, which aroused in me the desire to acquire as soon as possible an understanding of them. As apprentices, each morning we received three groschen with

[2] *Ibid.*, pp. 25-27.

which to buy ourselves rolls for breakfast. I went hungry, begging the old cook to keep my allowances instead. As soon as I had a few groschen saved up I went to a second-hand bookseller who lived near by and bought books. Imperfect as these old books were, they were a real treasure to me and must still be in my library. I studied them with joy. In order to learn to write German correctly I studied Gottsched's German Grammar. There was no better at that time. Gellert's writings, which I read eagerly, especially his *Letters*, were of great use to me. I copied his style of writing in short sentences just as one speaks. . . . I also took great pains to achieve a strong and good penmanship, since nothing else so commends a merchant. . . . For practice I wrote more than two hundred pages of merchants' letters to make myself fit as a correspondent in an office. For this reason also I taught myself double-entry bookkeeping, about which I learned from an old book that came into my hands. It left me somewhat puzzled in the beginning, but I was soon able to grasp the material. Later commercial arithmetic, coinage, and exchange and banking. May's *Science of Business* was my first foundation for this knowledge. But I did not stop with that; I studied all the laws of money and even political science or national economy; I read Büsch's writings and learned Adam Smith's *Wealth of Nations* almost by heart.

In order to train myself practically, in my own mind I set up my own business, in which all the merchants' transactions and occurrences that I could think of took place, and for two years I kept complete books and correspondence about them with fictitious business acquaintances.[3]

The story of Nathusius' life might have served as material for a novel by Horatio Alger; for Nathusius was completely self-educated and self-made. He read useful books, very little literature, and that of rationalistic and cosmopolitan character. He paid more heed to morality and conduct than he did to things intellectual. He attended carefully to the business in hand, learned the importance of detail, and entirely accepted bourgeois casuistry. In addition to these traits, which had been the standard equipment of merchants in all ages, Nathusius manifested inter-

[3] *Ibid.*, pp. 31-33.

ests and qualities which undoubtedly foreshadowed the emergence of the capitalistic industrialist. He loved to experiment. He was active, aggressive, and restless. During his later life he developed the interests and capacities which he showed as an apprentice. He was to become a combination—in some respects a confusion—of merchant, industrialist, experimental scientist, and engineer, an innovator in every field of business. The joy of action, of novelty, appealed to him even apart from the pecuniary returns to be expected. As a practical disciple of Adam Smith he was rapidly becoming a misfit in the society of the paternalistic, caste state.

After serving for some years with the merchant to whom he had been apprenticed, Nathusius accepted a position with a firm in Magdeburg. The history of his material success need not be told. He seized several opportunities which required considerable daring, emerging victorious each time. On one occasion it was a matter of purchasing and salvaging a boatload of rice which had been shipwrecked in the river. On another, he acquired cheaply a large quantity of wet tobacco. After having treated both the rice and the tobacco properly, he sold them at a large profit. When his employer died, he and a relative of the employer took over the business, and although it was almost bankrupt, Nathusius' intelligence and his partner's able administration saved the firm. When the Prussian state abolished the tobacco monopoly, Nathusius established a snuff factory. Although at the time he knew nothing about making snuff, he quickly experimented until he found out; and the excellent quality of the article made the reputation and assured the pecuniary security of the firm. The snuff factory later enjoyed the unique honor of being the only steady money-maker among Nathusius' numerous business ventures. By the turn of the century he was the most prominent merchant in Magdeburg and one of the wealthiest men in Germany.

It is significant that Nathusius' material success rested upon the withdrawal of the Prussian state from one of its mercantilist activities. In his youth he had been eager to become a Prussian official, and at the time at which he had moved to Magdeburg he had just been badly disappointed in not receiving a position in the state bank. Chance had prevented him from following a career which might have led him in the same direction which Stein and other reform-nationalists took. Private business trained him in a different manner. It taught him to distrust the state, to wish its functions restricted to the bare minimum. Although he cultivated cordial relations with officials for reasons of expediency and was willing to use the government whenever he could, he rejected the mercantilistic conception of the state. He closed the avenue to an appreciation of the state as a vital political body, which men of theoretical minds or men intimately associated with the state kept open. Except in so far as the freedom of the individual to pursue his own advantage coincided with group interest, he was not group-minded. As a self-made businessman he saw no proof, either actual or theoretical, of the dependence of individual welfare upon that of the state or the nation. It is doubtful whether the theoretical problem of the individual versus the group, which troubled Fichte so greatly, ever occurred to him.

The structure of the Prussian state and society was unsympathetic to Nathusius long before the Battle of Jena disclosed the weaknesses in it. His political, social, and economic ideals were the contrary of those which the Prussian state practiced. When one recalls his devotion to Adam Smith's *Wealth of Nations,* the trend of his economic thought is clear. He could not participate in Prussian political life because he was not connected with the bureaucracy. Socially he was barred from association on terms of equality with the aristocracy. Then came a time when the Prussian government restored the tobacco monopoly and Nathusius found even his economic independence menaced. He protected his snuff industry by securing an appointment as an official in the administration of the monopoly, and upon the speedy collapse of the project, he was put in charge of its liquidation. This experience increased his distrust of bureaucratic handling of economic matters and strengthened his belief in individual effort. His contempt for government grew with its prohibition of several of his enterprises, while he was never absolutely safe against a renewed attempt to establish a tobacco monopoly. One can understand why, after he became wealthy, he refused all offers of appointment in the Prussian bureaucracy, why for years he rejected all decorations, and why he said that it was better "that one distinguishes oneself than that one lets oneself be distinguished by others." [4] His superior efficiency in economic affairs over that of the bureaucrats enhanced his self-esteem, and, true to the developing bourgeois type, he desired social position and political influence somewhat commensurate with his economic power. Why should not his judgment in political matters be considered equally with his economic views?

The Prussian defeat at Jena did not surprise Nathusius. He had long agreed with his colleagues among the Magdeburg merchants that there were far too many officials in the Prussian government and that they were too poorly paid. Unlike Frederick the Great, who suspected all officials of being thieves and accordingly paid them low salaries, he believed in respecting an individual by rewarding him with a just salary and by permitting him the freedom to advance as far as he could. The liberal of the nineteenth century stands in sharp contrast to the despot of the eighteenth century. Nathusius' opinion of the Prussian army did not differ from his opinion of the bureaucracy. The boasting of the officers, he thought, covered a similar incompetence. Although Magdeburg was a fortress, he saw that it lacked in 1806 all the necessities for defense. After Jena the burghers, in wanting to defend the city against the French, proved to be braver than the army, whose commandant surrendered.

The defeat at Jena did not drive Nathusius to prophecy, to political philosophy, or to nationalism. He could not acquire nationalism through books, for he had no interest in literature. He was almost equally cut off from the exposition of the new idealistic philosophy. The intellectual activity of his countrymen was entirely unknown to him so that he failed to comprehend that which was so clear to Fichte, the superiority of the German people over the rest of the world. It is doubtful whether it ever occurred to him to fear the total destruction of civilization, of the German folk and its culture at the hands of the French. As a

[4] *Ibid.*, p. 199.

businessman and a man of peace, he had had no opportunity to develop a political sense of either internal or foreign affairs. He was not a very ardent Prussian, and the defeat of the old order in Prussia did not fill him with regret; he had wanted it changed anyway. He weighed the situation in Prussia after 1806, and when by the Peace of Tilsit Magdeburg was incorporated into the Kingdom of Westphalia, he easily accepted the fact. The desperate plight of Prussia counseled him against moving his factories into its poverty-stricken areas, where he would be unable, so he argued, to sell his products, would be burdened with enormous taxes to pay the French demands and would probably lose his extra-Prussian customers. Neither was he willing to accept an offer from the Prussian government to establish and direct a royal snuff factory. Although he still had a sufficiency, he had suffered severe economic losses from the political changes. He reasoned that the Kingdom of Westphalia promised him the opportunity of larger markets than did Prussia, that it might permit him more economic freedom, that it offered him an opportunity for political activity.

Nathusius' associates in the business center of Magdeburg, a town noted for its materialism and complete lack of literary or artistic interest, reacted to the French domination in the same realistic way. Once they perceived the compulsion of it, they accepted it easily and by acts of inexpensive friendliness to the French succeeded for the moment in escaping heavy contributions. They took the oath of allegiance to King Jerome in German because they knew no French. Their fate was not bound vitally to that of any particular state or to any one political authority. They adjusted themselves to the new situation, as they would upon necessity return to the former one. They did not fear the loss of their market as Fichte did the loss of a sphere of activity for his philosophy or Kleist for his dramas. They felt no urge to impose their ideals upon others; they held to facts, the business of daily living. Their dreams were about business, not about socio-political or military affairs.

Nathusius spent some of the happiest years of his life in the short-lived Kingdom of Westphalia. His snuff factory prospered as before, and he continued to experiment with many kinds of economic undertakings. He felt freer than under the Prussian rule. When money became short because of the forced contributions to the French, he was instrumental in establishing a bank and in securing a promise from the French not to confiscate the funds. He bought a monastic estate which the French had secularized, and by other purchases became in the course of a few years a large landowner, hoping in this way to assure the preservation of his fortune for several generations. Commercial and industrial enterprises still lacked the survival power which the corporate type of organization gave them. In agriculture and in industry he loved to experiment and to innovate. He greatly admired the English for their economic enterprise and tried to imitate them. From Albrecht Thaer he learned the English methods of stall-feeding and rational management of an estate. He built factories to utilize the raw materials of his estates, producing sugar from sugar beets, distilling rum and liqueurs, making vinegar, bricks, and pottery, opening up a quarry and a mill. His hope was to keep industry in intimate contact with agriculture and local natural resources; like Adam Smith, he believed that thereby the most efficient production could be achieved. He also founded commercial houses for the sale of his wares, thus joining industry, commerce, and agriculture in a way foreshadowing the trust movement.[5]

In 1808 the Kingdom of Westphalia received its new constitution and administration. Both were modeled after the French and put an end to the inefficient methods of the former Prussian regime. Along with many others in Magdeburg Nathusius praised them enthusiastically, and experience confirmed his first judg-

[5] Nathusius could have made "fantastic" profits during these years. The finance minister of the Kingdom, von Bülow, an incompetent aristocrat, leaned heavily upon him for advice and besought him to rent all the crown lands, to purchase from the state the secularized religious lands and to accept government contracts. Nathusius had numerous opportunities for gouging the state, but refused them all. He was too honest to graft, and he lacked courage or inclination to take up the other offers. The continental blockade favored his own ventures and he found in 1815 that he had weathered the Napoleonic period without loss; but he regretted later that he had not accepted the chances offered him to make a fortune.

ment. The establishment of a representative assembly opened the political field to him and he was immediately elected as a delegate. The assembly had slight power and Nathusius scarcely knew what to do with that little. He did not campaign for election or agitate for any issue and, apparently not conversant with political questions and certainly not excited over them, he never spoke in the assembly. When he wished something done, true to his Prussian training, he worked through an official rather than through parliament. He therefore failed to develop during these years a political sense and easily accepted the restoration of autocracy in Prussia after 1815.

His political apathy notwithstanding, Nathusius thoroughly enjoyed the experience with politics and often recalled with nostalgia the years of the Napoleonic regime. He liked the French officials and found them efficient and considerate. His early respect for King Jerome waned somewhat upon experience; but he never lost his admiration for the French, whom he liked because he resembled them. During these years he played a role in society such as he never enjoyed before or after. Social distinctions were loosened, wealth and intelligence opening the world of society to persons even of low birth. Nathusius' self-respect and feeling of independence were greatly enhanced; for the first time in his life his economic power was rewarded by social prestige and political influence. He recognized that the Kingdom was unstable, that the maintenance of the French troops placed heavy burdens upon the population, that Napoleon was an uncertain factor whose power would not endure; but he persistently hoped for peace.

When the War of Liberation began, Nathusius did not favor it. He opposed further upsets in commercial life, and felt quite content in the Kingdom of Westphalia. He feared that if the French rule was overthrown his title to the secularized church property which he had bought might be questioned, and he disliked the prospect of returning to the domination of Prussian paternalism, autocracy, and caste. The Kingdom of Westphalia favored the burghers and the incipient bourgeoisie, the Kingdom of Prussia, the aristocracy. After the Battle of Leipzig he felt the first stirrings of Prussian loyalty in him. As French power declined, his Prussianism grew. By the end of 1813 he was so patriotic that he feared the French might seize him as a hostage. Since the French troops remained in Magdeburg until May, 1814, he dared not show his Prussianism too plainly. But in January of that year he joined a commission for organizing and clothing the militia in his district, and soon thereafter had to flee from the French. The lack of Prussian patriotism among his neighbors and friends is illustrated by the fact that the commission met among merchants and landowners alike the greatest difficulty in raising funds for the army. Nathusius, however, seized the occasion to recover his former good standing in the Prussian state. He was once more a wealthy, intelligent burgher, whose advice was sought on financial and economic questions by the autocratic government, but who was otherwise ignored. He became again a subject instead of a citizen, a tool instead of a governing element. He returned to private life, and except when specifically consulted, left the settlement of political questions to the bureaucratic autocracy which he intensely disliked. He never again enjoyed the political and social liberty of the Kingdom of Westphalia.

By temperament Nathusius was well suited to become a nationalist. He thought and acted with enthusiasm and imagination and possessed courage. He had to cease going to the theater, where he often became so excited that he vocally joined in the performance. He was the first man in Magdeburg to cut off his pigtail. Being himself an original person, he admired women who ignored the strict rules of social etiquette and tried to marry one of that kind. He was a social liberal, associating easily and gladly with all types of people from all classes and possessing the imagination to see that caste distinctions were antiquated. Nonetheless, he refused to allow his business subordinates to take liberties with him or to practice equality; to that extent he failed to believe in fraternity, the social ideal of nationalism. He presents a perfect example of the burgher who, in becoming part of the capitalistic bourgeoisie, used the principle of social equality to abolish the bonds of caste and to rise to the top of the new social ladder. He would have denied this snobbishness without, however, ceasing to practice it. His frequent travels and his lavish entertaining brought him into contact with people of high rank and made for him a place on the periphery of aristocratic society.[6] He had sufficient social prestige to prevent him from wishing to transform quickly the present social organization into the democratic one of nationalism.

In the field of economic action Nathusius had been even more successful than in that of social life. He had proved by example that it was not necessary to become a nationalist in order to abolish the conditions of poverty of his youth. He had made money, had helped others to do so, and had assisted many young men to receive the education which he lacked. He chose capitalistic individual activity as the means best suited to effect slow but solid social reform and accepted the institution of private philanthropy as a necessary adjunct thereto. He never faced the problem of thorough social reform, and the ideal of a society based on the nation and imbued with the spirit of fraternity never crossed his mental horizon.

A short time after the beginning of the new century Nathusius had written that one kind of action gave him pride, "to transform a hitherto useless work into one which is useful and beneficial to the state." [7] His economic enterprises aimed at putting men to work, at creating instruments which would enable more people to live comfortably and to improve their intelligence and social-mindedness while doing so. He foreshadowed the ambitions of many industrialists of the next generation who believed that a factory would raise the moral and intellectual level of mankind as well as the economic. Whenever he could, he delegated authority over one of his enterprises to some man who had grown into his business, not necessarily the one in hand, and he often made these men partners, or even sold the undertaking to them outright. He enjoyed starting a business which would call into being other businesses. He often set up a factory and per-

[6] He had learned to conduct himself easily in these circles, he said, by imagining his aristocratic acquaintances to be naked. Then he did not feel shy in their presence.

[7] Von Nathusius, *op. cit.*, p. 93.

suaded the peasants to raise the raw materials or to utilize the by-products. After 1815 he experimented for some years with the construction of steam engines and established a machine shop on his own estate. When the men whom he employed failed through ignorance to build an engine, he stopped the work and never returned to it. If he had persisted, he would have become more than a mere industrial pioneer. It was his misfortune to be an experimenter who immediately preceded the era of industrial and engineering success in Germany. He kept a large garden and collected a number of strange animals, throwing both exhibits open to the public. One can say that he tried to fill the place which was later to be taken by public museums, technical schools, and corporations. In his papers were found membership cards to twenty-five agricultural, technical, and learned societies and one to the Society of Friends of Art in the Prussian provinces.

The social purpose of Nathusius' economic endeavors was unmistakable, but his method of acting was that of the liberal rather than of the nationalist. As a practical utilitarian, he liked to realize something on his economic enterprises while benefiting society. And society to him meant not an organic unit, not a blood-brotherhood, not a mystical body, but a collection of individualists. The way to serve society was to develop more individualists, each able to perform well his task. Nathusius thought in terms of a specific factory, a particular farm, a special product, a unique Herr Schmidt or Herr Krause; he wanted to assist the particulars; he was a nominalist, not a nationalistic realist. His way of thinking coincided with his way of acting—it dealt with the individual and ignored the group except in so far as the individuals with whom he came in contact were part of the group. Like the liberal capitalist, he let the group take care of itself.

The social nature of Nathusius' economic interests might have led him to nationalism if the general conditions of the age had been more favorable. He lived in the period of budding capitalistic industrialism, when locality or province was still paramount as the geographic unit for business. His enterprises sought to build on local materials for local wants; and even in the case of the snuff factory Nathusius did not find that particularism greatly obstructed his market. He was able to sell this product so widely that he did not experience the need the next generation felt for the economic unity of Germany. The south and west of Germany remained relatively unknown to him both economically and personally. Like his French contemporary, Saint-Simon, he perceived the advantages to the social whole of new economic enterprises such as a bank, a factory, or a rationally conducted estate, and realized that these enterprises demanded coöperation among the individuals involved. But the number of persons of similar perception was small and even Nathusius did not associate this social whole with so large a group as the nation. His enterprises lacked the size and scope necessary for teaching him the value of a unified nation. He defended his freedom to act within a limited territory untouched by the possibility of a national sphere of activity.

Nathusius was more concerned with production than with distribution. He enjoyed experimenting with new seeds or machines or materials. He had the mind of a scientist or an engineer, not of a merchant or an industrialist eager for an ever-larger market. If he had been born thirty years later he might have been more concerned about finding buyers for his wares. Industry had then passed its infancy and the battle for survival had begun in a period in which a unified market and a strong central government run by liberals seemed necessary. He might, like Friedrich List, have turned then to propaganda or, like Gustav Mevissen, to an active, pressing interest in politics. Instead of passively acquiescing in autocracy, he might have opposed it vigorously and demanded national unification and self-government. He might have perceived what the idealists and a few officials saw at his time, that man must be more than free to guide his private affairs, that in order to realize his maximum abilities he must share in political decisions and feel himself a part of the nation-group, a responsible citizen. Nathusius had grown out of the economic and social ideals and organization of the *ancien régime* and had made for himself ideals of liberalism which were to serve as the social and economic basis of early nationalism. But he lived a generation too early for the political implications of these ideals to become so clear to him that he would demand their realization. Although he understood that liberalism implies social duties, he never perceived that by a proper balance of liberty and of social responsibility for the individual nationalism might result. He remained a compromiser, rebelling against the existing order just so far as his own needs dictated. He was not a theorist; he was not a state official; he had no cause for confronting the problem of the relation between the individual and the nation-group. The ideological implications for nationalism of his beliefs and actions remained concealed from him.

Nathusius represented the burgher attitude toward the state and toward public questions which the reformers hoped to overcome. By liberating the population from caste restrictions and from state paternalism, by encouraging it to individual enterprise, by associating it in public affairs and making it an active part of the whole the reformers aimed to stimulate the people, whether a Nathusius, a selfish aristocrat, or an ignorant peasant, to defend their state, their culture, and their nation. They desired to prevent a repetition of the easy acquiescence in the Napoleonic domination which so many Germans had shown. They were fighting a losing battle just because the material and institutional conditions were still lacking that would unite men like Nathusius with the state and the nation. The reformers were political idealists living in an age of social, economic, and political provincialism. The social groups exemplified by Nathusius were mildly interested in political questions, but were still too modest, too uncertain, too economically sufficient to demand a share in state power. Within a half century after Nathusius' death they gave to nationalism the force to realize itself.

VII. MARWITZ

THE subject of this essay never became a nationalist. As a result of family background, training, and profession he fitted so well into the existing social system that he never wanted to transform it. An aristocrat, happily situated in the first rank of society, he firmly believed to the end of his life that God and nature had created the caste-state as the best possible order for mankind. During the critical years between 1805 and 1815 he felt loyal to the German nation and proposed reforms for strengthening its political power, while despising nationalism as a threat to his whole way of life. He did not act against it out of material interests alone, but he opposed it because it implied an antithesis of the social ideals and practices which he approved. He fought for the defense of caste society against foreign and domestic enemies, his relation to the nationalist movement typifying that of most agrarian aristocrats during the succeeding century.

Friedrich August Ludwig von der Marwitz, born on May 29, 1777, at Berlin, began a life sharply defined by the traditions of family, caste, and state. The decisive influences which guided him were set before he ever came into the world. His role awaited him as soon as he showed an inclination to assume it. While his mother was descended from a French Huguenot line prominent in Prussia, on his paternal side he belonged to one of the oldest families in the Mark of Brandenburg. Marwitz's father acted as an official at the royal court and in 1786 became court marshal to King Frederick William II. But the Marwitz family inclined more toward the military than the civil service, and as an old man Marwitz wrote proudly in his autobiography that in the last one hundred and forty years his family had provided Prussia with several hundred officers for the army, among them seven generals. He was to provide the eighth.[1]

The training for life which young Marwitz received conformed to the aristocratic pattern. He learned French, his mother's tongue, perfectly, for during his early years his parents spoke only that language at home. He endured the usual assortment of private tutors who knew little and who only succeeded in fortifying his aristocratic mistrust of knowledge found in books. Although he read widely, learning never impressed him as important; he succeeded without it; or, as he declared later in life, he succeeded because he had not stuffed his head with theories. No aristocrat needed academic knowledge, he said, particularly if he were intended for a military career. Marwitz learned most from social intercourse, including how to deport himself in aristocratic or royal circles, how to converse easily, how to bow, how to kiss a lady's hand, how to look superior without self-consciousness, how to dance, to ride, and to defend his honor. He received, on the whole, a practical education suitable to his station. He picked up some acquaintance with history by listening to the stories told by members of aristocratic families about their ancestors. When he saw or met a famous person, as he often did, he took note of the lesson to be learned from the life of such a person. He never forgot these meetings, assimilating history, ethics, politics, and government from them as he would never have done from books. Upon three occasions he saw Frederick the Great, once when the king, worn out by maneuvers, was returning to Berlin. After describing Frederick's progress on horseback through the streets of the capital, Marwitz in his memoirs portrayed his own reactions:

> Nothing happened! No display, no fireworks, no salutes from cannon, no fife and drum, no music, no preliminaries. One saw only an old man of seventy-three, poorly clad, dusty, returning from his day's hard work. But everyone knew that this old man worked for

[1] Friedrich Meusel, *Friedrich August Ludwig von der Marwitz* (Berlin, 1908-13), I, 49. The figure of eight given by Marwitz is inaccurate. There were actually eleven generals before him.

him, that he put his entire life into this labor and had not neglected it a single day for forty-five years. Everyone saw the fruits of the work about him, and when one looked at the king, he felt stir within him respect, admiration, pride, trust, in short, all the nobler feelings of man.[2]

This kind of experience demonstrated to a receptive mind like Marwitz's the importance of personality, of the exercise of the will, and of action, all factors in the development of a nationalist. But through his aversion to theories he destroyed the potentiality of his acceptance or creation of a new cultural ideal for his nation. He agreed with Goethe, "Life educates man and words signify little." [3]

Childhood did not last long for Marwitz. At the age of thirteen he entered the Prussian army, serving as Junker in the regiment which two of his uncles had led. He learned to obey, to command, the bases of conduct for the Prussian officer-aristocrat. His character was early molded by the most efficient instrument of caste-action then existing. At the same time, becoming aware of the French Revolution, he took a more serious interest in the preservation of the prevailing order of society in Prussia. At the death of his father in 1793 Marwitz, then sixteen years old, assumed responsibility for the family and henceforth supervised the management of its estate, not an easy task in view of the financial difficulties which his father had left behind. He matured early into a strict, conscientious aristocrat of the type of the eighteenth century.

The choice of friends and acquaintances manifested the essential conservatism of Marwitz's nature. In 1805 he confessed to his sister-in-law that "from my youth upward and even in childhood I have always sought the company of older and more intelligent persons; in the army I formed about me a circle of these and always chose as close acquaintances only the so-called best society. Even in general social life I never bothered about

[2] *Ibid.*, I, 28.
[3] *Ibid.*, p. 36.

most people, only seeking the small group in the larger, which otherwise often was not to be found."[4] Although he set high standards, he never thought of breaking with the aristocratic life of his time. He disliked the young rebels, the dreamers, the idealists, the wild and happy livers; he conformed and learned from those who had conformed.

In 1795 Marwitz, then eighteen years of age, fell in love with one known to us from his memoirs by the sole name of Irene. Irene emerges from the memory of her lover as a beautiful, soft, blushing, modest young lady, unusually well educated and remarkably self-effacing and considerate of others. The two loved each other devotedly until her death six years later. Marwitz never proposed marriage; his acute respect for propriety deterred him from taking a wife almost five years his senior. Irene influenced his life as no one else ever did. She encouraged him to study, to observe people, and to try to help others. During the years of their intimacy he grew to manhood. He read Klopstock, Herder, Kant, Goethe, Schiller especially, and other authors; he studied history, Latin, logic and, in addition to making long excerpts from his favorite writers, wrote essays for his own use. Through Irene he learned about the Enlightenment and the emerging Romanticism; but the effect of the reading upon him should not be overemphasized. The study of Herder did not prevent him from writing at the time, "One could call history a systematic arrangement of facts."[5] The imaginative Herder, who had difficulty in distinguishing real facts from unreal and who could never put either in "systematic" order, would have found this young student an exasperating factualist. From Kant Marwitz derived corroboration of his own inclinations.

> God created everything to some purpose [he wrote]. The fulfillment of this divine purpose is the destiny of man on the earth. The purpose of human existence consists in its daily task of being what practical understanding (*Vernunft*) demands of it. The design of this practical understanding commands that man obey God and fulfill his daily duties. Duties are general laws given by God to man.

[4] *Ibid.*, II, Pt. 2, 531.

[5] Walther Kayser, *Marwitz* (Hamburg, 1936), p. 29.

> What duty orders, as it speaks through the inner voice of conscience, is always the right thing, which must be done under all circumstances and before all other considerations. Whoever fulfills his duty toward himself deserves the title of wise. Whoever fulfills the duty toward those nearest to him should be called a friend of man.[6]

In accordance with these words Marwitz concluded that God had created the existing social order for a divine purpose, that French revolutionists and social radicals were opposing God. He felt assured that in performing his daily tasks he worked for God, whereas those who wanted to change these daily tasks did not. He derived the conviction that he must act as he did because God stood on his side and that, by so acting for the preservation of the *status quo,* with perhaps a few reforms, he deserved the title of a wise friend of man. He supplemented the justification of his way of life by an apology from Kant for severe restriction by law of the functions of the state. He wished thereby to take precaution against the possibility that either an autocrat or a revolutionary nationalist might try to extend authority over him by disrupting present society.

During this period, 1795 to 1801, Irene and Kant, love and the categorical imperative, struggled for control over Marwitz, and the outcome of the conflict proved to be of lasting effect. The manner of resolving it is evident in an essay which he wrote for his sisters upon the subject of the difference in function and character between man and woman. The young ladies had alarmed their brother by reading Jacobin literature, and he wished to impress upon them their place. The course of his banal argument need not be reproduced. Interspersed in it, however, were a few characteristic and significant remarks:

> The male must strive forwards, using every force to reach his goal and recognizing no other commanding principle than the directing reason, the consciousness of "I must." . . . But should the delicate feeling [of woman] rule the world, how quickly it would be destroyed. . . . Therefore it is necessary that a rigorous righteousness rule and in public affairs that understanding and right triumph

[6] *Ibid.,* pp. 27-28.

over feeling. . . . The result can easily be perceived . . . that nature herself has wisely marked out for each sex the sphere of its activity and has wisely given each the gifts necessary to it.[7]

Marwitz actually practiced these ideals in life. He was a hard-headed, ruthless, persistent advocate or opponent. He permitted feeling to affect his conduct only after understanding and right had determined the course of "strict justice." He assumed that right and understanding stood on the side of the existing social order. God had divided the sexes according to the nature of their functions. God had also, Marwitz believed, divided society into castes according to function, and he would assist God in preserving them.

After the death of Irene, Marwitz began in the winter of 1801-2 to frequent the home of the von Brühl family in Berlin. The Brühls were noted for their strict observance of old social forms and their opposition to Jacobinism, possibly because Countess Brühl, a member of an English bourgeois family, wished to prove her devotion to aristocratic Prussianism. Many of the patriots of Prussia, including Queen Louise, Princess Marianne of Prussia, Marie von Kleist, Prince Louis Ferdinand, Prince Wilhelm of Prussia, the two Counts von Dohna, Scharnhorst, von Gneisenau, von Clausewitz and others, often gathered in the Brühl home. Marwitz liked the family, their etiquette, and especially one of the young daughters, and in June, 1802, after judicious consideration, he became engaged to Fanny Brühl, another shy, beautiful, young girl. (Marwitz's ideal of a woman is singularly monotonous.) In the next year they were married.

The obligations of married life caused Marwitz to retire from the army and to assume the direct management of the family estate. The experience brought new contacts and new duties which acquainted him with the ideals and practices of agricultural and even social reform. For a time he participated in the movement, from which emerged later the Stein-Hardenberg reforms, liberalism, and nationalism, but within a few years it

[7] *Ibid.*, p. 32.

became anathema to him. After a careful study of the proposals made by Arthur Young and Albrecht Thaer for improving agricultural methods, he introduced some of them on his estate, characteristically rejecting others as impractical. He sought to make his estate as productive and modern as possible, although he did not wish to encourage the growth of capitalism lest it disrupt the social order, as it threatened to do. He soon transformed his land into a model farm. Furthermore, he even felt the current winds of social reform and endeavored to execute privately some of the proposals. Foremost of these was the emancipation of his serfs, which by 1805 he thought that he could carry out. Since he intended to preserve control over the serfs, they perceived nothing but disadvantages to be derived from this kind of freedom and refused it. Marwitz had read Pestalozzi and approved of his ideas; hence, in spite of the vigorous opposition of the local pastor, he also established schools for the peasant children. He forbade the whipping of his serfs and the use of cruelty toward animals. According to his own words, he created on his estate "the harmony and mutual coöperation which, as in all affairs, is also necessary in this one if the intention is to be realized." [8] We do not know the peasants' side of the story. Marwitz enjoyed the activity of managing affairs himself and alone with Fanny lived one of the few happy years of his existence.

In March, 1804, Fanny von der Marwitz died within a few days after bearing a daughter. Her husband placed a stone on her grave with the inscription, "Here lies my happiness," and to an intimate relative he wrote:

> I stand alone in the world, only twenty-seven years old but with the look of an old man. I am as alone as a creature on God's great, wide earth can be. . . .
>
> After all this is destroyed and the home tie broken which should bind me to the good and intelligent, I cannot tell you how indescribably empty it has left me. . . . What is more depressing than constantly to create out of oneself alone? [9]

[8] *Ibid.*, p. 38.

[9] *Ibid.*, p. 40; see also Meusel, *op. cit.*, II, Pt. 1, 3-4; Pt. 2, 524-31.

The loss of his best friend, Count Schwerin, a short time before and the successive deaths of Irene and Fanny made Marwitz suspect henceforth that he brought misfortune to those whom he loved most. He tried in vain to fathom the purposes of God in so dealing with man and concluded:

> Often it takes thousands of years for the light of truth to show that we have not suffered for centuries in vain. What is one life span in comparison with this? What the sorrow of a few short years to the suffering through centuries of the people who must agonize for the sake of the great cause?
>
> The goal is often perceived only after thousands of years. In a short lifetime could the human goal, or better, the goal of the individual, likewise perfection, be reached and joy and reward follow immediately thereafter? The appearance of most things shows us that much is still lacking for perfection.[10]

With a conception of so gloomy and insecure an individual life, with so little confidence in the power of man, Marwitz could scarcely have become a nationalist. He lacked belief in man's ability to achieve the kingdom of heaven on earth in the immediate future, finding peasants stupid, burghers circumscribed, and aristocrats not what they should be. Back of all his future actions lay doubt, which made him averse to change.

To label Marwitz as a passive fatalist would be maligning him. His independent, strenuous nature compelled him to act in spite of his pessimism. In 1805 he rejoined the Prussian army, hoping that war would break out with France and that he could find an honorable death on the battlefield. "I must confess," he wrote his sister-in-law three years later, "that had I not had Fanny's memory and felt so keenly the burden of living without her, I would perhaps have remained at home." [11] The death of a loved one afforded Prussia and Germany a great patriot. Marwitz concentrated all his feelings upon the war with Napoleon; he longed for it as a release to his emotions. He could purge himself of his private despair by throwing himself into that of

[10] Meusel, *op. cit.*, II, Pt. 2, 525.

[11] *Ibid.*, II, Pt. 2, 547.

Prussia and Germany and into hatred of Napoleon and the French. Suffering formed a prelude to the period when Marwitz approached nationalism most nearly.

From the last months of 1805 until Prussia finally opened hostilities Marwitz eagerly advocated war with France. He wished Prussia to coöperate with Austria, Russia, and England in 1805 and believed confidently that such a coalition could crush Napoleon. After Austerlitz he still longed for Prussia to enter the war and wrote to his brother-in-law:

If outwitted or from a shameful spirit of compromise Prussia wavers, and if from fear or *raison d'état* she deserts the battlefield which her army has entered with so much patriotism, I shall lay down my sword and bury it in dung. Confound any scoundrel who draws it again; accursed be every spark of patriotism still alive in a German breast. The Franks and Slavs rule the world and the only solution the Germans can find for it is to crawl. Hence nothing is done just when everything was ready for the heroic deed, every heart, every breast ready for great things—and nothing but the usual do-nothingness follows! [12]

Marwitz believed that victory over Napoleon and salvation for the world depended entirely upon Prussia. When Frederick William III continued to cling to peace, as early as December, 1805, he proposed to force the king's hand by the united action of all castes led by the officers. If Prussia, he thought, would take the initiative in war, even after Austria had made peace, Austria, Russia, England, and many of the lesser German states would combine against the French. Since a divided Germany only permitted Napoleon's success, Prussia must do so for her own preservation, as must Austria and the German states.

. . . that there is any other advantage than a German one in Germany is the main source of misfortune which has struck Prussia. Since Bonaparte's power began to be so frightful each has sought its own advantage, not only Prussia, Hanover, Austria, or Bavaria, but even Nassau, Hesse-Darmstadt, Schwarzburg-Rudolstadt. How could this interest exist in opposition to the will of the great tyrant, espe-

[12] Kayser, *op. cit.*, p. 54.

cially since Prussia has given up her erstwhile leading role. Now one hears everywhere, for example, in Mecklenburg-Strelitz, the complaint: "Alas, we have to suffer too! We are a neutral country (they even call themselves a Power). What does the war between France and Prussia matter to us?" As if any state in North Germany could stand or fall without Prussia. Oh, Germany, are these the descendants of Barbarossa? We Prussians have brought this ignominy to Germany! [13]

Marwitz recognized the source of Germany's weakness and proposed to change her boundary lines in order to strengthen her defensive power. The initial step lay in enlarging Prussia, an objective which the Hohenzollerns had pursued for centuries. Prussia should establish a North German empire, including Holland, in order to defend Germany against France. Archduke Charles of Austria must retreat into Hungary, refuse to accept the treaty with Napoleon which his brother had made and continue to fight. Czar Alexander must help him save Europe and humanity. When the king of Prussia persisted in remaining neutral, Marwitz blamed his "treacherous" advisers.

It is a pleasure [he wrote] in the midst of these horrible events to observe the spirit of the [Prussian] nation. Not only the army and the better part of the respectable people feel the humiliation, but the entire opinion of the upper burgher class, which once was completely pro-French, and the lower classes, which unconditionally and shortsightedly naturally want peace, is changed. Their indignation arouses patriotism. Nothing like it has yet been seen in Prussia. If only Frederick the Great still lived! [14]

Marwitz wished the patriotism of the Prussian people to be aroused to the flaming point. The king should use every means which was offered him and should lead, not fear, his people. "Empires rise and endure, not through their size or because of their boundaries," Marwitz wrote, "but because of the spirit of the people and the strength of the government." Prussia would fall, not because of lack of material, "but only because the hand

[13] *Ibid.*, p. 81.
[14] *Ibid.*, p. 85.

of the artist is lacking to synthesize the materials."[15] Marwitz realized that Prussia suffered from historic defects and he wished to overcome them.

The Prussian state up to now has held up [he wrote], not by reason of its internal strength, not because of its population, not through the communal feeling of the nation, not through inexhaustible resources, but by means of order in its domestic administration and through its army. The former has made possible the support of the latter. The latter has founded, strengthened, increased and protected the state. This state is merely a work of art; if all or even one of its foundations crumble, the whole building will fall. As soon as the bureaucracy says, "I cannot maintain the army any longer (or even "at this moment," since the moment could be a decisive one) in a position to march against the enemy and to sustain itself there," as soon as even once and for one instant the generals or a war council declares, "our war strength is not equal to that of the enemy; it is best for us to surrender," then all is over with the state—it stands as a rotten bulwark, victim of every wind, which will not delay in coming. There is nothing more easily noticed by an opponent than the suggestion or proof of any weakness, however hidden, and to fall upon the insecure is a pleasure for all opponents and envious men. What is then to be done when such a dishonorable opinion is expressed by the two officials who are supposed to be the support of the state? To save by extraordinary means the state extraordinarily brought together! The usual means will not suffice. Away with the civil servants who have made the price of food high by mistaken legislation. Off with the head of the general who shall say a word about the powerlessness of the army which after ten years of peace and maneuvers is to leave its garrison for the first time. Let unlimited power be given—no restrictions—command to feed the army off the enemy's land—whoever hesitates, to be executed before the front. Then talent will awake and the energy of despair will return to the weakened state its lost strength.[16]

That was to Marwitz's taste—unlimited power, desperate onslaught, popular dictatorship. Then an aristocrat could accomplish something, then he could destroy Napoleon! Prussia should

[15] *Ibid.*, p. 86.
[16] Cited by Kayser, *op. cit.*, p. 81.

be united in spirit, a devoted tool in the hands of her leader. But nowhere did Marwitz urge the transformation of society in order to create a nation. He relied essentially on the methods which Frederick the Great had employed. Leadership, for him, held the key to success. When the Holy Roman Emperor laid down his crown in August, 1806, Marwitz denounced this "complete overthrow of the constitution of our fatherland and its laws." [17] He was ashamed of the princes who formed the Confederation of the Rhine and still further broke up the old Empire. In the emergency he proposed desperate remedies.

> Since Francis II has resigned the Imperial crown, there is an interregnum and consequently, so long as he [the Elector of Saxony] is Imperial administrator through the power given him by the Golden Bull, he should declare immediately a new election; but temporarily and until this can happen, because of the divisions of the Empire, he should ban the revolting princes who want to separate from the Empire, and should give over to the Elector of Brandenburg the execution of this sentence against them. At the same time let him announce it as his Imperial will that the continued stay of the French army in Germany is no longer to be endured. He should give it fourteen days' time to get out of Germany. But after this time every Frenchman in Germany is to be looked upon as outlawed and to be shot down by anyone without punishment. At the same time let him call on all the guarantors of the Peace of Westphalia to help him carry out these decisions.[18]

In the summer Marwitz endeavored to persuade the provincial estates to petition the king for war. The king was to be thanked for preserving peace, but reminded that the mere preservation of peace was not "the highest good for a nation." [19] The aristocrats to whom Marwitz showed the petition disapproved of it. He was disgusted with them. Just before Prussia at last declared war on France, he said that only a miracle could save the sunken state, and the outcome of the Battle of Jena confirmed his worst predictions. He advocated turning the cavalry under Blücher toward northwest Germany, where it would arouse a

[17] *Ibid.*, p. 89.
[18] *Ibid.*, pp. 89-90.
[19] Meusel, *op. cit.*, II, Pt. 1, 133.

popular war while Prussia restored her army, but his advice remained unheeded. When a remnant of the army with which he was associated under General Hohenlohe capitulated a few days later at Prenzlau, Marwitz knew that the Prussian state had collapsed. Shortly after his capture by the French, he was freed on his word of honor not to fight against them and he hurried into East Prussia to his king. Upon his exchange for a French prisoner a few months later he returned to active service.

During the tedious period of his captivity Marwitz tried to explain to himself and his colleagues the Prussian collapse and to plan the revival of Prussia and Germany and the defeat of Napoleon. All three problems were closely related, for the choice of means to assure success against the enemy depended upon the nature of the weaknesses in the Prussian state.

Marwitz blamed Prussia's defeat upon the moral decline of the people, the habit of peace, the failure to reform the army, and the incompetent leadership in the army and in the government. He condemned the egocentric action of the Prussians and the Germans in the face of the French: each person had sought his own welfare and the lack of feeling of responsibility toward others and toward the state and its ruler had enabled Napoleon to conquer. The king had weakened, not to say benumbed, the warlike vigor of the nation by his determined policy of neutrality; when he did go to war, he found his people thinking only of peace. He had not kept the army in shape; he had neglected to learn from Napoleon how to wage war; he had not eliminated inefficient officers and he had permitted a division of military leadership. The army, like the nation, had succumbed to the curse of egoism and aversion to responsibility. The officers lacked personal contact with the privates and failed to act as true leaders. The strategy employed at Jena and afterward had been completely mistaken owing to the fact that the advice of Colonel Massenbach, "a theoretical fool," had been accepted rather than that of able officers. (Years later after Marwitz had read the conservative critics like Adam Müller, he added other explanations of a philosophic nature. I give the reasons which he used at the time.)

It is characteristic of conservatives to attribute failure primarily to incompetent leadership. In this manner they preserve their confidence that victory can be achieved by the change of a few persons rather than by transformation of the entire system. They prefer a personal explanation rather than a social one. The problem is kept simple, as is suited to the conservative type of mind, and the threat to the superior position of their caste or group is eliminated. The conservatives also make the charge of moral decline, but they take care not to condemn everyone or to accuse society too strongly. Otherwise, institutional reforms may appear necessary. They hold in reserve a number of leaders untouched by moral failings and competent, they assert, to guide the people (who, alas, err easily), and to save the situation. The gravity of the menace to Prussia and Germany forced Marwitz to advance other explanations which a conservative would otherwise not have given; but in the main he adhered to the conservative pattern. The proposals which he offered for saving Prussia and Germany reflected the limits to his thinking.

> At the head there should be a leader who understands war [Marwitz wrote, repeating the proposal which he had made prior to the Battle of Jena], is young and active, and who knows how to inspire this rabble with a scorn for death and a passion for the cause of the fatherland, which makes of every individual a hero. In this hour, when everyone sees his destruction before his very eyes, this is by no means difficult if one only wants it enough.[20]

He was describing the ideal of himself. Although he never reached for a position so exalted, he felt that he embodied the qualities necessary for filling it. But Marwitz also knew that the leader must have a worthy following and to that end he advocated measures of reform.

The state, Marwitz wrote, existed in the hearts of its true subjects and every subject in months like these should follow the king and leave to the enemy only empty houses. It was still thought, he said, that the state and the king were synonymous, that what the king commanded must be done, that in return for

[20] Kayser, *op. cit.*, p. 114.

taxes the king must protect. The citizens thought that once they had paid their taxes nothing else could be demanded of them. Like the cobbler for making shoes and the tailor for making clothes, the soldier was paid for defending the fatherland. When there were no more soldiers, the defense must end.

But this view, Marwitz wrote, was a false one. These three parts, the state, the citizen, and the soldier, were interdependent. The soldierly caste was not a caste of itself in the state, at least, no as the educated, the handworkers, and others formed estates; rather, it should be the part of all citizens to belong, just as every soldier also belonged, to a caste. The soldier was merely the most self-sacrificing of citizens, and everyone must be obligated to be a soldier. Moreover, every province must maintain its soldiers, who should be regarded as brothers in arms. Where this principle was disregarded, the state swayed, falling at the first storm unless it was held up by the giant arm of a genius. The pressure of such an arm was, however, he thought, seldom other than tyranny and Europe now saw a horrible example of it.

Marwitz's conception of the relation of king and people was as follows: (a) the state consists of the united forces of its citizens (*Bürgher*). The king is the head and directs these forces, not for his own good but for the best interest of the whole. These forces are directed (b) against an outside foe, that is, they are to defend the state and are soldiers. These work on behalf of all their fellow citizens. They gain nothing for themselves by it. On the contrary, their life is constantly endangered. Such service cannot be remunerated. The soldier is of the first and best caste. As long as outside foes menace the state, this caste cannot cease to exist. It must continually be recruited. If the attack is warded off, the soldier can give way to others and carry on civil pursuits (c) for developing the commonwealth, citizens, craftsmen, and peasants. These contribute to the state, but work for their own advantage. While the soldier risks his life, they remain at home. . . . But his work cannot be of advantage to him when he no longer has security at home. Then security must be restored. Each citizen must become a soldier. (d) Only in this way does a state exist: by the union of all, that is, that the citizen becomes a soldier and the soldier a citizen (*Staatsbürgher*). But the king must be the first soldier and the first citizen of the state.[21] Of the king he said also: "The head and soul of the fatherland is the King and he is the rallying point in time of danger." [22] Thus in time of need every member of the nation was to oppose the enemy "morally and politically and, if possible, militarily, in every village and town." The nation was to be composed of historically self-conscious and self-reliant burghers united as in one big military camp.[23]

In spite of Prussia's defeat at the hands of Napoleon, Marwitz insisted that the tyrant could be overcome. First a military leader must be found, then an "East Prussian national militia" must be organized, the remnants of the army collected and guerilla warfare inaugurated. Napoleon must be lured deep into Russia and the way destroyed before him as he penetrated. Thereby Napoleon would find his communications cut and would not know the strength of the opposition to him in Germany or even in France.

> Then the time will have come [Marwitz wrote] to expand the war by light troops in the rear of the French into a regular insurrection of the folk and to call the entire German nation to arms. . . . For that the most important weapon perhaps is that used and mastered hitherto only by France, propaganda with pamphlets and newspapers. In a war of nation against nation public opinion is as decisive as military power. And that nation will be victor who knows how to mobilize most effectively its own spirit, that of neighboring nations and of the opposing nations for the achievement of its objective. This point is vastly more important than one commonly believes. For years the French have controlled all political writing and it is scarcely believable how great the power of the printed word is on the masses.[24]

[21] *Ibid.*, pp. 111-12.

[22] *Ibid.*, p. 117.

[23] *Ibid.*, p. 113. Strictly, *Staatsbürgher* should not be translated as "citizen," for the latter word carries a democratic meaning alien to Marwitz's intention.

[24] *Ibid.*, p. 116. This is a translation of Kayser's summary of the document which is not itself published. The pronounced nationalistic terminology arouses suspicion. It is not found in such extreme form in the direct quotations from Marwitz's own writings.

How was the war to be carried on? Marwitz believed that once regular troops were sent to Berlin, the oppressed Germans would rush by the thousands to the standard and England and Sweden would land troops on the northern coast. He wished to organize a regular propaganda service among the German people. He wanted to advance every officer (not privates or noncommissioned officers) according to ability, thereby benefiting himself and his friends as well as the fatherland. He thought that success or failure would be decided by the personality of the leader, and he proposed to provide the latter with dictatorial power of appointment and command, of life and death. Such measures, he thought, would once more restore the fatherland, enabling it to take its former place among the peoples of Europe.

Marwitz tried in vain to interest the king in the plan. He then turned to Prince William and urged him to restore the kingdom to the ruler even against the latter's will. But Prince William hesitated and finally did nothing.

In the meantime Marwitz endeavored to initiate action by organizing, with the king's permission, a volunteer corps. He knew that the townsmen and the better classes disliked military service because of the humiliating treatment which soldiers received at the hands of the officers. A volunteer group, he thought, would afford an honorable medium for their patriotic activity and even aristocrats would enroll. He succeeded in organizing the corps, appointed his own officers, took in a large number of footloose peasants as soldiers, and was ready for service. The chief action which he saw, however, consisted in quarrels with Blücher, for the latter disliked a volunteer body and wanted the troops himself. Marwitz handled his corps admirably and won the affection of his men, but he had to report the desertion of soldiers.

In July, 1807, the king signed the Peace of Tilsit. Marwitz's dreams collapsed. In September he resigned from the army and said farewell to his soldiers. "We assembled in the happy hope," he told his men, "of participating in the emancipation of the fatherland. . . . The conflict has been ended without our aid and Europe lies at the feet of the conqueror. . . . If God has determined that our common German fatherland should some day be torn from the power of the enemy and from lamentable servitude, His invisible might will lead us together again in better, freer times."[25] With this last declaration of devotion to the "common German fatherland," Marwitz departed for home. He had done his best. The first period of his patriotic activity was concluded.

In estimating the quality of Marwitz's feeling for the nation during the years before Tilsit, one must first answer the question why he hated Napoleon and the French so intensely. A clue may be found in the most complimentary adjective which he could use in describing a person, the word "proud," a genuine aristocratic expression.[26] Since the French had defeated Prussia, they had humiliated Marwitz, the Prussian aristocrat and officer. Since they had captured his ancestral home and then himself, they had cast shame in double measure upon him. How could he be proud without independence? His honor was violated with that of Prussia and Germany. Furthermore, wherever the French conquered, they did not respect the traditional order; they destroyed old customs, rights, and institutions, toppled over monarchs, states, and constitutions, and menaced the aristocracy. When aroused, Marwitz's passionate temperament led him to extremes and, as his happiness seemed buried with his wife, he concentrated his bitterness upon the victorious French. Economic motives seem to have been absent.

Between 1795 and the outbreak of the war against Napoleon in 1806 Marwitz read much of the literature which nourished German nationalism. After 1801 he attended the military school

[25] *Ibid.*, pp. 152-53.

[26] Marwitz's pride was in no sense mere egotism. It came from the deep feeling of self-respect of a member of an old and prominent aristocratic family and of a high-spirited individual. It was not offensive to others; it was backed by accomplishment and ability. The following may be given as an example: "There exists a certain inner feeling of one's own worth of which no one should let himself be robbed who wants to keep his joy, power and courage in fulfilling his profession. Whoever loses this self-respect, upon which honor rests, will only with difficulty find it again. I live only in it and through it and therefore cannot serve behind such a network of underlings without morally destroying myself and my whole ability." This he said when in December, 1815, he sought to resign because he was passed by in promotions. He was subsequently promoted and served until 1827 (*ibid.*, p. 304).

directed by Scharnhorst and associated closely with figures who later became ardent leaders of nationalistic reform. About the time of his first marriage (1803) he declared that a person's achievement depended solely "upon his heart and upon his will to do good." [27] Had he lived by this assertion, he would have wished to break down caste privilege and in his devotion to the heart would have been able to align with the nationalists.

Before most of the nationalistic reformers realized the gravity of the Napoleonic menace, the emotional state induced by the death of his wife enhanced in Marwitz a sensitivity to the international situation and to the danger threatening Prussia and Germany. Marwitz appreciated that all German states shared a common lot, that only the union of all Germans could defeat Napoleon. In addition, his deep sense of humiliation turned him to Germany as a whole for salvation, making him wish to arouse all Germans, to unite them in spirit, to arm them, in order to restore his own honor and that of Prussia and Germany. Better destruction than the loss of self-respect, he argued. He interpreted the conflict as one between French, German, and Slav. The vast scale of the wars made him nation-conscious. In view of the nature of Marwitz's reading and associations and of the intensity of his feelings about the humiliation of Prussia and Germany, one wonders, not at the concessions which he made to the new social ideals, but at their meagerness.

The fact that Marwitz felt as a German, instead of merely as a Prussian, by no means proves that he had become a German nationalist. At no time did he advocate the abolition of the existing social order in favor of a society organized solely for the national good. The reforms which he proposed—peasant emancipation, establishment of popular elementary schools, universal military service, promotion of officers in the army according to merit—did not entail, so he thought, a thorough transformation of the institutional framework of the state. The peasants should continue to serve the aristocrats, the elementary schools should train them for practical work on the landed estates, universal

[27] *Ibid.*, p. 38.

military service should last only during the crisis, the officers of the army should continue to be drawn from among the aristocrats. The reforms and the revival of Prussia and Germany should be accomplished with the coöperation of the estates, that is, under the direction of the king and the aristocracy. Marwitz lacked the type of mind and the interests, material or otherwise, for appreciating the ideals which moved the nationalists to reform. Factual, rational, careful, measured in his assertions except when defending the existing order, more inclined to preserve the old than to create anew, he was wanting in the vigorous imagination of a nationalist. He neither admired nor respected mankind enough to have confidence in the effectiveness of quick institutional reform. He did not believe in the responsibility of society for man's stupidity or wickedness. The Marwitz family, having lived in Prussia and having served the Hohenzollerns for centuries, did not need to improve its social position; it was satisfied with the constitution of society. It served Prussia first and searched for the active, enthusiastic aid of the masses in Germany only when the Marwitzes and the caste-state of Prussia were endangered. The Marwitzes looked toward the past for their ideals, while their interests lay with the present order, which they expected to preserve for the future. Although Marwitz wished to force the king to war, he never dreamed of nationalistic republicanism. Since he could not love the cautious, cold Frederick William III, he gave his devotion to the fatherland, Prussia or Germany; but he remained a staunch monarchist and a loyal member of the caste-state. The fact that his mother was descended from the French and that his wife was half English may have helped to prevent him from becoming too exclusively German. His national feeling acted as a preservative of the nation as then organized. Such national feeling as he possessed demanded the defense of aristocratic privilege in a caste-state. An aristocrat without independence, he thought, would no longer be an aristocrat; but he wished independence in Prussia to be kept within the strict limits of caste. Marwitz's pride compelled him to desire the preservation of the institutional basis for his pride and the German people should help him to do so. One cannot call this nationalism. At most it was a feeling for the German nation provoked by a crisis; but it did not go so far as nationalism.

When in October, 1807, Marwitz returned to his home not far from Berlin, he found his house burned, his land pillaged by the French, and French troops quartered there. He had to play host to the hated guests for over a year. During this time he married again and settled down to rural occupations. Hardships did not deter him, and within two years he had restored his estate so efficiently that even Thaer, the agricultural reformer, praised it. Nonetheless, his material existence continued to be precarious. Although his brother joined the Austrian army, he refused to believe that an insurrection against the French could succeed: the German people remained too disunited. He did not become excitedly patriotic again until the French disaster in Russia in 1812.

During the period before 1807 Marwitz had read and associated with persons sympathetic with the new social ideals of liberty and love of nation. Service in the army had afforded him a milieu favorable to national feeling and to a desire for the reforms necessary for victory. After he returned home, he allowed this interest to give way to a concern with the management of his business affairs; his contacts with staunchly conservative aristocratic neighbors and the influence of his outspoken, strong-tempered, conservative wife helped to turn back the clock. He had been far too occupied heretofore to think about the ultimate effects of his own reform proposals or those of others. Stein, Hardenberg, and Gneisenau had seemed to him admirable characters and bulwarks of the state. Now, face to face with the question of how to achieve patriotic ideals, he began to study the social implications of nationalistic reforms. To clarify his thinking he read among others works by Montesquieu, Hertzberg, Luden, Burke, Fichte, and Adam Müller. Of them all Müller exerted the greatest influence upon him, both by way of his writings and through personal intercourse. From these authors, heterogeneous as they were, he took the ideas which suited his own inclinations and interests. He quickly concluded that far from emancipating the Prussian and German fatherlands (he referred to them both as his fatherland) from Napoleon, the Stein-Hardenberg reforms would ruin him and society. The social ideal which he arrived at has frequently been called that of conservatism rather than nationalism. If all Prussians and Germans had acted as Marwitz did during these crucial years, Prussia and Germany would not have cast off the French domination. It required nationalistic enthusiasm to keep up one's hope, and since he lacked the one, he lacked the other.

The criticism which Marwitz offered to the Stein-Hardenberg reforms and his own counterproposals must be examined briefly in order to clarify the distinction between the two sets of ideals. Marwitz maintained that by their reforms Stein and Hardenberg were destroying the spirit of unity and patriotism in Prussia. He accused them of borrowing their proposals for reform from the French and imposing them upon the Prussians, to whom they were unsuited. He recognized that elements of liberalism had penetrated into Prussia and that moral disintegration had already begun before Jena and the reforms. Greed had induced even the aristocrats to sell their estates, break the personal bonds uniting them with their peasants, and speculate, just as it had led the burghers to object to guild restrictions and the separation of economic functions between town and country. When he discovered that the aristocrats lacked courage in fighting the social reforms pushed by the government, he bitterly and sadly complained that even his own caste had lost its former independent spirit. Prussia was morally destroyed, he wrote, not merely by the Napoleonic victory but by the "complete dissolution of all internal bonds." [28] In fighting the reforms of Stein and Hardenberg Marwitz believed that he was defending Prussian morality and unity against the domestic enemy, as in 1806 he had fought the foreign enemy. He considered that only he and his friends understood and practiced patriotism.

Although Marwitz frequently referred to Prussia as a nation, he acknowledged that at present she was not one. She was "a patchwork of many provinces, varied in laws and habits," he wrote, not a nation with her own language, customs, and laws.

[28] Meusel, *op. cit.*, II, Pt. 1, 314.

In fact, he continued, "she can never become a nation like the one delineated above because each province has alongside it foreign provinces, to which it feels fundamentally more akin than to the distant and unfamiliar provinces in the Prussian state. . . ." [29] Marwitz distinguished between the new nationalism and his own national feeling. The new type he considered to have been borrowed from France and to demand the leveling of everyone and everything within the state. It stressed equality and used liberty for the sake of securing equality. It wished to make everything alike, to rob it of its peculiarities, to transform "a living body into a dead mass." [30] Adam Müller wrote him in February, 1811:

> You will already have heard of the warnings of the president over yesterday's explanations by the chancellor. The debt situation of the country is exposed, but after tomorrow there are to be no more provincial boundaries, because there is to be only one nation. The way in which quite different parts of the state are mixed up and kneaded together so that one does not know whether bread or cake will be the result shows the beauty of the new principles [of national feeling]. We do not understand the art of preserving the particularities of locality, of harmonizing them to make a living whole.
>
> The idiot of a legislator in today's *Vossische Zeitung* appeals to the divine law or to nature, although the great creative art of nature consists in guarding the differences of the individual species to produce a whole.
>
> This nationality which has been given us is called up by the cudgel of necessity, by the anxiety and worry of the weak-minded. They want the deputies done away with: there are no provinces, no counties, so no deputies! Consequently departments, new geography —*Departement de la Spree, de l'Oder,* etc. He is an idiot, who calls that concoction the future Prussia. . . .[31]

Marwitz agreed in every detail with the distinction made by Müller. He hated the French idea and practice of nationalism and opposed to it his own ideal, or rather that which he thought

[29] *Ibid.,* II, Pt. 1, 323.
[30] *Loc. cit.*
[31] *Ibid.,* II, Pt. 1, 265-66.

had united the country under Frederick the Great. He expressed his views in remarks which he made in 1811 on a speech by Hardenberg:

> To every province the idea of Prussia means something higher. Such an idea is perhaps the strongest bond which can hold a state together; the Prussian state has proved it, the Austrian proves it today. It would long since have fallen if it had tried to shape Bohemia, Austria, Hungary, and Croatia to a pattern and to eradicate the peculiarities of each. But to preserve these and with them the whole there must be a government which understands more than how to formulate a scheme on paper in order comfortably to cut up and destroy provinces and subjects.[32]

The analogy between Prussia and Austria rested on false premises. Except in her few Polish subjects Prussia did not confront the nationality problem which Austria had. Marwitz foresaw the disruptive effect of the new ideal of nationalism upon Austria; he had no right to apply the same standard to Prussia. The German nationalists would have endorsed his admonition to serve the ideal Prussia—they would have said Germany—but the harmony of views would have ceased there. The nationalists wished to reorganize society and its structure in order to enable, persuade, or force everyone to become nation-conscious and serve the Prusso-German ideal. They would have broken old loyalties in order to clear the way for complete loyalty to the nation. Marwitz manifested more alarm over Prussia than over Germany, and Prussia meant to him essentially the old Prussia. He did not want to make her over; he wanted to preserve or restore her. With his literal mind he conceived Prussia only as she was or had been. He thought of loyalty to an ideal as coming by way of loyalty to the parts of the object of one's ideal with which one had contact and in which one had interest. He was a pluralist. He wished the ideal to exist apart from the separate items composing the material form of it; but, because he connected the ideal so intimately with the individual's interests, he offered no way for one's perceiving the ideal as a whole. Hence he could not

[32] *Ibid.*, II, Pt. 1, 323-24.

realize the ideal or appreciate it fully because he had no means of doing so. He did not care to arouse everyone to the ideal Prussia; he thought of the few upper classes.

Let one not forget [he wrote] that the will of the nation cannot be determined by the majority of heads and opinions; let one remember that the nation consists of those individuals who are able to think the idea of fatherland and are capable of enthusiasm for it, that all those who are not capable of it are nothing but an inert mass necessary for use for the state and for the idea, that therefore the will of the nation is to be recognized in very few individuals and that these can be discovered in a short time in the different estates if one permits them to share in the functions and the needs of the state. The inert mass will separate itself immediately from the others; the living, the true *Staatsbürgher,* will remain.[33]

The most significant point of Marwitz's statement lies in his unconcern with the inert mass and his restriction of the nation to the few. No nationalist would have tolerated the division between the inert and the alive: he would have striven to arouse the lifeless at any cost, for since each possessed German blood, spoke the German language, belonged to the German culture, he ranked among the hallowed and must be saved. Marwitz lacked any respect for these animals and was indifferent as to whether they ever became nationalists or Prussianists. The nationalists loved all Germans as brothers, Marwitz only the select.

Marwitz lamented the want of public spirit in the population of Prussia and blamed it upon the failure of the Prussian state to permit any public life among its subjects. So far his language sounded like that of a nationalist. How did he propose to preserve or revive public spirit? Again, part of his answer might have come from a nationalist who had not quite clarified the meaning of the terms he used.

Patriotism [Marwitz maintained] could be aroused solely by conceding to every estate its own interest, that is, by allowing manifold interests to speak out in a state. . . . Through this activity alone can a true glimpse into the nature of the state be given and

[33] *Ibid.,* II, Pt. 1, 318-19.

only through it may its citizens be convinced that they are everything in this state of theirs, that without them it is nothing, that they must live and die for it and must sacrifice all they possess to it, because only in and through it do they possess anything. The salvation and revival of the state cannot lie in the tax system [he was fighting Hardenberg's proposal to tax the aristocrats] but it lies in maintaining the existing laws and putting life into the constitutional forms through which the state is revealed to its citizens and recognized by them.[34]

The first part of this statement resembles the ideology of enlightened selfishness—let each fight for his own interest, as he, Marwitz, was doing. He forgot or ignored the enormous advantage which the aristocracy enjoyed over the other castes or groups. He also neglected to describe how the struggle of each against each would develop idealism among the competitors with respect to the state. The nationalists concerned themselves primarily with this problem, taking the nation and not the state as the object of their endeavors. The second section of Marwitz's statement, that about the complete dependence of individual welfare or even existence upon the state, would, if referred to the nation, have satisfied the most ardent nationalist. The ultimate that a nationalist wished was to have the individual recognize that apart from the nation he was nothing. The third section of Marwitz's assertion discloses the pure conservative who defends the existing legal and constitutional forms and, if these have been permitted to decay, demands that they be brought back to vigor. The present and the past, not the future, interested him and furnished him with an ideal; he must preserve or restore, not create a new model, nationalistic society.

The contract theory served many purposes in the eighteenth and nineteenth centuries. Marwitz used it to justify aristocratic privilege. He maintained that the existing castes looked back upon a past as long as that of the monarchy, that they had a divine right to defend themselves, that between the castes and the ruler contracts had been made which could not be abrogated or modified without the consent of both parties. In this manner

[34] *Ibid.*, II, Pt. 1, 315.

he endeavored to assure to the aristocracy its social and legal position. He even went so far as to declare that the king had signed a contract with each province and that each change made by the government in the constitution must be approved by each province. The practice of this theory would have broken up the state. It implied a reversion to the conditions in Prussia before the Great Elector and his successors compelled scattered and rebellious provinces into something like a state. A more anti-nationalistic view can scarcely be imagined. Marwitz warned that a constitution could not be appreciably modified without breaking all the bonds holding society together. One change would encourage another, he said, until a constant state of revolution would ensue. Nothing would be sacred; each person would strive only for his own interest; society would degenerate into anarchy.

> In these matters [he wrote] nothing can be discovered, nothing done and nothing created from the beginning. An old state like the Brandenburg-Prussian one, which grew of its own accord and was not founded on ruins through the caprice of a conqueror is not possible without a constitution; likewise it needs representation and such exists here. If this representation lies in shadow and is not recognized, it can be brought to light, be revived and something better attached to it; but it cannot be made.[35]

Marwitz maintained that only two estates existed, the landowning aristocracy and the business middle class. These two represented all the rest of the population; because they alone possessed knowledge about soil and industry, they alone could assist in the governance of the state. He jeered at the practice of deciding by counting noses and reserved the political rights, as he did the social privileges, to the few, to "the nation." The provincial estates must be kept or, wherever lacking, be restored and their power extended. In addition, a central representative assembly must be created. To all these assemblies only the two estates were to send delegates. Although Marwitz in general restricted the assemblies to advisory functions and studiously neglected to define these functions precisely, he included among the powers

[35] *Ibid.*, II, Pt. 1, 316.

the right to veto tax legislation, constitutional changes, or any other important measure disturbing the *status quo*. When Hardenberg took over the supreme control and direction of the administration in 1810, Marwitz approved so long as Hardenberg kept in agreement with the estates. When he did not, Marwitz, while preaching the necessity of unity against the French, waged a private civil war against him and the government. For Marwitz aristocratic interests in actuality took precedence over state or national interests. Marwitz declared that he approved necessary reforms, but he did not describe them at this time. Most of his thought and energy was devoted to criticizing and opposing the reforms which the government adopted. He protested violently that destruction of the lords' police and financial power and the emancipation of the peasant from the control of his lord had loosed the bonds between lord and peasant. He denounced as bitterly the abolition of restrictions on the sale of land and of distinctions between town and country. Censuring such freedom as vicious in its effects, he prophesied that the substitution of the jurisdiction of state officials for that of the lord over the peasant would destroy all patriotism and lead ultimately to the disruption of the state. He could not conceive that a peasant might comprehend the nature of the state; rather, regarding the state as a tax collector and source of interference, he might come to hate it. Marwitz stopped far short of the nationalists' vision of the free peasant as an active, patriotic citizen. In his praise of former relations between peasant, lord, and state, Marwitz overlooked the fact that Prussia had fallen partly because of indifference on the part of her subjects to the common welfare. In opposing the Stein-Hardenberg reforms he ignored the additional fact that reforms of this kind had inspired the French nation to fight first for its defense and then for the expansion of its power over Europe.

When Hardenberg proposed to diminish the tax burden on the peasants and to tax the aristocrats, Marwitz tried so hard to arouse widespread resistance that in 1811 the government imprisoned him for several weeks. He maintained that no one objected to the present system of taxation (probably true in view of the control which the aristocrats kept upon the peasants), that the introduction of a new system in a time of crisis would ruin public finances; and he expressed his willingness (his colleagues did not share his generosity) to accept heavy temporary taxes provided they were abolished after the crisis had passed. If any changes must be introduced, he said, let them apply solely to the aristocracy and the ownership of land. He formulated a program, which need not detain us here, for strengthening the aristocracy and its control of the soil.[36] At the same time he proposed the thesis that the preservation of an aristocracy (he called it the middle class) was necessary for the preservation of the monarchy and that the decline of the aristocracy entailed revolution and the decline of civilization. He tried to close every loophole to liberalism and nationalism. At the utmost Marwitz was willing to apply some of the social ideals of the nationalists to the aristocratic landowners and the upper class of burghers. He would give to them alone those duties and rights which the nationalists wished for the whole body of citizenry. In so far as he approached the ideals of nationalism, he did so for the defense of the interests of his caste and himself. He fought the government because its nationalistic reforms menaced or, rather, would destroy the caste-state. He defended the old order of privilege, which he idealized in order better to protect it, against the new order of nationalism, to which he denied all idealism. This was a social conflict between two ideals resting on different premises.

Like an efficient soldier, Marwitz practiced the proverb that attack is the best defense, and as the battle between him and the nationalistic group became fiercer, his prediction of doom grew more positive. He wrote in 1810:

[36] Marwitz wrote: "Kind cannot separate from kind. Many more characteristics of the father descend to the son than the new pseudo philosophers and sophists allow to be the case. In agreement with the law of nature the root of the aristocrat is maintenance of the family. The striving for learning and talent is for individual glory without consideration for the family. The former live in time, the latter only for the moment" (Kayser, *op. cit.*, pp. 187-88). He also wrote: "Agriculture is an office and a duty for the people of the land; it is laid upon them by God through the caste in which He causes them to be born; they cannot give it up, even when they carry it on at an apparent loss" (*ibid.*, p. 197).

> The scribblers, blinded by the false light of philosophy, and the young people, trained in their school, are trying to stamp out everything which formerly made up the intermediate group between prince and people. They heap upon this caste all blame and all the sins of these hard times. But experience will hardly teach us that parvenus, who have neither an honorable name to uphold nor hereditary and landed property which binds them to the fate of the state, will be more loyal and more enduring in suffering with this state than those whose rights are to be destroyed.[37]

Among the scribblers were to be found the nationalists and many of the reformers. Marwitz hated the lot of them and denied them every virtue. In 1812 he condemned the entire achievements of Stein and Hardenberg. Stein had started a social revolution, he said, and Hardenberg continued it. He accused the latter of hypocrisy, lies, despotism, of destroying by his acts the last remnants of public spirit. Hardenberg was proposing, Marwitz avowed, to regenerate the people by encouraging them in the craving for riches which had brought about their downfall and that of the country. Marwitz prophesied that as a result of Hardenberg's grievous mistakes the king would lose his throne, Hardenberg's own plans would fail, entailing the complete ruin of the country. "And so he [Hardenberg] is like all regenerators of our time, each in his own way a true copy of the great regenerator [Napoleon], whom in their hearts they all worship. They feign creation and only know how to destroy." [38]

The years since 1807 had gone hard with Marwitz. In private life he had experienced happiness and tragedy. He had failed to find in his second wife, with whom he shared too many traits, a congenial companion. In 1810 she had borne him a son, but while he was in prison in 1811 both the son and a young daughter had died. Marwitz felt convinced that fate was pursuing him. The failure of his colleagues to assist him in opposing the government revealed to him the egoism and materialism of the caste which he idealized. His own financial position continued to be

[37] Meusel, *op. cit.*, II, Pt. 1, 178.
[38] *Ibid.*, II, Pt. 2, 33.

unfavorable, not to say precarious. He felt so discouraged that he wrote:

> You can not believe how indifferent I am to everything since the illusion of freedom, honor, and country has disappeared and I seem only destined to live on. I am beginning to believe in predestination, else why, if I was not predestined to vegetate further, did death spare me when it was so near under hostile bullets or staring me in the face from the abyss of the Baltic Sea? Yes, to vegetate, since fate has cut me off from every greater task in the world or in the Empire of freedom almost as fast as I had undertaken it.[39]

Marwitz wrote a few months too soon. Napoleon marched to Moscow and lost an army. Early in the next year Prussia entered the war. Marwitz found existence more satisfying as soon as he could be active, and, as he honestly tried to realize his ideal of an aristocrat, he reëntered the Prussian army. By way of manifesting disfavor the king did not assign him to the regular army but put him in charge of organizing the militia in his home area. When Marwitz executed his duties admirably, he quickly received orders to take charge of the militia of all Prussia. The excitement of engaging in several small battles evoked from him a cry of pleasure, "It is a hard but a good time!"[40] To arm the peasants, to command them, to defend home and fatherland seemed to him the fulfillment of his dream of the nation in arms —a nation organized according to caste. The initiative taken by General Yorck (1813) in preserving the neutrality of the Prussian troops in East Prussia and not joining the French as treaty demanded, the measures for defense started by the East Prussian estates in the same year, thrilled his soul; at last the aristocracy was active. When the king delayed, Marwitz vigorously approved of forcing the "fool" into war and threw himself into the work of preparing the *Landsturm*.

> The *Landsturm* [he wrote] is a necessary measure and must not be neglected. It is so important that, in a case where victory

[39] Kayser, *op. cit.*, p. 231.
[40] *Ibid.*, p. 271.

might be given our enemies, the salvation of the country depends on it alone—and without fail must come from it.

If the enemy nowhere finds any support, housing, care for the sick or transport for its needs, but is attacked from all sides as soon as it appears, it cannot stay in a country but must evacuate.

It is, however, not enough that these [the men of the *Landsturm*] should hasten together leaving children and the old at home with their herds—so that, as a current expression has it, "business may not be disturbed"—but it is especially important that in such an extreme case the economy be completely destroyed. It is the continuation of daily life which gives the enemy sustenance and attracts our defenders, the members of the *Landsturm,* from us toward their homes, that is, over to the enemy.

The source of our success lies in having, as soon as the moment approaches when the enemy is to invade our country, all the villages and towns completely evacuated, the women, children, old people, and herds driven away.[41]

In advocating the *Landsturm* the conservative patriot of the caste-society joined hands with the most fiery nationalist. Both sought to rouse and arm the entire folk, both craved victory at any cost, both saw this as a moral war demanding the employment of every force. When advancing to action they met on common ground. Marwitz read at this time some of the nationalistic literature and undoubtedly felt the impact of it. During the crisis he even borrowed from the nationalists the practice of giving to the war a universal significance: Germany stood for certain ideals, France for others. The peculiar nature of the combination which he made is disclosed in a memorandum which he wrote in November, 1813. The memorandum manifestly borrowed from the writings of Arndt, but it nonetheless preserved the whole of Marwitz's conservative ideal.

The present war [he wrote] is no struggle of princes for the holding or gaining of a piece of land; it is likewise not the war of Prussia or Russia or Austria against French hegemony; but it is the struggle of freedom against tyranny, of law and order against

[41] *Ibid.*, p. 264.

force and arbitrariness, of truth against deception, virtue against sin.[42]

He continued:

> The struggle is over the question whether in Germany and in all countries which wish to take Germany as their model it is to be held, as it has formerly been held in France, that a people can be happy by means of words when it is deceived by deeds; that man must always bow to the mightiest and accept silently whatever he does; that everything is allowed to the rich and powerful; that the greatness of a people or a person consists in the horrible and dreadful rather than in the steady exercise of right; that the state and the government are the same thing; that all which proceeds from the rulers must also be regarded as if it proceeded from the state. . . .[43]

Marwitz cut the nature of the war according to his own pattern. In his battle against the French and in his struggle with Stein, Hardenberg, and the other reformers, imitators of the French in Prussia, he was fighting for freedom against tyranny, for law and order against force and arbitrariness. In this Janus-headed struggle he placed truth and virtue on his side, lies and evil on that of his opponents. He showed that all those practices and ideals which were anathema to him had originated in France—royal absolutism at the expense of the aristocrats and other natives (he used the word *Landsleute,* not *Untertanen*), the exchange of rights for money and material advantages, the desire for gain and for power over others, "the denial of belief and religion, the clinging to the temporary and earthly, the acceptance of appearance for truth, words and deeds, the use of hypocrisy and lies when they bring advantage."[44] The list sounds familiar: it included those "evils" which he attributed as well to his enemies in Prussia. As Marwitz frequently complained, the battle had to be fought on two fronts, the one against the French, the other against the reformer-enemies within.

Germany represented to Marwitz deep attachment to an old

[42] *Ibid.*, p. 272.
[43] *Ibid.*, p. 274.
[44] *Ibid.*, p. 272.

constitution, a beloved emperor who did not encroach on the rights of his vassals but achieved strength through their aid, a nation of firm believers who would fight to the death for these beliefs, a people devoted to the role of law and justice and the preservation of rights, a people who despised materialistic gains at the expense of principles or beliefs, a nation which left others in peace. Belief, right, law, antimaterialism were the key words of embattled conservatism. Belief strengthened the arm to defend the rights as established in law and the denunciation of utilitarian interest freed the conscience. The German, the conservative (the one implies the other), was ready for action, that is, only for defensive action to preserve that which time had hallowed.

> If we consider in addition the geographical situation of Germany in the center of Europe and that Germany is the homeland of the greatest part of its [Europe's] inhabitants as well as the center of European learning and culture, and compare the powerlessness of the Italians, the enslavement of the Magyars and Poles, the extra-European character of the Russian Empire, the unimportance of the Danes, the isolated position of the Swedes, the English, and the Spaniards, we know immediately that if the evil principle widely spread in the heart of Europe from France is to be effectively opposed, it can only be so by Germany, the heart of Europe, the source of the opposing principle of law, truth, and virtue.[45]

The exalted nature of his thought scarcely suited his blunt style; he showed embarrassment at writing about Germany as the heart of Europe, Germany as the place where civilization must be saved. When he wrote of law, of rights, he felt more at ease; he was defending the caste-society, or as he said, "truth and virtue." The rest was useful to convince him and others that all nations must help save the "heart of Europe," where caste-society was threatened with ruin.

In the next paragraphs of his essay Marwitz declared Providence to be on the side of the German cause. Providence had placed on the Russian throne a prince of German blood with German conservative ideals and prepared to fight for Germany.

[45] *Ibid.*, p. 273.

Providence was inciting "the entire Prussian nation," even the king, to war; the Austrians, other Germans and their neighbors, were entering the conflict.

> In such form is . . . a principle of right and truth again mightily revived in Germany and has successfully begun the struggle with the French principle of evil, and as the evil came over us and was there and grew until it was so powerful that it almost consumed us, so, we hope, will the newly aroused principle of right grow and flourish ever more gloriously.[46]

In this war between spiritual principles, he said, one must conquer and destroy completely the other. He was confident of the outcome.

If one identifies the principles of truth, law, and justice with Germany, one must be able to distinguish Germans from other peoples. No one was to believe that he could become a Frenchman simply by crossing the Rhine or a German by returning. "There is an inner, essential, and unchangeable sign," Marwitz wrote. "Each carries his Germanism or his Frenchism about with him wherever he goes. It is language, which conditions and limits the ideas of man, which shapes for him all his concepts, which imposes upon him from youth all its characteristics and determines his entire way."[47] This Fichtean tone should not deceive one. Marwitz used language more to differentiate Germans from Frenchmen and to establish a boundary between them than to unite the Germans. He never attributed to the Germans a peculiar quality and power because of their language. Language was to Marwitz on the whole a means for conveying thought rather than a mystical creator. Marwitz also wrote: "In so far as we truly love freedom and right, no one of us must be allowed to be a servant." But "our German brothers" was in the main a rhetorical phrase. Marwitz would have liked to bring to them his conception of freedom and right; he did not contemplate adopting theirs. Whether they would all have welcomed it seems decidedly doubtful. Marwitz did not love these brothers, but

[46] *Ibid.*, p. 274.
[47] *Ibid.*, p. 275.

he wished to use them in order to oppose Napoleon. If brotherwise they had wished to share alike things other than the privilege of fighting Napoleon, Marwitz would quickly have damned them as French in their views. The fact that he employed a phrase or two from some nationalistic tract does not outweigh the effect of the blunt manner in which he handled these expressions.

The matter-of-fact, live-and-let-live nature of Marwitz's thinking during these exciting days characterized the program which he offered for making peace. No people, he said, should try to conquer another people; each people should act as it pleased within its boundaries without any interference from another; each people should be distinguished from all others by its language and no people should serve another. The negative quality of these demands conformed with Marwitz's conservatism. He indulged in no exalted expectation, in no extravagant description of the German folk or prophecy about the future of the German nation. In order to insure the permanence of peace he demanded:

> Let every province, every town of both countries [Germany and France] send their representatives to the place of assembly; let the kings appear with their ministers. After holding divine worship, let the peace be made known and solemnly sworn to, first by the kings and their advisers. Afterwards let the representatives of both nations swear to it in the same manner.[48]

Marwitz called the procedure one by which the nations would participate in the peacemaking. By nation, however, he meant the aristocracy and the upper class of the burghers, the leading groups in the caste-state. Even in peacemaking he still endeavored to assure the preservation of aristocratic society; for by associating representatives of the upper castes in this work he would diminish the authority of the domestic threat to their privileges, the absolute monarch and his ministers. One cannot term him a nationalist when he excluded most of the nation from participation in so vital a national matter. A nationalist would have denounced this haughty disregard for the vast body of his brothers. He would have argued that, while this aristocrat might

[48] *Ibid.*, p. 277.

be patriotic toward Prussia and Germany, his sense of superiority and the weakness of his fraternal feeling put him in the group of those whose military aid was acceptable but whose social ideals were offensive to nationalism.

As the War of Liberation drew to a close and the Congress of Vienna met to decide the fate of Europe, Marwitz longed to see Germany united. The sincerity of his wish cannot be doubted, but it should be recalled that the desire implied a mere shift in political frontiers without any social transformation. The difficulties lay in finding a plan for unifying the nation and in discovering leaders to execute it. Marwitz proposed several means. One called for the coöperation of Prussia and Austria but withheld details. According to another, Austria should leave the rest of Germany, at least North Germany, to Prussian control. Marwitz discovered to his surprise, however, that a large part of North Germany hated and feared Prussian control much more than it did that of the French. Since the Germans wished national unity, he suggested that the Prussian king win their favor by changing his title to "King of the Germans in Prussia, Brandenburg, and Saxony." Marwitz predicted confidently that within fifty years it would also include the Germans in Franconia, Swabia, the Rhineland, and elsewhere. One should not mistake this concern about German unity for nationalism; during these days Marwitz still referred to Prussia as a nation.

The treatment of Germany at the Congress of Vienna saddened and angered Marwitz. "This Germany is a genuine chaos," he wrote in 1814, and he contrasted the unity and high spirit of the French with the disunity of the Germans and their recession into egoism and materialism. "The war was a holy one for which the nation became enthusiastic. . . . The enthusiasm is gone and many who then pushed forward now long for rest." [49] Marwitz complained and advised to the end without any effect.

As years passed Marwitz grew more conservative and more bitter about the course of history. Whereas Napoleon had previously shared honors with the Prussian reformers, liberalism,

[49] *Ibid.*, pp. 286, 289.

democracy, and nationalism now received the full blast of Marwitz's attacks. He fought them in the ethical, economic, political, social, and administrative spheres and defended the ideals and practices of a patriarchal, caste-society. Hating absolutism almost as much, he strove to restore the conditions in society prior to the age of autocracy. In his struggle he employed the conservative, agrarian ideology formulated by Adam Müller and others and mustered theory in defense of a manner of life dependent primarily for its justification upon the irrational factors of tradition and the brute power to survive. When he died in 1837, he could look back upon a life of consistent adherence to caste ideals, of struggle to maintain Prussian aristocratic, agrarian conservatism, to retard the growth of capitalism, and to preserve the traditions of the eighteenth century against the nationalism of the nineteenth and twentieth centuries.

In contrasting Marwitz and the nationalist one recognizes sharply defined differences and similarities. Both judged the world as moralists and wished to reform it; both believed in strong will power and positive action. Although both preferred deeds to words, they loved to read and learned in part from the same works. In sensitivity to affront either to themselves or to their country they were alike, the nationalist probably holding a slight edge. Both accepted a semiorganic conception of society and shared a common aversion to rationalism and the Enlightenment. Marwitz stressed the value of a hierarchical structure of society such as nationalists were later in part to advocate. Both felt as Germans, longing to overthrow the French domination and to unite the Germans. Both wished to inflame the people to war and to a better life. Both spoke bluntly and honestly and hated authority over themselves. Both inclined in a crisis toward dictatorship, although Marwitz did so much more than the nationalist. By temperament difficult to work with, by inclination hostile to bureaucratic ways, they believed dogmatically in certain ideals, were independent and easily aroused. Both of them cloaked self-interest with their idealism and both despised their opponents as immoral, cowardly, and imitative of foreign ideals. Both had vitality and ambition and loved to struggle, but both lacked patience. They knew absolutely that they served a vital cause to which God was lending aid. As is often the case with the two extreme parties in a social conflict, they were sufficiently similar to fear and hate each other.

In spite of similarities the differences between Marwitz and the nationalist were fundamental. The one mistrusted mankind, did not believe in progress, rejected the ideal of social equality; the other had confidence in the capacity of each person to become a model nationalistic citizen. Whereas the nationalist loved and admired and had faith in the common man, Marwitz wished to keep him in his place. Marwitz disliked emotionalism unless previously directed by reason and interest: his aversion to rationalism did not extend so far as that of the nationalist. The latter used rationalism to support an emotional ideal of a future society. Marwitz preferred measured words, cool praise, facts, the truth; the nationalist poured forth words like raindrops and lived in a world of dreams. Fundamentally Marwitz suspected books, ideas, and intellectuals; the nationalist nourished himself with ideas. The one saw relations in a personal way, relations between the individual and the government, between lord and peasant, between master and worker. The nationalist conceived these relations primarily if not altogether in ideal terms of how they should be, not how they were. The one clung to religious orthodoxy, the other subordinated God and religion to work for the nation. Marwitz felt as an aristocrat, Prussian, and a German; he was loyal to all of these forms and conceived his Prussianism and his Germanism as including the preservation of caste. He turned his patriotism to a Prussia or a Germany in which he, von der Marwitz, the descendant of seven generals, would continue to be an aristocrat and leader over the folk. He was satisfied with his social position and the structure of society, wishing only to be let alone. When Napoleon threatened this society, Marwitz resisted, sought the aid of all Germans and of other nations and proposed to change the political boundaries of Germany for the security of existing society. He adhered to the tradition of political reckoning after the model of Frederick the Great and bitterly opposed social transformation. Looking to the past for his ideal he believed in only one kind of social organization, that of the caste-state, and thought it competent, with proper leadership and more public spirit, to defend itself. The nationalist did not share his confidence. The latter maintained that a thorough social transformation was necessary to revive and keep up public spirit and defeat the French. He wished to introduce movement into society. A social organization was valid to him only if it permitted the nation to flourish; when it had ceased to do so, it must be changed. The nationalist subordinated every interest to the welfare of the nation. That his own interest in part would be served best by the new nationalism does not detract from the fact that he devoted all to the nation. Marwitz wished freedom for the aristocracy, some freedom for the burghers, very little for the peasants. His concept of freedom was a negative one, synonymous with privilege of caste. The nationalist demanded freedom so that each person could realize the maximum of his abilities and serve the nation to the utmost. Freedom to him meant the destruction of caste and privilege in the interest of uniting the individuals with the nation. Marwitz wished only the few to be united with the nation and those few to decide and act for the stupid and incompetent remainder. He respected tradition in every case; the nationalist scorned it if it interfered with the welfare of the nation. Marwitz loved law, order, rights, justice; the nationalist heeded these only in so far as they conformed to the national advantage, considering that order as such, rights as such, law as such were of no value and that even injustice to some might be necessary for the sake of the nation. Marwitz conceived of reform as reform of the existing structure; the nationalists meant by reform the transformation of the structure of society to a new kind, one based on the full development of all individuals and their integration into a national society.

If Marwitz had wished for German unity above all else, if he had devoted all his resources to the cause of the nation, he would have joined forces with the nationalists, the only strong ally which he might have had. Instead, because he hated and feared them, he remained isolated, thus lacking support for an attempt to unify the Germans. The fundamental differences between the two groups prevented their union. Marwitz and the aristocrats like him became German only in so far as consistent with their social position. They never understood the nationalistic ideal of a complete submerging of the individual in the nation. Their social position, family, and past always stood in the way of their becoming nationalists.

VIII. FREDERICK WILLIAM III

PRINCES have played a minor role in the rise of nationalism. The more autocratic they have been, the more they have combated nationalism. The throne stands apart from the people; the monarch cannot merge with the common mass or accept the ideals of equality of opportunity, rights, and duties, and of the full participation of all in a common cause which are characteristic of nationalism. He is a power demanding devotion not merely as a symbol of the nation but as a separate and complete unit. If he claims authority by the grace of God, he assumes a religious character identical with that which nationalists claim for the nation. The conflict between autocracy and nationalism is one for supremacy between divine rights. The autocrat feels the responsibility to God for his subjects and claims special knowledge commensurate with it. He must rule autocratically in order to fulfill this duty; his subjects must revere and obey him because he governs by God's grace. What he says is true; what he does is proper. The subject must remain a subject and not claim as a citizen a share in the direction of public affairs. Those below the king must maintain distance from the state and avoid trying to merge themselves with the nation. By violating these principles they will limit the authority of the king and set up a power, the nation, greater than his. No longer a ruler by divine right, the king will be subject to the will of the nation. The character of his position will be entirely changed. He must then sacrifice the religious quality of his office and transform his entire way of thinking and acting. Instead of being responsible to God for the welfare of his subjects, in the role of first citizen he is responsible to the nation for his actions. He may no longer decide issues with unquestioning assurance, but must subordinate his judgment to that of the citizens acting through their representatives. In nationalism the absolute monarch faces a rival who threatens the bases of his power and may in time even accomplish his destruction.

At the top of the structure menaced by nationalism sat the king. Since he associated most intimately with the state and possessed a monopoly of political power, he felt the danger of nationalism immediately, for his position was, politically speaking, most exposed. As the leader of the *ancien régime* he had to assume the initiative in defending that regime against the new and dangerous competitor. And yet, as the head of the state, he felt obliged to accept or initiate reforms which would benefit it. These reforms might turn in the direction of nationalism; to preserve itself and the state the absolute monarchy might have to associate with itself the forces of public will. In order to enable the state to live the people might have to be aroused to political thinking and acting, to public participation in state affairs. A dialectic might be set in motion.

Such was the dilemma which confronted the Hohenzollerns from the period of the French Revolution until the German Revolution of 1918. The first Hohenzollern seriously to be disturbed by this issue was Frederick William III. Like all of his successors he failed to find—perhaps one should say, to accept—a satisfactory solution. The evidence of this failure is manifest in the unsteady course of German history from that day to the present.

The most revealing remark which Frederick William III ever made was the following:

> I often wish I could envy others their self-satisfied, contented feeling. I am entirely different; the more seriously I regard affairs and myself, the more discontented I am and remain with myself. I know from the word of God what I should do and wish to do it; but I never entirely succeed, I never satisfy myself. Something unripe and deficient sticks to everything; everything is inferior to the Christian idea. God has graciously preserved me from gross sin, but I do not know a single act in my entire life of which I can say that it is

completely pure and without flaw before His holy face. Therefore praise and acclaim of men are so repulsive to me.[1]

This unhappy king formed his picture of man and society according to his own limitations; and his subjects and the other Germans had to suffer for the shortcomings of biology and education. The combination of a warped and defective personality exercising autocratic authority was unsuited to the exigencies of the period and enhanced the difficulties of both the ruler and the state.

By temperament Frederick William III differed from the nationalists as daylight differs from dark. He was of a dry, reticent, calm nature to whom enthusiasm, daring, and vision were anathemas. Self-control became to him almost an end in itself. The occasions on which he flared into a temper were so rare that they have in the main been recorded in history; and he always grew angered against something rather than on behalf of a cause. He was noted for his kindly and considerate manner, which made it difficult for him to be firm in any personal matter or to dismiss an incompetent official. Although at times he exhibited obstinacy, he usually felt uncertain and as long as possible postponed arriving at a decision. He hated change in any form, whether in personnel or policy, and he would hesitate for years before agreeing to it. "I dislike new and strange faces," he often said,[2] and he clung to advisers sympathetic to him with a loyalty which, except when it was undeserved as was often the case, redounds to his credit. The art of discussing serious problems was beyond his capacity. Disliking intensely arguments or quarrels, he could think only when reading memoranda in his own study with at most a private secretary present. The written form was more natural to him than the verbal: it was calmer, more rational, more impersonal. He was the first bureaucrat in the state, not the first public figure or statesman. While he knew the military personnel, he was acquainted with few of the civil officials, even from the higher ranks, and came into more intimate contact with his private secretaries and adjutants than with his ministers. The former

[1] R. C. Eylert, *Charakterzüge und historische Fragmente aus dem Leben des Königs von Preussen Friedrich Wilhelms III* (Magdeburg, 1843-46), I, 381-82.

[2] *Ibid.*, II, Pt. 1, 140.

undoubtedly exercised more influence on him, especially before 1807, than his ministers did. In his choice of advisers, whether ministers or otherwise, Frederick William preferred mediocrities like himself. He had an intense aversion to men of brilliance and vigor, like Baron vom Stein, and avoided appointing them to office as long as possible. Experience showed, he wrote in 1797, "that talented men seldom harmonize with one another, and that naturally much evil and injury arises therefrom. The common goal is forgotten and the caprice of the individual member ruins the whole and has the worst results."[3] Bishop Eylert, courtier and friend of Frederick William, who has written the most interesting memoirs about the king, has asserted that Frederick William placed in office more able men than almost any other Hohenzollern.[4] While the Bishop was correct in the fact, he should have added that Frederick William did not wish to appoint them, that necessity forced their selection upon him and that as soon as conditions permitted he either dismissed them or forced them to govern after his fashion. The two possible exceptions to this statement were Scharnhorst and Hardenberg, and their abiding in favor confirms this severe criticism of the king's character. Scharnhorst preserved Frederick William's good graces by virtue of his quiet, unruffled manner, his gift of silence, and his willingness to adjust himself to the royal will and bide his time. Hardenberg was the model courtier who clung to office and practiced successfully the advice which he gave Stein:

> Avoid completely the appearance of wishing to govern. He [the king] possesses the good quality of being willing to be contradicted and of thinking well of whoever tells him the truth, provided it be with the respect due to a sovereign, without bitterness, and in an affectionate manner.[5]

With personalities like Stein Frederick William was always in difficulty. The quality of the latter's mind and character pre-

[3] Georg Küntzel, *Die Politischen Testamente der Hohenzollern nebst ergänzenden Aktenstücken* (Leipzig and Berlin, 1911), II, 134.

[4] Eylert, *op. cit.*, II, Pt. II, 348.

[5] Georg Winter, *Die Reorganisation des preussischen Staates unter Stein und Hardenberg* (Leipzig, 1931), Pt. I, Vol. I, p. 219.

vented him from understanding or trusting men of the nationalistic type. Whereas the king was critical, Stein was creative. The king stopped at the comprehension of details, while Stein, not particularly precise in this respect, used the detailed information supplied by others for the formulation of policies. The king once said that "opinions" are "the most dangerous thing in human society when they contain a wrong trend"; [6] and to him almost if not all new ideas or principles were alien and dangerous. For Stein ideals, because they expressed the highest in life, guided action. The king possessed intellectual energy and strength of will, but primarily with respect to objects long familiar to him. In times of crisis he became confused, uncertain, and bitter. Unlike Frederick the Great, he apparently harbored no ambitions toward fame, no desire to expand the power of the state or to place his personal imprint upon the state or the age; he wished merely to preserve that which existed, to reform conditions only in so far as necessary for the restoration of former excellence. With Stein, if allowance is made for the difference in position, the contrary was true. Stein found happiness in meeting emergencies and overcoming difficulties. Blessed with magnificent energy, courage, and self-confidence this imperial knight, who considered his family at least as ancient and well-born as the Hohenzollerns, spoke and acted vigorously. No obstacle, not even Napoleon, deterred him. If radical reforms were necessary to preserve the nation, he demanded that they be pushed through immediately and did not spare the king, his colleagues, the people, or himself in the pursuit of his ideal objective. The king was a pedant, Stein a statesman. The king faced toward the caste-state of the previous century, Stein toward the nationalistic state of the nineteenth century. Neither understood the other. When the king first appointed Stein minister in 1804, he doubted the wisdom of his act: Stein, he feared, was "genial and eccentric" and liked the Westphalian government organization too much. He foresaw that Stein might endeavor to introduce Westphalian liberties, few as

[6] Friedrich Meinecke, *Das Leben des Generalfeldmarschalls Hermann von Boyen* (Stuttgart, 1896-99), I, 207.

they were, into the eastern part of the state. The stormy course of their relations bears out the king's predictions to a degree which even his pessimism had not foreseen.

The limitations fixed by his general nature would have sufficed to prevent Frederick William from becoming a nationalist. His education unfortunately in part enhanced his dry, critical negativism and, even where it endeavored to combat these qualities, scored only modest success. In his early years Frederick William received the personal attention of his famous grandfather. Frederick the Great wished to develop in the boy those traits which his father, Frederick William II, lacked; but Frederick could not replace the defects of nature, and his overemphatic efforts only transformed the boy's good qualities into defects. As one critic has said:

> Training in economy and simplicity smothered his feeling for a kingly style of living, while military drill led to his exaggerating the value of military externalities. Rationalist philosophical teaching hindered the growth of imagination and the regard for ideas. His education, which sought to develop a Spartan and heroic vigor, lacked, as Hardenberg said, vitality.[7]

The early tutors of the young prince seem to have been a morose, incompetent and unsympathetic lot and to have had a similarly bad effect upon him. They drilled into the boy a cold, utilitarian rationalism and the importance of details. Enthusiasm and imagination, in so far as they were present in him, vanished, never to return.

Frederick William's conception of government derived from the Hohenzollern tradition. He accepted it as unquestioningly as the sun or the stars. It was compassed by the single word autocracy, which, however, carried with it a sense of duty. The ruler, wrote the king in his *Gedanken über die Regierungskunst* (1796-97), must devote the public funds "to the welfare of the state."

[7] Karl Griewank, *Briefwechsel der Königin Luise mit ihrem Gemahl Friedrich Wilhelm III, 1793-1810* (Leipzig, 1929), pp. 8-9.

> Money [he continued] is not the private possession of the sovereign; it belongs to the country, and he has only the administration of it; he must be regarded as the first official of the state; therefore he is not justified in extravagant expenditure, because he is responsible to the country for it. He must use it to make his country happy and prosperous, and this is accomplished when not only the wealthy and respected, but rather the more useful and more ordinary working half of the population enjoy his favor and recognition. At all times more consideration must be paid to the whole than to individual private advantages.[8]

This conception of a ruler's duty was a pure inheritance from the theory and practice of enlightened despotism as illustrated by Frederick the Great. Alongside the sense of responsibility to the state and its people occur the words "favor" (*Gnade*) and "recognition" (*Aufmerksamkeit*). The king must do all. Frederick William never forgot the last admonition which he received from his revered grandfather. "The foundation stone," Frederick the Great said to him, "is the united people. Hold with them so that they will love and trust you. Only thus can you be strong and happy."[9] The tutor whom he received as a young man emphasized this need. By a fortunate choice the famous lawyer and legal reformer, Suarez, was entrusted with the care of the crown prince, and he taught him the humanitarian practices of the eighteenth century. It is doubtful whether Frederick William ever understood and accepted Suarez's idea that a prince should rule his subjects as free men rather than as machines; but at least this tutor acquainted him with the reforms approved by the Enlightenment and practiced to some extent by despots like Joseph II. He learned to respect mankind, particularly the individual, and to wish to avoid humiliating or degrading any person. He perceived the offense of serfdom to human dignity and wished to abolish this evil. Although denying the validity of the abstract idea of equality, he recognized the practical justice of it to a certain degree—a case in which his rationalistic, religious instruction supported his other training; and he accepted the need of more

[8] Küntzel, *op. cit.*, II, 115.

[9] Eylert, *op. cit.*, I, 455-56.

liberty than had hitherto been allowed. All men, he believed, were equal before God, and he practiced this idea in the church. While he held himself responsible in part for the moral conditions among his subjects, at least prior to 1815 he refused to exert any unusual pressure upon them in matters of religion. Although not so free in this respect as Frederick the Great, he abhorred the thought of forcing his subjects into hypocrisy. In social relations he wished to preserve castes, and accepted it as an eternal truth that some must be subordinate to others; nonetheless, he disliked snobbishness and exclusiveness and recognized a certain equality among aristocrat, burgher, and peasant. Preferring each person to remain in his station, in occasional individual cases he approved of emancipation from caste. He was particularly willing to accept burghers as officers in the army, and several times issued an admonition which speaks for itself.

> I have been very displeased to learn [he instructed the army in January, 1798] that especially young officers by reason of their caste have tried to assert themselves before the civilian caste. I shall know how to make the soldier's authority effective when it brings to him important advantages, and that is on the field of battle, where he must defend his fellow countrymen with his life; otherwise, whatever his rank or caste no soldier shall be rude to one of my burghers. It is they, not I, who support the army. The army of troops confided to my command is maintained at their expense, and arrest, loss of rank, and sentence of death will be the fate of anyone who acts contrary to my unbending sternness in this respect.[10]

These blunt words attest to the sincerity of Frederick William's intentions and manifest the profound change which had occurred in the conception of the relations among the army, the civilians, and the king. An enlightened conception, however, does not mean an immediate change in practice.

The extent to which Frederick William actually proposed reforms after he ascended the throne depended upon the actual need for them. He could rarely if ever rise above the specific situation and set an ideal to be realized by means as yet unknown to him.

[10] *Ibid.*, III, Pt. 1, 113-14.

Theoretically averse to any methods other than that of practical experimentation, he disliked experimenting itself for fear of destroying existing advantages. The first period of his reign, from his assumption of power to the Battle of Jena, teemed with the work of committees of investigation for reforms, and most of those actually carried out later by the nationalistic officials were taken up. Social and economic reforms, changes in the military system, educational revisions, improvements in administration, even reforms in the organization of the church were carefully considered. Yet, except for the emancipation of the crown peasants and some changes in tariff policy, nothing was done. To borrow a statement made of Austria before 1848, Prussia wished to prove to posterity that she knew of what she was dying. The king meant well, but lacked the self-confidence and force with which to overcome the opposition to reform. He consulted and weighed and hesitated, and Napoleon caught him still undecided.

It may be doubted whether the king ever heartily favored the thorough institutional reforms which became necessary after Jena. (A Prussian minister said to the French chargé d'affaires in 1799:

> The revolution which you have made from below will come about gradually in Prussia from above. The king in his way is a democrat: he works unceasingly on plans for the limitation of the privileges of the nobles and will follow the plan of Joseph II but with slower means. In a few years there will no longer be any privileged class in Prussia.[11]

The assertion greatly exaggerated the truth.) This mild, conservative patriarch was stirred from his normal condition of petty routine, official indolence, and conjugal happiness less by the few humanitarian ideas which he had been able to master than by the fears aroused in him during the French Revolution. In advising him to preserve the love and trust of his people, Frederick the Great had prefaced this admonition as follows:

[11] Cited by Paul Haake, *Der preussische Verfassungskampf vor hundert Jahren* (Munich and Berlin, 1921), p. 25.

> I fear that after my death *pêle mêle* will break loose. Things are everywhere in ferment. The ruling houses, especially in France, nourish this condition instead of calming and stamping it out. The masses are already beginning to exert pressure from below, and when they break out, the Devil will be loose. I fear that you will have a difficult and bad time of it. Prepare yourself, be firm, think of me. Watch over our honor and our fame. Commit no injustice and allow none.[12]

The outbreak of the French Revolution confirmed the prophecy and taught Frederick William to be cautious. "We live in a time of change," he wrote his wife in 1794;[13] and although he was thinking apparently less of internal relations in Prussia than of international boundary lines, he nonetheless perceived to some extent the social implications of the events in France. This recognition was attested to in three significant assertions by him. Since he spoke and wrote comparatively little and weighed his thoughts carefully beforehand, these words reveal much. In a document concerning reforms drawn up immediately after he ascended the throne, he stated his intention of restricting court expenditures. "It is often true," he said, "that courts are seats of lavishness, which the country detests. As a result it makes all manner of false judgments, thinking this lavishness due to monarchical or princely constitutions of government, when it is not."[13a] In the same memorandum he stated that the French Bourbons almost deserved their fate. He felt that he must refute the accusations made against royalty by proving the value of this form of government.

> Healthy, clear reason, correct judgment, and the most rigid love of justice [he said] are certainly the chief characteristics of a ruler. Since these are absolutely necessary, no good government can exist if the sovereign himself does not possess them or if he makes himself despised by laziness, vice, and weakness. Such a ruler does not deserve to rule and it is no wonder if his hard-pressed subjects in the

[12] Eylert, *op. cit.*, I, 455-56.
[13] Griewank, *op. cit.*, p. 153.
[13a] Küntzel, *op. cit.*, pp. 117-18.

end, tired of such a rule, join together in order to secure a better one. The French Revolution gives a great and fearful example for all bad rulers who do not rule for the good of their country like good princes but like bloodsuckers drain it dry and exact money from their subjects for their our sensuous pleasures and waste it when they should use it for the true good of the state.[14]

Experience had shown him that particularly in this age a "ruler can and will never really make himself respected by ceremony and display but only by deeds and acts." [15] While he did not fear the fate of Louis XVI for himself, he wished to prevent disorder or outbreaks in his state. The second occasion on which he revealed his understanding of the change inaugurated by the French Revolution and its ideology had to do with his building a clubhouse in Potsdam for the mutual use and enjoyment of aristocrats and burghers. He wished the two classes to come closer together. When someone praised his freedom from social prejudice in this matter, he replied in his abrupt fashion, "That is not worth speaking of; in our day it is understood." [16] Even more striking was the king's statement in 1800-01:

In the present crisis in which all Europe finds itself it is undeniably of the greatest importance that every state which still exists should look ahead and neglect no measures which, if it is to escape the fate that has already overtaken other states, may anticipate and prevent the revolution more or less threatening the entire world. I therefore consider it absolutely necessary and of the greatest importance that the Prussian state make it its business to examine in great detail all the possible means, both within and without the monarchy, and to use everything possible wherever possible in the world to multiply and complete them. In so extraordinary a war as the present one, in which everything is at stake and which either today or to-

[14] Frederick William's *Gedanken über die Regierungskunst, 1796-97,* cited by Küntzel, *op. cit.,* pp. 101-2. It is doubtful whether Frederick William believed much of the latter part. The ideas are all those of Suarez, and the crown prince, as he then was, probably borrowed them without much thought. Nonetheless they disclose the profound effect of the French Revolution upon his thoughts about the duties of royalty.

[15] *Ibid.,* p. 117.

[16] Eylert, *op. cit.,* III, Pt. 1, 117-18.

morrow threatens us also, one must seek aid in extraordinary measures, even if up to now we have not put some of them to use.[17]

This statement contains the key to an understanding of Frederick William's entire efforts for reform before Jena. He feared the French, but he also feared the effect of their seductive ideas. Although he saw that he must make concessions to the age, unfortunately, with his aversion to change, he never could decide what measures should be taken. "Conserve," "appease," "calm" were favorite words with him even during these years, as was "fatal." He wound himself in a web from which only Napoleon could free him.

The king wished to make his subjects happy and was willing to sacrifice personal pleasures to that end. His conception of happiness, however, was limited to that which he himself could comprehend, depending upon moral conduct and material prosperity. He often remarked that he did not want to rule over a people without religion. He did not mean that they should attend church regularly, although he himself did so except in winter when the churches were too cold. Rather he thought of morality in the manner of a small-town burgher. A person should be honorable, thrifty, and industrious; he should not overindulge in food and drink; he should be faithful to his wife and a good father to his children. Frederick William emphasized the thou-shalt-nots of the Ten Commandments. He judged people and to a certain extent chose his advisers in accordance with their moral deportment rather than for their knowledge or ability. When misfortune occurred, he explained it ultimately on moral grounds. He manifested his own mediocrity and his belief in the basic value of material success.

The most important object for a ruler [he wrote in 1796-97] is the administration of finance and its corollary state economy. . . . To the finance administration belongs everything which is connected with the domestic welfare of the state, including the right use of the products raised or manufactured in the country. The more one can

[17] Freiherr von der Goltz, *Von Rossbach bis Jena und Auerstadt* (1906), pp. 277-78.

get from the country without oppressing the subjects, the more advantageous it is for the state. The ruler must direct his whole care to this, since true statesmanship consists in it.

Above all, one of his first and most important duties is to advance the cultivation of the land and all that is connected with it. . . . The further one develops agriculture, the happier and more flourishing the state, since from this all other advantages flow.[18]

Agricultural prosperity, he continued, brought also prosperity for manufacturing and commerce, these items forming the second main object of the ruler's attention. In all economic respects Frederick William was a confirmed paternalist, willing to recede from his mercantilist views only when the cost of adhering to them became too great for the state.

"True ambition and a feeling of honor maintain a state; therefore these become some of the main objects of the ruler's concern," Frederick William wrote in the same memorandum. In his plans to keep these alive and active he did not set his standards very high. "One must take men as they are and not as they ought to be," he added.[19] He proposed to encourage ambition by rewarding with promotion and decorations those who accomplished something—not too many rewards or too often, for they would then become less enticing. With respect to the army he confronted a difficult and immediate problem. How could he arouse loyalty among the soldiers and revive among the officers the will to serve? He was troubled over the ill-will felt among his subjects toward military service, the increasing number of resignations from the army of officers, and the decline in the number of aristocrats wishing to enter service. His proposals for correcting the military evils consisted entirely in material improvement, more pay and better treatment, and for the officers a little practical military instruction.

Education meant to this royal materialist training in the "useful arts and sciences." He despised philosophy and theology and recognized no value in theory. His own feeble attempts to read in these fields had not carried him beyond the point of find-

[18] Küntzel, *op. cit.*, II, 110-11.
[19] *Ibid.*, p. 108.

ing that all theorists disagreed; therefore their works were useless and their efforts should be curbed. Almost as soon as he came to power, he expressed his convictions as follows:

> To protect useful arts and sciences and to develop them must be one of the chief concerns of the ruler. I say useful, that is, such as have the land and the welfare of the state in mind, as, for example, the improvement of agriculture, domestic economy, trade, commerce, and industry.
>
> Abstract sciences, which touch only the academic world and serve only to enlighten this group, are of course without value to the welfare of the state; it would be foolish to restrict them entirely, but it is healthy to limit them. I may go so far as to say that a regent would do well [he later did so] as soon as he comes to power to direct the notice of the learned men and of the academies more to the aforesaid and other useful things rather than to let them fill their heads with speculative reasoning, from which no good to the common welfare proceeds. The subject for prizes should be set in the same way. Prizes are often given for the most absurd things and should each time be for something of value to all so that one could expect from such an academy . . . at least some good.[20]

It would be too much to hope that this king would know any economic, social, or political theory. He was totally unacquainted with the writings of Adam Smith and his German followers, and if he ever read Montesquieu or Rousseau, he left no evidence of it. He knew about Kant, Fichte, and Schelling, as well as of Hegel and of lesser philosophers without understanding at all their epoch-making work. He knew almost nothing of Goethe, Schiller, Lessing and the writers who were founding a culture worthy to be ranked with the best of all time; the works, the humanistic ideals, the search of these men for the beautiful meant less to Frederick William than the peasants around Paretz, his favorite home. The peasants lived in the same world of moral and materialistic values as Frederick William, while Goethe and Schiller did not. When Queen Louise endeavored to live in the culture of her own age by reading the works of these men, her royal husband was disgusted and complained. He told her bluntly

[20] *Ibid.*, pp. 109-10.

that he did not wish his wife to read this literature; he feared, so he said to her, that she might grow out of his cultural sphere, that she might no longer be so intimate with him and see her duty in amusing him. It never occurred to him that he could have joined her in the cultivation of their minds: he despised literature too much, calling it "eccentric, popular scribbling." [21] For his own entertainment he preferred light novels, and he went to the theater only when comedies or farces were played. Life, he often said, contained enough tragedies; "One does not need to exaggerate them in the theater; that deadens and makes one indifferent. One must strengthen himself for the coming sorrows of every day by making merry." [22] The fact that he was mainly responsible for his unhappiness did not suggest itself to him.

Frederick William lacked the capacity for appreciating greatness, whether in an ideal or an action. The course into nationalism which the rising German literature and philosophy opened so brilliantly for others remained closed to him. With the aid of the small amount of reading in this literature which she was able to do, Queen Louise could glimpse this realm of national feeling. She possessed a far richer personality and a deeper understanding and sympathy than her husband and, a Prussian by marriage only, had a deeper appreciation than he did of the common qualities of all Germans. A woman so sympathetic and imaginative as to be blissfully happy with Frederick William was able to conceive a German nation.

The king had determined to keep the peace as long as he possibly could. In his view the most dreadful calamity that could befall his people was to become involved in war like the other peoples of Europe. Yet he realized the danger of remaining pacific and late in 1805, with the fatal clarity of vision often characteristic of him, said, "More than one king has fallen because he loved war; I shall fall because I love peace." [23] In the next year he was often seen weeping; he longed to run away from state

[21] Karl Griewank, *Königin Luise, Briefe und Aufzeichnungen* (Leipzig, 1925), p. 21.

[22] Eylert, *op. cit.*, I, 78.

[23] Von der Goltz, *op. cit.*, p. 497.

affairs and join his wife at the quiet resort of Pyrmont; he felt confused, apathetic, and helpless and only through despair declared war. The general whom he put in charge of his troops, the Duke of Brunswick, suffered from old age and habitual indecision, and when out of a sense of duty as the grandson of Frederick the Great Frederick William joined the army, he enhanced the confusion. The history of his reign to this point had been that of a series of careful investigations and consultations, each ending in disagreement and further consultation. The practice continued before, during, and after the Battle of Jena. The duke was undecided and consulted the king; the king was uncertain and consulted the duke; both were uncertain and consulted the staff officers. They were still discussing the proper strategy when Napoleon attacked. Further consultation was not necessary to establish the fact or even the degree of defeat. King, officers, and privates, individually or collectively as convenience dictated, fled northeast and every Prussian who could, particularly the officers in the fortified towns, either joined the rout or surrendered quietly to Napoleon.

In these chaotic days and with his kingdom falling to pieces Frederick William preserved the even temper of a plaster cast. The diary of Countess Voss, chief stewardess of the court, contains time after time during these days the significant remark, "The King remains the same." Occasionally the Countess's astonishment boiled over into disgust; "It is unbelievable," she wrote.[24] During his flight the king even organized a hunt, an event so rare in his life that his associates should have perceived in it his confusion. During the weeks following Jena he could not decide whether to continue the war or to sue for peace. Thoughts of abdication occurred to him as a way out of his dilemma; but since the war was a fact and since he hoped for rescue by Czar Alexander of Russia, he let events more or less take their course. After Alexander deserted him at Tilsit, he despaired and again thought of abdicating. Although courageous under fire and in no degree a

[24] *69 Jahre am Preussischen Hofe. Aus den Tagebüchern und Aufzeichnungen der Oberhofmeisterin Sophie Wilhelmine Gräfin von Voss* (Berlin, 1912), pp. 105, 107.

coward, Frederick William feared his own incompetence. He dreaded decisions and the war was forcing them on him. Even his wife grew irritated over his attitude.

The course of events would have thrust greatness upon Frederick William, but he refused to let it. The historian can imagine the heroic exploits of Frederick the Great in this emergency—the reassembling of his troops, the arming of his entire people, the quick marches and sudden attacks, the fire and enthusiasm of the king arousing his subjects, the negotiations with the other enemies of Napoleon, the calling and organizing of all Germans for a holy war against the new Satan, a king at the head of a nation. The reality under Frederick William was otherwise. He wished peace and retreated from state affairs as much as he could into the indolence of family life. He found in intimacy with the queen, the only person whom he completely loved and trusted and with whom he was as nearly happy and free as his nature would allow, the relief and solace which the nationalists sought in the ideal of a new nation. Instead of spurring the king on to action, the presence of the queen really served as a hindrance. So long as the king was with her, he could forget his troubles. The outside world of affairs seemed petty.

Religion furnished another source of comfort for the king. Frederick William had always believed in a personal God, but he had accepted from his tutors the rationalistic view of religion. After Jena he reinforced this rationalism with a degree of mystical trust in God. In Königsberg in 1809 he met the staunchly orthodox Pastor Borowski, who, so the king said, used the language of an Old Testament prophet and who fixed the religious change which the king had been undergoing. The king later expressed his debt to Pastor Borowski as follows (the formulation is Eylert's; the king never spoke such fluent language):

No one did so much as he to strengthen me by religion. He helped to bring me to a certain, definite and positive firmness without taking from me my respect for and toleration of general free and liberal views. By turning my thoughts constantly toward the Highest Borowski especially helped me to lessen the bitterness which threatened in the terrible year of 1806 to fasten itself on my soul, and thereby he made me inclined and able to forgive even my personal enemies and to do good.[25]

One may question how tolerant the king became toward liberal ideas, even in religion, and it is noticeable that he felt more indebted to Borowski for having calmed him than for having changed or deepened his religious trust. However, religious strengthening did occur. The king remained true to religious rationalism, but supported it by new faith. In 1810 he stated as the purpose of the government in matters of religion "the furtherance of true religiosity without compulsion and mystical enthusiasm—freedom of conscience and tolerance without public offense." [26]

Frederick William, like the nationalists, rejected the rationalism of the eighteenth century as the sole guide for man. He loved simplicity and quiet life in the country as did the romantic and nationalistic Arndt. He believed that man was guided not merely by reason but by his heart and soul and by the ideal of the necessity of developing character and personality. Like the nationalists, he sought refuge in faith and belief. Frederick William was not an abstract thinker who systematized his ideas or grew out of one body of ideals into another. He preserved rationalism alongside mysticism without uniting head, heart, and soul to form a complete personality; the three remained separate forces, each governing his actions in turn as occasion demanded. His standard for man remained essentially that of eighteenth-century rationalism, to which he added just enough mysticism and emotionalism to satisfy the wants of an ordinary, limited, practical man. He never believed that the world needed a new personality or synthesis of man's qualities, that the heart must guide man, that reason was the surface manifestation of man's richest source of wisdom, his emotions. He never reached the ideal for the individual which the nationalists set up and tried to realize. He never combined his ideals sufficiently to permit even a shadow of the nationalistic type of personality to arise in him. Even if he had, the ingredients would have been weak and

[25] Eylert, *op. cit.*, I, 222.

[26] Walter Wendland, *Die Religiosität und die kirchenpolitischen Grundsätze Friedrich Wilhelms des Dritten* (Giessen, 1909), p. 71.

disproportionate. Furthermore, for all his love of rural simplicity, Frederick William never acquired that passionate devotion to the people and to the soil which fired Arndt. Paretz appealed to him because there, isolated from ceremony and state affairs, he could live as a petty burgher. He loved it not for itself but for what it was to him. He was too self-controlled, too unimaginative, too dry and pedantic to become a nationalist. He could not conceive of himself as one of a nation or merged into any group. He could not give way to his emotions or forget himself in devotion to a cause. Since ambition did not trouble him, he felt a primary duty to maintain the *status quo*. He was first a Hohenzollern, secondly a Prussian, and scarcely at all a German. As a Hohenzollern he must preserve as much of Prussia for the dynasty as he could; but to nationalistic urging he replied several times between 1808 and 1812 that he would not risk a war, that he preferred to rule over a small piece of Prussia rather than not to rule at all. Occupying the highest position in the state, he felt no personal need for reorganizing society so as to permit more social freedom for himself. The existing structure suited him entirely, subject to small improvements which would enable it again to function smoothly. Certainly he had no occasion to dream of a society of the future built on the ideals of freedom and nationalistic fraternity. Even if he had had the capacity, he lacked any interest in becoming a nationalist. In the time of Prussia's defeat and Germany's threatened annihilation, Frederick William sought solace in the arms of Louise; the nationalists lusted for action, pulling down their weapons and demanding a leader; the king softened his despair with religion, by which the nationalists strengthened their confidence.

Although Frederick William never had a high opinion of his own ability, when misfortune came, he found an explanation which would exculpate him. Prussia's collapse, he said, was the "natural and deserved result of past conditions,"[27] the effect of moral decline. Some years later, apparently in the period after 1815, the king was talking with Bishop Eylert about the merits

[27] Cited by Wendland from a letter of Queen Louise, *op. cit.*, p. 66.

of education. In the course of their discussion the king remarked upon the general condition of the age as follows (the formulation is the bishop's):

The earthly destiny of man is determined according to the position in which he is born, according to the conditions in which he finds himself, according to the abilities given him, and according to his inclination for a particular profession. For his profession he must be aroused, taught, and trained so that he may acquire all the knowledge and technical information and (I have here in mind especially the middle and lower classes) that he may know, whether he be a merchant, manufacturer, craftsman, economist, farmer, day laborer, servant, what he ought to know in order to be content in his calling and able to be of use to others.

One does no good to him and to society when one educates a man beyond the bounds of his class and calling and gives him knowledge which he does not need, when one stirs up and awakens demands not in conformity with his position. A man cannot learn everything, for there is too much to know and life is too short. Each should learn thoroughly only what is needed in his work. More is not necessary for the ends of life and only proves disturbing and hindering. More only destroys peace and quiet, which all mechanical work, if it is to succeed, requires. Knowledge beyond the bounds of class and calling makes a man forward, overbearing and argumentative. It leads to that unhappy habit of making comparisons and, if these are based on the idea of the equality of man, causes injustice and discontent. Instead of resting happily in his condition of life, he widens the area of his demands and life becomes unsteady and disturbed. He misses what he does not have and does not enjoy what he does have. There can be no order in the world without subordination. If one does not like this arrangement and thinks himself suited for something higher, the bond between the upper and lower orders, which holds together public and private life, grows looser and becomes a burden to all those who with increased demands do not like to subordinate themselves.

Apparently a troubled spirit of unrest and excitement hovers over the present generation. One class wishes to be like or better than another and everyone wants to break his bounds. Whence comes this urge with all its stimuli?

With the ever-increasing inclination for sensuous enjoyment of life and the ever-increasing poverty which must result therefrom, a fermentation is going on below which is already taking on a threatening form. I should not like to live through the explosion of it.

If a feeling of the equality of human rights is aroused, must not in like measure the power be aroused and developed for honoring duties as well as rights? If the one happens without the other, what will be the result? The greatest danger of our time is the simultaneous growth of intelligence and pauperism.

The cultivation of intelligence in all directions by means of the common school is not to be censured; but it must not be the highest aim. Everything depends and depends entirely in the long run on diligence in one's work, on character, and on life.

The diabolical power in the nature of man is a terrible thing. What has not happened and is always happening to prevent its breaking out and to hold it in check! We have scaffolds, prisons, houses of correction, officials of justice, police, guards and arms, and yet I read to my great dismay in all the monthly reports from all the provinces of the realm that the prisons are full and will continue to be so.

When I do not see the fruits of the education of the masses, I cannot have confidence in it. The schools are not alone to blame; the trouble also lies elsewhere. It is not true, at least not altogether true, when men say that it lies in the crudeness and ignorance of the people, that they should be taught and trained, their feeling of honor aroused, they be made happier, that then they would of themselves grow better. Improvement must come from elsewhere.

I have found the greatest moral depravity among the upper classes, among those who are called the cultivated and in whom one finds plenty of intelligence. I have found it not in the class as such, but in many individuals who belong to it and even who excel in it, clever, well-informed, versatile, useful, and charming people. I have chosen them out, given them posts, attached them to my person, given them honors, decorations, and lands and, forgetful of their duty, they have treated me with ingratitude, treachery, and malice. When all went well they seemed able to do anything and everything; in misfortune they were exposed and disloyally deserted.

When ambition and greed seek satisfaction and are satisfied, they appear to serve their country with energy and zeal and with complete devotion to their work; but in time of need and danger it is clear that they only served and intended to serve themselves.

When they must make sacrifices their prick of conscience becomes dull and they are no longer so zealous when there is nothing to be gained.

Cleverness is not wisdom nor braggadocio courage; the pretty phrase has no meaning; attentiveness is not loyalty nor suppleness love; efficiency is not devotion. The true, unadorned, real virtue in man lies deeper and arises out of another source which, if it does not flow within, cannot be created by the goodness of the best of rulers.[28]

The disloyalty of trusted members of the upper classes during the years of Prussia's humiliation inclined the king to regard the simple burghers and peasants with favor. He had always shown more affection for these classes than was usual for a king and liked to be among them. He approved of their naturalness and lack of ceremony, their direct speech, their silence, their religious faith. He shared by nature more traits with them than with the upper classes. Like Fichte, Arndt, and other nationalists, in the crisis he placed his trust in the common folk and wished reforms to be made for their benefit. In 1810 he said: "Whence shall help come? I no longer expect anything from those who up to now have been called my friends and the support of the Throne and who have looked upon themselves and been regarded as such. Only through the honest folk, the upright burgher and the simple peasant, can things improve."[29]

Disappointment in many persons of the upper classes did not blind the king to the fact that other members remained devoted to him. His practicality and aversion to change would not permit him to dispense with the aid of these classes. He never thought of merging them into the body of the nation. As he said to Bishop Eylert, men were not equal; some must be masters and some subjects. He needed class distinctions as a support to monarchy. Furthermore, in reality the king saw little difference between the moral state of all classes. That of the upper classes was most depraved; but the same tendencies were manifest in the others. The king had never put much confidence in mankind; after 1806 he had even less. "As for belief in humanity," he said

[28] Eylert, *op. cit.*, I, 375-79.
[29] *Ibid.*, III, Pt. 1, 117.

to Bishop Eylert, "one cannot push it very far; mine has become terribly shaky." [30] "Do not try to teach me anything about mankind," the king said to the bishop on another occasion. "I have seen through all kinds. The truth of the story is that man has turned his heart away from God, and if he does not seriously and earnestly return to Him, everything will be only shadow-boxing without reality." [31]

The collapse of Prussia forced the king to realize that the state needed immediate reforms. His bitterness at the conduct of the aristocracy and the intellectual upper middle class facilitated his approval of reforms at their expense and his increased affection for the common folk inclined him more than ever to assist them. He appointed reformers to office and in general accepted their decisions. He freed the serfs, abolished the main restrictions between town and country, permitted the towns a large degree of self-government, canceled the aristocracy's monopoly of the officers' posts in the army, approved other military reforms, and was even willing to associate laymen with the government by introducing a system of representation for the provinces and for the whole state. He hoped that the nation (he meant Prussia) would participate more actively in the welfare of the whole and would thereby firmly establish its "feeling of community and love of country." [32] He approved the founding of a university at Berlin in these words: the state must replace with intellectual prowess what it has lost in physical.[33]

The king seemed even to be speaking the language of the nationalists. In accepting the reforms he recognized for the moment the power of ideals and of spiritual forces, acknowledging the necessity for awakening the "feeling of community" and "love of country." Yet it would be a mistake to credit him with much enthusiasm for reforms; the emergency alone induced him to assent to them. At most he wished those which would not reduce

[30] *Ibid.*, I, 85.
[31] *Ibid.*, I, 375-79.
[32] Haake, *op. cit.*, pp. 29-47, *passim*.
[33] Max Lenz, *Die Geschichte der Universität-Berlin* (Halle, 1910), I, 78. The statement is not a direct quotation but it reproduces the king's thoughts.

his own authority and was loath to put additional burdens upon his subjects, since their discontent was already great. His secretary, Beyme, suspected the French in 1807 of oppressing the Prussians heavily so that they would repudiate their king. Frederick William showed that he also feared this when he wrote the czar in July, 1809: "A sovereign fortunate in war can demand without danger the greatest sacrifices of his people, especially after a revolution like that in France; but a prince who has suffered only reverses during the war risks a revolt of his subjects if he makes such demands." [34] The king was afraid to ask his people for further sacrifices. The reformers had no throne to lose, whereas he did. Furthermore, what might he expect if he were to call a representative assembly to discuss the acts of reform? What if he introduced a permanent system of representation? The king kept vividly in mind the result of convening the Estates-General in France in 1789. He wished to take no chances on a repetition of those events in Prussia. When West Prussian aristocrats requested a constitution based on the estates system, he replied: "The aristocracy will not need the sanction of a general Landtag because His Majesty without that will lend a willing ear to their reports." [35] Only the emergency and the insistence of Stein and later of Hardenberg induced him to propose the introduction of representative assemblies, and he did so under the condition that they should be advisory bodies on those matters alone which the king submitted to them. He never entirely fulfilled his promise.

Frederick William fought the reformers most bitterly over the question of the relationship between himself and his ministers. The king wished to keep the ultimate authority in his own hands. He was convinced that he knew how to judge conditions better than his ministers or anyone else. From the first day of his reign he had sought to obtain full and impartial information and to arrive at his own decisions. He once said that if he were to act against his own conviction he would commit "a sin against the

[34] Paul Bailleu, *Briefwechsel König Friedrich Wilhelms III mit Kaiser Alexander I* (Leipzig, 1900), p. 194.

[35] Haake, *op. cit.*, p. 26.

Holy Ghost which cannot be forgiven"; [36] and the long hours of labor devoted by him to state business attest to his conscientious adherence to this strenuous rule. The king requested memoranda on each question from his ministers and his many other advisers and then decided on the basis of them. This procedure suited his own calm nature and catered to his indecision. The entire machinery of government ran loosely and inefficiently because, although the king was unfitted to govern, particularly in times of crisis, he would not permit his responsible ministers to govern. The monarchical authority was ruining itself and the state as well. The fact that, especially after Jena, he clung obstinately to one incompetent foreign minister and two secretaries hated by the public added to the confusion. That one of these secretaries, Beyme, was a highly intelligent and able person did not diminish the disastrous effects. When the reformers demanded that the king depend entirely upon the advice of his ministers before making decisions, he felt his authority threatened. This was a constitutional crisis of the deepest concern to him and he never gave in. Temporarily he hedged and compromised. In 1810 he named Hardenberg, the perfect courtier, prime minister with power over the other ministers and the right to be heard on every issue; but he continued to heed his secretaries, and after 1815 he returned as soon as possible to the previous method of personal rule.

The king drove the reformers to fury after 1806 by appointing opponents of change to the reform commissions and to state offices. He felt it his duty to hear both sides before deciding what was best for all. He must try to reconcile all opinions and not alienate one large and powerful element among his subjects by definitely declaring against it. When pressed to the limit he must compromise. In a sense he performed functions like those of a responsible political leader in a parliamentary government. The reformers and nationalists constituted in his eyes only one group pressing for immediate action. Frederick William felt uncertain, the reformers knew that they were in the right; Frederick William remained calm, the reformers grew passionate and com-

[36] Eylert, *op. cit.*, I, 70.

bative. He found difficulty in coping with these strenuous men and felt his power of judicious decision wrested from him. When controversy arose and arguments grew hot and one side positive, he was likely to lose authority. Since this period was full of passionate controversy, he was especially unhappy; and the more passionate the arguments became the calmer he tried to be so that he could preserve his power and the *status quo*.

The years between 1806 and 1813 witnessed repeated conflicts between the king and the reformers and nationalists and caused Frederick William on occasion to fear rebellion. That he was himself responsible for the decline of royal prestige did not detract from his fear. The first of these conflicts occurred before the Battle of Jena when several generals, high officials, and even members of the royal family signed a common petition to him to dismiss several of his incompetent officials. Frederick William was angry at this act of insubordination, punished those who he thought were the main offenders, and forbade its repetition. Even more serious in his eyes was Minister vom Stein's refusal to carry out an order. The king countered with one of the famous letters in history. After relating the difficulties which he had had with Stein since the latter's appointment as minister, he declared:

> I have realized with sorrow that I did not err in my original opinion of you. You are an obstinate, perverse, stubborn and disobedient servant of state, who, flaunting his genius and talent, is far from having the best interests of the state at heart, is led by caprice and acts from passion and personal hatred and bitterness. Such state officials are just the ones whose manner of working is most disadvantageous and dangerous for holding together the state. I am indeed sorry that you have put me in a position where I must speak so plainly to you. Since you maintain that you are a man who loves truth, I have given you my opinion in good German and must add that if you are not willing to alter your disrespectful and improper attitude, the state can put no great value on your further services.[37]

It would be unfair to the king to assert that this letter contained his ultimate opinion of Stein. Frederick William recognized the

[37] Winter, *op. cit.*, p. 114.

minister's capacity, and a few months later restored him to office. Whether he would have done so except in a time of despair is doubtful. After the Napoleonic ban on Stein was lifted, the king never recalled him to office. The truth seems to be that the letter expressed Frederick William's emotional estimate of Baron vom Stein but not his rational one evoked in a situation of necessity.

The next crisis and the severest of all occurred in 1809. The Spanish people had rebelled against Napoleon with amazing success and Austria once more went to war. In Germany the bitter hatred against Napoleon broke loose in Schill's famous raid. Many of the king's officers, officials, and members of the royal family begged him to declare war, and even the modest and quiet Scharnhorst almost threatened him with rebellion. The grandson of Frederick the Great would not budge. He had tried war once; he refused to risk his state and his throne again unless practically certain of victory. At length he agreed to aid Austria if she defeated the French army and if Prussia were allowed plenty of time to arm. That the first condition failed to be fulfilled is of less significance here than the king's reaction to the nationalists.

When Schill's advance to action against the French was reported to him, Frederick William was horrified and berated the weakness of the officials in Berlin toward the "spirit of frivolous unrest." [38] Thus he characterized one of the patriotic acts of German history. To his cousin Prince William, who had besought him to go to war, Frederick William replied: "Since I have a view of the whole, I am best able to decide what measures are needed for the good of the state and I do not need any bidding from my subjects to execute them." [39] This is the classic formulation of an autocrat's omniscience and the limited intelligence of an autocrat's subjects. The king is always right; he knows more and has better judgment than any or all of his subjects, even though they be of the same blood as himself. This he held at a time when the patriots were trying to recover his state for him and free him from Napoleonic domination, when the intelligent leaders of Prussia almost unanimously demanded war, when the head of the police

[38] Bailleu, *op. cit.*, p. 312.
[39] Max Lehmann, *Scharnhorst* (Leipzig, 1886-87), II, 278.

of Berlin reported to the king that the populace and army were so eager for war that, "it is a question of the peace of the country, the throne of the King—the army is wavering in its obedience." [40]

That the king felt less sure of himself than his reply to Prince William would indicate is evident from a memorandum of his thoughts which he made in this crisis. The summary of the document given by Max Lehmann (the document has never been published) deserves to be quoted in full. Frederick William declared that he wanted to help his people live happily and contentedly. He complained

that his hope of finding a loyal, peace-loving, willing, obedient people able to be improved has been disappointed, his efforts to save his people by his own example from the paths of atheism, immorality, and pleasure have been in vain. These evils have even increased. His acts—he thinks of the years 1805-6—have been ruthlessly criticized and intentionally misrepresented, his most loyal servants have been called incapable weaklings, even traitors, while men who often had nothing but the favor of the misled mob have been all the more praised; even intrigues which had so long been banned from the annals of the history of the fatherland have begun again. Unfortunately no change of mind has resulted from the catastrophe of Jena. What is called patriotism is only self-righteousness, since bitter hatred and frivolous passion to blame exist in place of unity. It is a thankless task to rule a people in this condition without unity and without obedience to the government [he said government and not king]. Doubtful of an improvement the king speaks of the significant fact that his throne is no more safe, either from abroad or even from within. "After all these experiences [he asks] would it be unheard of and quite unexpected if the spirit of partisanship should aim at bringing about sooner or later a change of government or at putting someone else more popular in the place to which I was destined and which certainly has brought me few happy moments and all kinds of trouble and worry?" In this case he is "firmly resolved and ready" to turn the reins of government without reluctance over to the one whom the nation recognizes as more worthy of controlling it and more worthy of the confidence of his unhappy and misguided people. All

[40] Bailleu, *Königin Luise* (Berlin and Leipzig, 1908), p. 312.

he asks is the privilege of living as an independent and undisturbed private person in his beloved fatherland. If he once resigns the throne nothing can induce him to take up this burden again. He expressly recognizes the nation's claim upon the members of his family. "God is my witness [Frederick William wrote] how often I have had the thought of turning over of my own free will the throne to one worthier, wiser than I am if I could thereby assure the happiness of my country. I have thought of it especially in these critical and decisive moments, when the difficult choice between war and peace upon which depends the welfare or woe of the whole people was made more difficult and more uncertain by embittered partisanship and opposing opinions. Perhaps I would have taken this step before if the belief in my calling had not held me from it and if I had not always hoped that I could perhaps still do much good." [41]

It is clear from this confession as well as from other data of this crisis that the king felt the menace of deposition hanging over him. He grew excited at the rumor of a plot, and even after the rumor proved to be false, he mistrusted his most intimate councilors among the patriots. When the queen read this memorandum, she found it shocking. One can scarcely conceive a ruler in a greater state of confusion. Determined to fulfill God's purpose, Frederick William would not give in to his desire to abdicate. He clung to peace even though all the patriots and all those who had fought most bravely during 1806 and worked hardest since then to revive the state craved war. His aversion to the reforms and the reformers stands out with appalling clarity. The reformers accused him at the time and afterwards of hindering their work; the king is herewith supplying the corroborating evidence. His description of them was scarcely flattering. "Self-righteousness," "bitter hate," "frivolous passion to blame," "partisanship"—these were strange words to apply to men like Stein, Gneisenau, Scharnhorst, men who were striving to save Prussia, Hohenzollern power, and Germany from Napoleon.

[41] Lehmann, *op. cit.*, II, 259. The author has also used the original in the Preussisches Geheimstaatsarchiv, Dahlem, *Repository 92, Friedrich Wilhelm III, B. Vlad. 24,* and expanded Lehmann's summary at certain points.

The slight understanding of the king for the nationalists and reformers was evident from many statements during these years. When the nationalists spoke of national devotion, enthusiastic sacrifice for the nation, liberty, the greatness and goodness of man, the king scoffed at their ideals. He called them "eccentricities," "castles-in-the-air and illusions," "brainstorms," "dreamings." "I do not like phantoms and fantasies. I cannot make use of fantastic persons. . . . Phantasus was a brother to Morpheus," he said.[42] In a memorandum of instructions to his ministers in March, 1807, just at the time when the work of reform and of arousing the national spirit was getting under way, the king wrote:

> Since this arrangement must certainly be for the best of the whole, I recommend the most conscientious reticence, public spirit and suppression of personalities, private opinion or theories. When partisan spirit, prejudice or animosity is mixed up in any undertaking, nothing comes of it.[43]

A more complete repudiation of nationalism can scarcely be imagined. The nationalists were to him all egoists and theorists; they lacked a feeling of community. In 1810 the highest praise which he could give his friend General Köckritz, a mediocrity after his own pattern, was as follows: "You have not indeed, as is the custom now, served me with plans, projects, theories and proposals, which no one can use if he measures them by reality; but your wealth of experience has often been valuable to me."[44]

One of the proposals, projects, or theories was submitted to him during the next year by Gneisenau. Gneisenau wished to arm the entire people, to use preachers and other public persons to stir up the people, to wage a national war against the oppressor. The king put no confidence whatever in the plan. He wished a true, peaceable, obedient, loyal people, not a nation in arms. He agreed heartily with Hardenberg, who in 1808 (later he changed his views, whereas the king did not) cautioned him about the proposals of the reformers as follows:

[42] Eylert, *op. cit.*, I, 48.
[43] Winter, *op. cit.*, p. 142.
[44] Eylert, *op. cit.*, I, 115.

> It is highly important to be extremely cautious about everything which has to do with the participation of the nation in matters of state, its defense, and so forth, so that this affair which is in itself excellent and in the present circumstances necessary shall be accomplished in a way befitting a monarchical constitution and not end in something revolutionary. In view of the ever-increasing danger, which should not be lost sight of, that Napoleon intends to destroy Prussia, the arousing and use of the national spirit is of course of the greatest importance; but it is above all necessary that it be done wisely and carefully in order that it may not even with the best intentions ruin everything. A fundamental principle of Your Majesty's policy must now be, in my opinion, to avoid all sensation. And what causes a greater and more dangerous sensation than an incautious and untimely arousing of the people? What matters is that this people be prepared and willing out of love and loyalty to its king and the constitution for any sacrifice, that one recognize and know its feelings, what one may demand and expect from it, that one in all stillness may plan as to how he can make use of this sympathy with the best possible advantage. Careful supervision of groups and of measures of individuals who with the best intentions might bring about irretrievable wrong is accordingly of the highest necessity.[45]

In these sentences one can perceive the ultimate reason for the king's aversion to nationalism, that it might lead to revolution; and his imagination was vivid in portraying the possible disastrous effects of this eventuality. Better to rule half or even a quarter of a kingdom than none, was his belief. He stood between two fires, Napoleon on the one hand, the nationalists on the other. If he acceded to the demands of the latter, Napoleon might invade his land again and dethrone him. In that case the Prussian people might rise and fight desperately; but even if they gained a victory, they might destroy the land. Furthermore, as Hardenberg cautioned him, no one could be sure that in the case of arming and rousing the folk against the enemy, this folk might not overthrow or diminish the power of its own king. Frederick William preferred to stay quiet, to adjust himself and wait for better days than to take so great a risk. A nationalistic war agreed

[45] Cited by Haake, *op. cit.*, pp. 36-37 from Paul Hassel, *Geschichte der preussischen Politik 1807-1815* (Leipzig, 1881), pp. 570-71.

neither with his interest nor with his nature. He abhorred it.

The king understood nothing of the deeper ideas underlying the reforms and mistrusted the thought of creating a new spirit in the folk and the army. He disliked the proposal for compulsory military service as one likely to disturb the economy of the land, as democratic and revolutionary, and he held out against it until the War of Liberation actually began.[46] In matters of educational reform he revealed his conservatism to an even greater extent. He wished the schools to remain subordinate to the church; the utilitarian and rationalistic nature of his view of education has already been indicated. Education should above all turn out loyal, practical, moral, and obedient subjects. He despised philosophers and nationalists who believed in the power of ideas and the greatness of the spirit. Frederick William preferred proficiency in making a shoe or a gun, in executing orders, in abiding by the law and the tenets of religion. He, as king, would take care of the ideas and things of the spirit—in so far as it was necessary; his subjects should perform their tasks and not concern themselves about such things as the common good, devotion to the nation, regeneration of man, a new order of society, nationalism. In his statement of 1807 that the state must replace by spiritual force that which it had lost in material power, he meant quite other things than the idealists did. He remained fundamentally the same throughout life.

Sometime during the years of humiliation, 1811-12, Eylert preached a sermon before the king on the text, "Blessed is he who endures persecution; for when he has been proven, he will inherit the crown of life which God has promised those who love

[46] This statement is made notwithstanding the fact that before 1806 the king occasionally, especially in 1803, spoke of modifying in this direction the method of recruiting. He was still far from wishing a national, that is, a Prussian army. In the same year, 1803, he stated: "Since the foundations of the Prussian military system rest above all on the strictest subordination and on the promptest obedience to the command of every superior," His Majesty expected all officers and men to observe this habit (*Die Reorganisation der Preussischen Armee nach dem Tilsiter Frieden* [Berlin, 1857], p. 277). This order reflected the ideas of the old Prussia and is an entire epoch removed from the ideal of a nation in arms, a nation of individuals fighting singly with initiative and enthusiasm for a common cause.

him."[47] The king was much affected by this text, fitting the words to his own case. He had suffered much from foreign enemies, from friends among the royalty, and from his own subjects. He had refused the counsels for war of his ministers and close advisers; he had slowed down the work of reform; he had suffered in patience. The death of the queen in 1810 deprived him of the one person on earth whom he completely loved. Just before her death he made the bitterest remark of which man is capable, "If she were not mine, she would live; because she is my wife, she will surely die."[48] Defeat at Jena, collapse of a great state for which he was responsible to his dynasty, French domination, the near exhaustion of his land, loss of the West Elbian territory and precarious control of the remainder, the condition of unrest and the excitement aroused among his subjects by the reforms—this long list of woes seemed climaxed by the loss of his wife. The king became fatalistic and melancholy. "There is no more misfortune for me," he wrote on the death of Queen Louise; "the worst has struck me; in comparison to it all else which may come is as nothing."[49] Nothing remained for him but the dry fulfillment of duty and the consolation of religion.[50] He soon overcame his fatalism by renewed faith in God; but at the time when nationalists were eager for action and determined to save that which was dearest to them, their fatherland, or to perish, Frederick William seemed more indifferent to affairs of this world than ever before.

In 1812 the king allied with Napoleon for the great invasion of Russia. He felt that he had no choice; but many of his officers were so angry that they quit his service. When Napoleon lost his magnificent army on the way to and from Moscow, Frederick

[47] Eylert, *op. cit.*, I, 435.

[48] Wendland, *op. cit.*, p. 67.

[49] *Loc. cit.*

[50] See the beautiful and touching memoranda which the king wrote about his wife after her death. They are masterpieces of character analysis, and give the reader a far deeper respect for this bottled-up king as a person than he has for him as a ruler. The memoranda are published in *Vom Leben und Sterben der Königin Luise. Eigenhändige Aufzeichnungen ihres Gemahls König Friedrich Wilhelms III*. Edited by Otto Meisner (Berlin and Leipzig, 1926).

William still would not decide to break his alliance and risk a war against the conqueror; as usual he mistrusted everybody. In this stage of indecision one of his hardheaded, reactionary, but ardently Prussian generals, Yorck, signed on his own initiative a convention of neutrality with Czar Alexander. This act marked the turning point from a French alliance to a Russian one and inaugurated the War of Liberation. The king denounced bitterly this insubordination, and when the East Prussian burghers and aristocrats organized resistance to the French without waiting for the royal initiative, Frederick William grew even more excited. He asked sarcastically if "Yorck wears the burgher crown already." [51] He was still not thinking in the same terms as the patriots, that it was "a struggle of the good against the evil" in which "form must be forgotten in the thought of the goal." He hoped that Napoleon's difficulties in Russia would lead to peace, with Prussia's independence and welfare assured. When the East and West Prussians sent him a memoir assuring him of their full support in case of war on Russia's side, he answered coolly on January 7, 1813:

> I honor the patriotic feelings which are expressed in your petition of December 29 and recognize with grateful heart the offer which you make me therein. Since you are ignorant of the exact situation of the political relations, your views must of necessity be accompanied by confidence that I shall take the best measures and choose the most favorable time for assuring the welfare and independence of the state. In this attitude and in the loyal devotion and the support of my subjects, when circumstances make it necessary, I shall always find my greatest satisfaction.[52]

"Be quiet, my children," he might as well have said, "the king alone knows what is best." He was putting a damper on enthusiasm immediately before the outbreak of one of the most popular and heroic wars in German history, when if he had not declared war, he undoubtedly would have faced a rebellion among his own army and people.

[51] Walter Elze, *Der Streit um Tauroggen* (Breslau, 1926), p. 15.
[52] *Ibid.*, pp. 9-10.

Just as humiliation at the hands of Napoleon had compelled him to tolerate reforms and reformers whom he disliked, so in 1813 Russia and his patriotic subjects forced him into a war which he feared. Once the king had made the plunge, he felt sufficient exhilaration to accept the nationalistic reformers' proposals for military reorganization. He approved the establishment of compulsory military service, although only for the duration of the war, and even agreed to the creation of the *Landsturm*, the most exalted demand of the nationalists. But he disliked it and in a few weeks destroyed its real character; since the French never reached Prussia again, the edict never came into actual operation. In these same weeks of activity the king established the decoration of the Iron Cross for heroism in war, whether of private soldiers or officers, thus recognizing the equality of all exposed to the dangers of battle. Even this king came to perceive that heroism was heroism, whether in aristocrat or peasant. Even he comprehended that the Prussian people must fight as a unit against the powerful enemy, that a common danger made brothers of all those exposed to it. Even he felt a slight stirring akin to nationalism and promulgated the first appeal to his people and to his army which a Prussian autocrat had ever made. He called the nation (the Prussian nation) to war, put himself within the nation alongside his people, and explained the necessity for war to the finish. He called it a holy war for the freedom and independence of the fatherland and the preservation of the most sacred goods of people and state. He admonished each man to sacrifice himself and his possessions for the common welfare, asking him by implication if not by actual word to use his own initiative, to act according to his capacity. The king urged his people to share and coöperate with him, not merely to obey him. He came as close to nationalism as he ever did in his life: he was excited and under such pressure from the enthusiasm around him that for the moment he forgot himself.

It would be too much to expect this crabbed ruler to maintain the pitch of even mild exaltation which he felt in 1813. He soon returned to his normal attitude of negative criticism, for he still thought of wars and politics in the dynastic manner of the eighteenth century, that is, that wars were won by maneuvering, not by losing lives. After Napoleon was driven across the Rhine, the king was disinclined to continue the conflict; his Prussia seemed safe. He opposed Gneisenau's plan of pursuing Napoleon as fast as possible. He hated to sacrifice men in battle and frequently showed his anger over the loss of them. In 1813 on the morning after the Battle of Culm, for example, he reviewed the reserve cavalry of Kleist's corps. He found the number of survivors of the battle very few and said to the commander: "You lost many yesterday. It was not really necessary; they [the French] would have had to surrender anyway. Your bravery is well known and needed no new proof of it."[53] Words of encouragement like these hardly made his soldiers fight like heroes. It was neither a pleasure nor an honor to be led by such an appreciative king. "With God for King and country" was the slogan which Frederick William had coined for this war. He might have added with more accuracy that his army was fighting as much against Napoleon as for its king, that it was fighting for the king in spite of his characteristics.

After Napoleon had been defeated, Frederick William returned immediately to the former order of things. At the Congress of Vienna he worked only for Prussia. It is doubtful whether he even thought of the existence of a German nation or of the possibility of German unity. He was vaguely aware that the Germans possessed a common culture; but Germany to him meant only a Central European body of independent states. He agreed entirely with the statement made by Ancillon, his adviser and tutor to the crown prince:

> I hear the cry, "Germany, Germany!" I answer that Germany should not be the principal end, the primary object, the absolute condition of all good for Prussian policy. The freeing of Germany would be a precious means of obtaining the national goal, of assuring our existence and our independence; but this means itself should not be our first concern, and in declaring for this means, one would not reach the goal. If a part of the German princes does not wish to cut the yoke and prefers it to liberty, if another part does not wish to

[53] Von der Goltz, *op. cit.*, p. 524.

cut it for lack of sufficient forces, if Austria refuses to let her banners float on the Rhine and to head a general movement, which the friends of humanity desire, let us remember that first and foremost we are Prussians.[54]

He was a Prussian "first and foremost." Nothing more need be said about his German national feeling; it did not exist.

Even with respect to Prussia Frederick William had no comprehension of public feeling akin to nationalism.[55] He sometimes referred to the Prussian nation; but he understood the term only as a name for an agglomeration of provinces united mainly by virtue of the royal tie. He opposed, for example, breaking down in 1815 the provincial basis of the army organization; for he trusted in provincial patriotism more than in patriotism to the Prussian state. He was still living in the world of the old territorial state. Probably he was correct in his view of Prussia. He realized that commercially or economically speaking Prussia formed no unit, but consisted of separate provinces. He actually disliked the thought of assisting it to become a political unit.

Some time after the Napoleonic Wars were over, Frederick William summed up his opinion of the age in which he lived. His assertions contain the conclusions which he had drawn from living in the most idealistic and heroic period in modern German history. The king said:

Our age loves extremes and moves in opposite directions. It separates and tears asunder that which belongs together, that which can have great results only by being together, and since that occurs in the Holiest and Highest, naturally this inner disunity has taken hold of almost the entire life so that everything is contaminated, jolted, and insecure. Partisanship and factionalism are added to this; prejudice prevails, mercy and justice have vanished, and from all sides one hears and sees bitter opposition. In view of the disinclination to everything which stands for authority, and where each man sets up his own, there is naturally no longer any point of unity. The

[54] Cited by Lehmann, *Scharnhorst,* II, 497. The king said specifically that he agreed with the memorandum.

[55] The term nationalism should be applied only to Germany, not to Prussia, although contemporaries sometimes referred to the latter also as a nation.

object of truth disappears and everything dissolves into a thousand different, subjective ideas, and opinions. Since that which up to now was of value is no longer of value, the new takes its place, only to be displaced by the newest. With the great number of thinking minds the end of all this is not to be foreseen. This number is not greater than ever before; but a great man, a hero, who overshadows all, is lacking. He will, however, come.[56]

The hero did not appear, but Frederick William substituted for him. Freed from the compulsion put upon him by the Napoleonic menace, he began to rule after his own heart. He eliminated all those reformers and nationalists who made him uncomfortable. In the case of some, like Arndt, he permitted them not merely to be dismissed from state service but to suffer the humiliation of state trial for their nationalistic words and actions during the War of Liberation. He allowed others, like Stein and Gneisenau, to live unmolested, while depriving them of any important influence over state affairs. Those men who before 1815 had been the patriots and heroes became suspect and were avoided. The king talked affectionately about his good friend Metternich instead of referring to Stein. He mistrusted any official who tried to exert power over him. The inefficiencies of the years before 1806 revived automatically. When Hardenberg in 1815 urged the king to grant Prussia a constitution, Ancillon wrote to the king as follows:

If the wearer of the crown should voluntarily limit his power now, he would easily incur the suspicion that he was doing it out of obedience to necessity or with the intent to create new sources of help. One must not allow the hotheads, those very active and loud groups of persons who for some years have set up as the nation and have cried for a constitution and through that wished to control Prussia, a gathering place where extreme ideas and feelings would be furthered, especially not after the arming of the whole people.[57]

The king was profoundly impressed by this warning; but under renewed pressure promised a constitution and then never fulfilled

[56] Eylert, *op. cit.*, I, 321-22.
[57] Haake, *op. cit.*, p. 65.

his word. Ancillon's assertions undoubtedly provide the key to the king's repressive actions against the nationalists and their proposals. He feared as before the diminution of his power and after 1815 was even more excitable over the menace of revolution than previously. Nationalism still threatened his authority and he could not fight it with impunity. When he read some new proposal in the newspapers which the author maintained expressed the general opinion, the king shrugged his shoulders. He knew that his peasants and burghers had never heard of it. So he lived on, unconcerned with the public opinion of a few scribblers and determined to keep down any attempt to question or defy the royal will. Nationalism in Prussia was a bad dream which had passed, and in his testament of 1827 and again in 1838 he admonished his son to rule autocratically, to grant no constitution, to change nothing.[58]

The counterpart of the king's repression of nationalism in internal affairs was his opposition to the intrusion of it in international relations. The king wished diplomacy and wars to be carried on under the guidance of royalty and gentlemen. He disliked having the masses become excited over these issues lest they desire a voice in international affairs. When he returned to Berlin in August, 1814, after the defeat of Napoleon, the populace prepared a great reception for him and covered the city with decorations. Although the king detested celebrations of this type, in view of the enthusiasm of the people over the defeat of Napoleon, he might have accepted this show of emotion with pleasure. Instead of doing so with the best grace possible, he was irritated, declaring that the city had wasted money, that the decorations were too elaborate, and continued:

[58] He even disliked the word Protestantism as applied to the church and endeavored to unite the Lutheran and the Calvinist churches in his own state and to fix definitely a ritual and a liturgy for them. Protestantism could easily become subjectivity and dissension and lead to the complete disintegration of the church and of all religious authority. As in the state affairs, so also here, he tried to impose authoritarianism and he fought the ideal of self-government in church as in state. See Wendland, *op. cit.*, and Eylert, *op. cit.*, I, 329-30, as well as elsewhere.

I do not like the trophies of victory, the captured cannons and flags heaped together at the armory opposite my residence. One must not and dare not taunt the defeated enemy. This is miserable boastfulness, and we do not want to begin again in our good fortune that haughtiness which made us unfortunate. It is against all rule of propriety to want to cause people with whom we have just made peace feel again humiliated by putting up cannons and flags, especially the Bavarians, Württembergers, and others, who in the end helped to fight as our allies, boldly and courageously supporting us. The festive victory arches, the elaborate trophies in the windows of the arsenal must be taken away again; tomorrow's festivities shall be a Christian feast of pious gratitude and humility before God. It is He who has done great deeds for Prussia; to Him alone belongs the honor.[59]

He added another act to the long list of those successfully dampening the ardor of his subjects. He did not hate the French and wanted to return as soon as possible to friendly intercourse with the French royal house. He was a king and alien to the passions of the masses.

In view of his love of peace and his moral outlook on affairs one can readily comprehend the king's approval of the Holy Alliance. This agreement expressed orthodox Christian, humanitarian, royal internationalism. It and the practical international politics of Metternich became for him the acme of astuteness and he clung to them as long as he lived. They were weapons for repressing nationalism wherever the power of these rulers, if one may place Metternich alongside Alexander and Frederick William, reached; and this power extended over most of Europe.

Frederick William reigned at the most critical period in modern German history. He can be credited with preventing Prussia from becoming liberal and from taking its place in the same movement of forces that was so strong in France and England. By tenacious defense of authority, by cautious weighing of reforms, by determined preservation of the old order of society, he kept Prussia in the class of the reactionary empires, Austria and Russia. His opposition to nationalism retarded the work of German unification and destroyed the German chance of keeping

[59] Eylert, *op. cit.*, III, Pt. 1, 209-10.

pace with the nationally unified states of Western Europe. The cleft in the standards and ideals between Germany and the Western European powers fixed by Frederick William III persists to the present day. The king was personally honorable and loyal, careful in financial matters and devoted to his subjects. As a ruler he brought Germany misfortune. If at this period Germany had undergone a French Revolution of her own on a scale suitable to her, she might have escaped many hardships. She owes the failure to do so primarily to Frederick William III.

INDEX